TEACHING 3–9 YEAR OLDS

YEAR OLDS

THEORY INTO PRACTICE

Marion Dowling

and

Elizabeth Dauncey

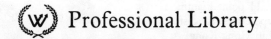
Professional Library

First published 1984
by Ward Lock Educational Ltd
T. R. House, 1 Christopher Road,
East Grinstead, Sussex RH19 3BT,
England.

Reprinted 1989

A Ling Kee Company

ISBN 0 7062 4338 2

British Library Cataloguing in Publication Data
Dowling, Marion
  Teaching 3–9 year olds
  1. Education, Primary
  I. Title   II. Dauncey, Elizabeth
  372.11'02   LB1523

  ISBN 0-7062-4338-2

Set in 10 on 11 point Plantin
by GRP Typesetters, Leicester
and printed in Hong Kong
for Ward Lock Educational
T. R. House, 1 Christopher Road,
East Grinstead, Sussex RH19 3BT.

CONTENTS

ACKNOWLEDGMENTS

We acknowledge with gratitude the many contributions from teachers and children without which this book could not have been written. Thanks are also due to our husbands whose encouragement and practical support have been invaluable.

The authors and publishers are grateful for permission to reproduce extracts from the following publications in this book:

Children's Minds by Margaret Donaldson, Fontana Paperbacks; *Education 5–9, Mathematics Counts,* and *Primary Education in England,* HMSO; *Inside the Primary Classroom* by M. Galton, B. Simon and P. Croll, *The Concept of Education* ed. R. S. Peters, Routledge and Kegan Paul; *Involving Parents in Nursery and Infant Schools* by B. Tizard, J. Mortimore and B. Burchell, *Purpose and Practice in Nursery Education* by Lesley Webb, *Under Five in Britain* by J. Bruner, Grant McIntyre; *Open Plan Schools* by S. N. Bennett, J. Andreae, P. Hegarty and B. Wade, Schools Council Publications 1980, NFER/Nelson; *Parent–Teacher Relationships* by I. Stout and G. Langdon, American Educational Research Association; *Primary Education: Issues for the Eighties* ed. Colin Richards, A. and C. Black Ltd.; *Record Keeping in Primary Schools* by P. Clift, G. Weiner and E. Wilson, Schools Council Research Studies, Macmillan Education Ltd.; 'Teachers in Partnership' by J. Rudduck, *Journal of NAIEA; The Practical Curriculum* from Schools Council Working Paper 70, pp. 9, 20, 42, 56, *Making the Most of the Short In-service Course* by J. Rudduck, Methuen Educational; *Written Communication Between Home and School* ed. J. Bastiani, University of Nottingham School of Education.

INTRODUCTION

In 1966 the Central Advisory Committee chaired by Lady Plowden suggested that children of seven years would be given a greater chance in their learning if they were kept in extended infant schools for an extra year rather than transferred to junior schools. This recommendation provided impetus for the development of first schools which accommodate children of five to eight years or five to nine years.

In 1982 the HMI survey of *Education 5 – 9* considered 80 first schools and stated that:

> The evidence of the survey reveals a number of both in-service and initial training needs. The majority of teachers come from other than first schools and these teachers need appropriate in-service training to help them translate the best schemes into good practice. . . .

We hope that this book will assist teachers' professional development at all levels. Although focus is on first schools the material is equally relevant to children of this age range in infant, junior and primary schools and Chapter 1 – 'The Youngest Children in School' – applies to nursery-age children in a variety of settings.

There is considerable evidence that the majority of teachers do not read professional literature: when they do read about their work it is most likely to be at a very practical level. Understandably teachers want helpful suggestions and hints to arm them to cope with the needs of a large class of children. At the same time the best practitioners are those who are well informed about educational theory and as a result have worked out a rationale on which to base their classroom practice. They can accommodate new thinking in the light of the theoretical framework of ideas which they have established.

This book is aimed at helping busy teachers to link educational theory to practice in a manageable way. If teachers can see the relevance of research and can develop their teaching from sound principles they will become more professional and better able to withstand uninformed pressures from society.

HOW TO USE THE BOOK
Each chapter has five sections:

Introduction
What the Theory Says
In the Classroom
Appraisal Questions
Further References

The Introduction gives the reader a broad overview and introduces the major headings under which the topic will be discussed – in terms of consensus of theory in 'What the Theory Says' and in terms of actual classroom practice 'In the Classroom'. In this way the teacher can see how attitudes, daily practices and activities can fit into an abstract framework, or how theoretical statements can be translated into action.

The Appraisal Questions aim to offer the teacher a simple way of checking on her effectiveness and help her to identify strengths and weaknesses. Bearing in mind that it was impossible to include all the detail we would have wished Further References will suggest additional useful material.

The book is designed to be used flexibly. Using the headings in each section the teacher should be able to find some practical refreshment without considering the theory. The material should be useful to an individual teacher, but can also be used as a document for staff in-service, e.g. a school staff may wish to look at how effectively each teacher spends her time in the classroom. The references and suggestions in the chapter on Organization should provide a starting-point for discussion and the appraisal questions on 'Time' will will help teachers to check their practice.

We are aware that suggestions can sound like a counsel for perfection; we also know just how demanding it is to teach young children and that teachers are unlikely ever to acquire all the resources to provide the service they would wish. We do not apologize for aiming high, however, because in our experience professional teachers expect a great deal of themselves and get the greatest satisfaction from their work. We hope each reader will take from the book what is helpful to *her*. (For the sake of clarity the teacher is referred to throughout as 'she' and the child as 'he'.)

The book confirms the complex nature of teaching and learning and emphasizes the tremendous responsibility of a first school teacher. We hope that it also gives a flavour of the joy, excitement and privilege of working with young children.

1

THE YOUNGEST CHILDREN IN SCHOOL

INTRODUCTION

In this chapter we will look at the varying provision for children under five years of age in school. Depending on where they live these children may be attending nursery schools, nursery classes or reception classes either on a full-time or part-time basis. (Others may of course still be at home, with childminders or attending day nurseries or playgroups.) Whilst recognizing that resources of staff, space and equipment vary tremendously in different authorities, our contention is that children of pre-school age merit special provision to meet their developmental and learning needs. Nursery schools and classes have in the main recognized this but young children entering infant and first schools do not necessarily face a similar environment. Sometimes there is pressure to develop the 3R skills early; sedentary activities may predominate as these are easier for one teacher to oversee; children may be required to record their work to the detriment of time spent discovering and learning. The result of these practices will be an image of children learning whilst in effect they are simply learning to make the correct responses to demands which they are unable to understand. Clearly a teacher who is solely responsible for a large group of under-fives accommodated in a small classroom is operating under severe constraints when compared to the teacher in a purpose-built nursery with a smaller number of children and support from a nursery nurse. We realize therefore that some of the theory and related practice will have to be considered in the light of necessary compromises. The main message must remain however: if we are to lay sound and reliable foundations for learning we must look very carefully at the environment that we offer children when they first start school.

We hope that this chapter will be useful, not only to teachers in the classroom but those offering support to feeder playgroups. For those schools who do not have attached nursery provision playgroups are a significant resource. The closer the links developed between playgroups and schools, the greater the benefits for everyone concerned with the young child's learning. When considering what type of provision is appropriate for these very young children, we need to bear in mind their developmental and learning needs. The following main principles provide a framework within which we can examine those needs.

PRE-SCHOOL/SCHOOL LIAISON AND CONTINUITY

As long ago as the Plowden Report in 1967, parental involvement was recommended as an important consideration for educators in the primary sector, and since that time information about home/school liaison has widened to become both more sharply focused and more objective. (In this chapter we will be concentrating on parents solely as key persons in the liaison between pre-school experience and the rising-five class.)

In her contribution to the Oxford Pre-school Research Project[1] Teresa Smith writes: 'The emphasis in involving parents, as we have seen from both parents' and staffs' interviews, was overwhelmingly on sharing the child's experience as a natural extension and continuity of the home experience and as a vital support for the child.'

The finding that parents are in the main eager to become involved in their children's school experience is reassuring. However, many more parents would like to become involved than are asked. Organizing parents so that all who wish to become involved have an opportunity to do so is a complex managerial task. 'Involvement' can have a variety of meanings. The Pre-school Research Project team identified two models around which a busy teacher can organize her thoughts or a school staff can formulate policy. The first kind of involvement is called 'professional'. From the parental point of view, 'professional' involvement means open access to the classroom and ready exchange of information, but simply hearing about or looking at their child's progress rather than becoming part of the educational process themselves.

The second kind of involvement is called the 'partnership' approach. Here trained staff regard parents as teachers of their children. Staff not only encourage parents actively to participate with their children, but offer them explanation about specific educational issues.

There is a very real difference between these two approaches. Although they have not been evaluated in terms of effectiveness they deserve thoughtful consideration. From time to time it may be useful to list all the activities which involve parents of the youngest children and make a note of which category they fall into.

INDIVIDUAL NEEDS

Each child is a unique product of genetic endowment and environment. John Brierley sums up the circular argument succinctly: 'We cannot easily apportion the extent to which a particular characteristic is inherited and how much is due to environment, simply because heredity and environment interact and the proportion of each is unique to each individual.'[2] If the child is to learn effectively, his or her individual needs must be catered for.

How is the teacher to cater for the large number of individuals who make up her reception class? Brierley suggests that 'nurture is vitally important'. The concept of continuing nurture for individual young children, whether in playgroup, nursery class or school, is not 'blanket' handling but shaping the environment to meet special needs. For example, coping successfully with the shy or noisy boy or girl, giving a child an outlet for individuality through real choices and decision-making, and helping him realize his intellectual potential.

Stages of development

Piaget's theories on the intellectual stages of development through which children pass, albeit at different rates, have had a massive impact on educational practice. Recent work has challenged some aspects of these theories in such a way that provision, especially for the youngest children, may need to be re-assessed.

Teachers have accepted that children from about eighteen months of age until approximately seven years old are in the pre-operational concrete stage of development. This means that from the first development of language until the point when the child can manipulate symbols his thinking is dictated by experience.

Because learning depends on action, it has been thought that reasoning (particularly deductive reasoning) and reflective awareness are not features of intellectual growth at this stage. How can a child reflect on his actions unless those actions have become part of his thinking? He is limited to the present both in time and space.

Margaret Donaldson has shown that pre-school children are not only capable of deduction but are capable of reflecting on their actions. She comes to the conclusion that 'At least from age four then, we must again acknowledge that the supposed gap between children and adults is less than many people have claimed'.[3] She also argues that pre-school children can learn much that was thought to be beyond them if that learning is put in a human setting which makes sense to the children. She draws her examples from language and ably demonstrates that children learn to understand language from the setting in which it is spoken – by inference, by body movements and by the whole logical situation. An example of the kind of situation she has in mind might be a grandmother with her two-year-old grandchild. The adult points to the bookcase, nods her head and says to the child, 'Fetch me the dictionary please, Rachel.' Rachel assesses the situation, looks from her grandmother to the bookcase and puts her hand on a book. Her grandmother then shakes her head and the child selects another book. At this the adult smiles and says 'Thank you.' Rachel does not know what 'dictionary' means but selects one succsssfully because she makes sense of the human situation.

Donaldson has coined the term 'disembedded thinking' to describe the thinking which is divorced from such a context. The important point to grasp, and one which has a tremendous bearing on educational practice, is that disembedded thinking is also desirable and should be nurtured by the teacher.

Structure

If we are endeavouring to give children, beyond the present pleasure and delight, learning that will serve the future, then we must offer them structure. Structure is 'knowledge in terms of basic and general ideas'.[4] A child who is beginning to read, or beginning to learn mathematics, should be engaged in the same basic ideas that any undergraduate is considering when tackling a subject. If we are dealing with mathematics, for example, the idea of order is basic to the discipline. It is through structure that principles and attitudes are learned. Structure 'is at the heart of the educational process'.[4]

A child cannot comprehend structure unless he is able to reflect, become aware of his own thinking, release his mind from present time and space, and make choices which are not the result of trial and error. 'However, the argument here is that you cannot master any formal system unless you have learned to take at least some steps beyond the bounds of human sense, and that the problem of helping children to begin to do this in the first stages of their schooling – or even earlier – has not been properly recognized and is not usually tackled in any adequate way.'[3]

We have greatly simplified some powerful arguments here. The message, however, is clear. If children are to succeed in the formal systems on which educational advance is based, then they must be helped to acquire those modes of thinking which we have described. This does not reduce provision for pre-school children to a cold, calculated regime, nor does it mean that all provision should be of this kind.

THE CHILD AS A PERSON

The younger the child the more impossible it is to separate intellectual growth from other aspects of development. Clearly, lack of physical well-being must affect learning. Michael was delivered to school daily in an uncomfortable state. He had not had an adequate night's rest, his clothes were filthy and his head was regularly infested with lice. Until the headteacher and welfare assistant helped Michael's mother to recognize the problem and do something about it the teacher's job was restricted to making the little boy feel welcome and needed in the classroom. Little more could be accomplished.

Children need a well-balanced nutritious diet so that the brain can develop and function well, plenty of sleep and relaxation so that it can be repaired and maintained, and protection from physical danger. Children also need comfortable, clean and warm clothes, and both space and time in which to learn. Every teacher of young children pays attention to these needs and sometimes calls upon the back-up services to help her. It is a comfort to know that even if a child has had a poor start, the brain has the facility to catch up. Children also need a consistent, caring adult who will play with them, talk to them, stimulate them, laugh with them, grieve with them and become a model for them.

The teacher needs to remember that she is educating a whole person, not merely an intellect. In order to do this any environment for under-fives must give priority to helping children to develop good relationships with their teachers and other adults; to provide the security and consistency of handling that aids emotional growth; and above all to offer praise and encouragement that will assist a child develop a sound self-esteem. If we are dealing with socially adept, secure, confident small individuals who are beginning to feel a sense of mastery over their own lives then the ingredients for mental development are there.

So the teacher of this young age-group needs to keep a vigilant eye on the physical needs of the children. She also needs to provide an environment where the child can develop as a person. But further than this, she becomes to some extent a model on which the child will base his view of the world and his place in it. If the rising five-year-old is housed in school or a nursery class he is learning what it is to have a teacher. Does she have high expectations of him? Has she patience, time and genuine delight in his achievement? How can she so order her day that she can give 'unhurried attention and provide a consistent, caring, continual model of his world'?[2]

The answers are not easy, but many of them can be worked out in collaboration with colleagues. We offer some suggestions but there is no substitute for a free exchange of techniques and ideas between experienced teachers.

WHAT THE THEORY SAYS

PRE-SCHOOL/SCHOOL LIAISON AND CONTINUITY

Continuity between pre-school and school

If we regard learning as continuous and sequential then it is imperative that at every stage of education we take account of the child's previous and subsequent experiences.

The nursery or reception teacher has a particularly difficult task in that she receives children from a wide variety of backgrounds – from enriched and disadvantaged homes, from childminders, or playgroups. Indeed provision for very young children is not seen as a matter for uniform state provision: 'Childhood in the years before school begins is, by conventional standards, a family matter. . . . We are repelled by the idea of a national policy for infants and toddlers, for it smacks of invasions of privacy, or worse, of totalitarian efforts to shape young minds.'[5]

The teacher needs information about these different environments in order to plan appropriate learning programmes for children and to arrange a smooth transition into school. And the child and his parents need to know about the school for, as the NFER project on Transition and Continuity stresses, 'familiarity with the school before he starts will give the child an idea of what to expect and may help him to cope more easily with change'.[6]

The First Schools Survey suggests that most first schools regard this as an important part of their planning:

A first school takes great care in and devotes much effort to introducing children and their parents to their first days in school. Before admission, children and their parents are encouraged to visit the school and spend some time taking part in an activity such as painting or listening to stories.[7]

Schools will decide for themselves the form of contact to develop with parents. (A conventional way of offering information to new parents is through letters and circulars. Whilst this is appropriate for some parents, schools need to be aware of the limitations of written communication.) What is important is to seize on the tremendous enthusiasm, interest and energy shown by new parents when their child starts school. Bruner describes the strength of this interest when parents were invited to be involved with their child's induction into school.

The sense of 'belonging' or 'shared experience' and a 'shared world' came over powerfully when parents were talking about what they had gained from being involved in their child's group and what they thought their role should be. It came over equally powerfully when they talked about their first visits to the group, their first conversations with the staff, the period of settling in the child, their contact with staff once the child was in the group, and the educational and social events provided by the group. Parents clearly wanted to know how the child had passed his day and whether there had been any problems.[5]

The process of acquiring information about children's pre-school experiences is complex and time-consuming. With limited staffing resources many schools understandably concentrate on developing home/school links. The First Schools Survey applauds the quality of parent and staff relationships and we look at this aspect more closely in Chapter 5.

Although the family may be the first line of contact, various other agencies have been involved with the pre-school child and teachers need to be at least familiar with their role, so that schools playgroups and nurseries can plan together to benefit the children. For example, an understanding of the difficulties of running a playgroup in a large open hall could lead to a teacher offering some advice and support in helping to break up play-space. (A small-scale study[8] looking at the effect of building design on the behaviour of staff and children in pre-school playgroups suggested that in an open space adults tend to oversee a range of activity rather than become involved with specific children.)

Bruner sees this type of contact as just one means of using nursery teachers' expertise to help develop other forms of pre-school provision. 'The more intensive and longer training of nursery-school teachers prepares them, I believe, not only for what they do but for more demanding work than many of them are now called upon to do.' He speaks of using them 'for developing new and better provisions for meeting the new child-care needs of a changing Britain'.[5]

However, the NFER study noted 'a fair degree of caution between staff in nurseries and playgroups and some views arose out of ignorance of what actually went on in the other setting'.[9] The present situation calls for nursery classes and playgroups to break down immediately barriers of prejudice by becoming more familiar with one another.

The NFER study also recommends that contacts should be developed with health and social services: 'What is required is a more concerted attempt on a wider scale to bring together everyone involved in early education and care so that they can learn more about each other's aims and work.'

Continuity in the classroom

Very young children need to relate to and learn with one adult. A secure environment is important for their confidence and sense of well-being:

The relationship that a young child establishes with his teacher is an important one; it is often the first strong link that is made outside his family. Most children starting school are helped by having one teacher with whom to relate and it is desirable, therefore, that teachers of young children should be responsible for all, or nearly all, of the day's work.[7]

Most teachers develop means of class control and ways of starting and ending the day which are understood and accepted by the children. These have a steadying effect on a group and are justified educationally. But Lesley Webb also warns of routines that are unthinkingly applied:

There is a higher proportion of time spent in some nursery schools on non-educative pursuits apart from socialization. . . . examples recently observed are: compulsory listening to stories (except that children do not actually listen when made to sit down and look as if they are): children desultorily looking at rubbishy picture books: constant interruptions of absorbed play, in order to get children to drink milk, change shoes, go outside, wash hands, . . . all could be corrected or eliminated at the cost of more thought about the intentions of nursery education.[10]

Whilst consistency of major routines will help group management, consistency of curriculum is essential to children's learning. If the teacher is to build on a child's past experience she will need to observe the child closely.

The seeing eye can be trained as can most senses, and the more we train ourselves to observe the more we see even when we are not actually making a child-study. Noticing what they really do, how, when and in what order, becomes a habit with the good teacher. Like all habits it can be encouraged by letting the novice practise it frequently. Once established, the ability to look without prejudice, to note detail, to assess a child's pace, needs and strengths makes for realistic goal-setting and consequent success and satisfaction for the child and teacher alike.[11]

The main area of observation will be the child's language. The teacher will want to find out how the child uses language and for what purpose. The Oxford Pre-school Research project team found that 'connected talk', i.e. talk that brings out the child's full linguistic capacities, flourished best when the children were playing in pairs at a pretend game. If the game was played in a place where distraction was avoided and where the children had some privacy, the conversation was 'rich and connected'. Good language was also fostered when a teacher joined a small group of children to participate in their play. Less structured activities, such as large motor-play, produced opportunity for more talking but of less high quality. Rather more difficult is the role of the teacher. Margaret Donaldson reminds teachers that they need to 'de-centre', that is, 'consider imaginatively what [her] words would mean to a small child'.[3] It is also possible for teachers to change their classroom style, and reduce their managerial role so that they have more time for conversation with children. This may be needed because 'Findings do not support the fact that helper parents provide "the conversational gap". Also 2/3 of the children's more elaborated exchanges are not with adults at all, but with other children'.[5] 'Talk is also far more likely to occur with an adult in those tasks involving the putting together of means to reach a goal'.[5]

Good connected talk occurs when the child is engaged on loosely-structured, intellectually undemanding activities (when a child is concentrating hard he is thinking rather than talking). As we have already mentioned, children come to an understanding of language in a real-life context where language and action are mutually supportive. Peter Lloyd found that although pre-school children do not often ask for explanation or further information when they cannot understand something, nevertheless when they were encouraged and shown how to do so, they did ask questions.

Now the principal symbolic system to which the pre-school child has access is oral language. If he can become aware of it, manipulate it, choose what to say, he is not just talking, he is in command of the structure, and is therefore making intellectual advance.[12]

Continuity with the receiving teacher

The NFER study *And so to School* found that the smoothest transitions from pre-school to school were the result of gradual change, when people, places and things were partly familiar and the child felt a sense of security.

In order to ensure such smooth transition the adults involved must liaise closely and yet the same study revealed:

Pre-school staff who do not know what goes on in other provisions, who would like more contact with schools and who feel their opinions are not valued. . . . Infant staff who know nothing of their new entrants' pre-school experience, who regard pre-schools with suspicion, who seem unapproachable to parents and non-professionals, and who are unaware of the cultural customs of their pupils.[6]

Pre-school staff and infant teachers need specific information about each other's provision. They need to be aware of the differences in the daily programme:

By far the most popular mode of operation in pre-schools is for children to have unlimited choice of the available activities while adults supervise or become involved from time to time. In infant classes the most prevalent mode is for children to be engaged in prescribed activities while the teacher is either actively involved with the class as a whole, or is taking the opportunity to hear individuals read or discuss their work while the rest are busy.[6]

Moreover the ratio of adults to children is likely to alter radically once a child enters the main school. Pre-school staff need to observe the reception teacher's day and possibly prepare their older children for certain regimes. The infant teacher also needs to be aware of particularly stressful times for young children when they first start with her. The NFER report observed children reacting unfavourably to being in large groups with few adults in the following ways:

impatience at having to wait for the teacher's attention,
covering the ears to shut out noise,
bewilderment and dismay in mass situations,
failure to respond to instructions given en masse,
inability to keep still and quiet for sustained periods, unwillingness to pool creative work.[6]

The NFER project emphasizes the need for a national move to enable everyone concerned in early childhood education and care to work more closely together. In the meantime teachers need to develop their own initiatives as far as the resources in each school will allow.

Special provision for non-English speaking children and ethnic minorities

Many societies, and Britain is no exception, tend to view the world in an ethnocentric way: people take their own cultural norms as the only possible ones and then use them for judging what may be quite different cultures. The result, of course, is that people from other countries and from minority groups are perceived as different, odd, strange, less virtuous etc. Ethnocentrism is part of the childhood socialization process so the bases for prejudice are available at an early age.[13]

This statement contrasts with the response of headteachers of primary and nursery schools who were confronted with evidence of early racial prejudice in young children.

In their schools, they insisted, matters were quite otherwise. Young children were oblivious of race and the different ethnic groups mixed and played together happily. Where an incident did occur, it was invariably an isolated one and the result of a maladjusted child mindlessly mouthing what he or she had heard at home.[14]

Alf Davey's study provides evidence that

. . . racial and ethnic distinctions are extensively employed by British primary-school children in their attempts to make sense of the world. Moreover, since they are being initiated into an implicitly discriminating society, this early classification process is often accompanied by frank ethnic prejudice.[15]

The teacher needs to be aware that the onus is on her to provide a model of tolerance and genuine interest in people from other races and cultures, in order to help shape her children's attitudes. 'All schools, whether they include children from ethnic minorities or not, should prepare children for life in a multicultural society and help representatives of each culture to appreciate what others can bring to the community.'[15] However, schools which admit children from ethnic minority groups have a special responsibility to receive their families in a manner which they can understand and appreciate and to provide for the children's needs.

The importance of a good self-concept for all children has already been emphasized but this is particularly so for children from ethnic minorities. Alan James, looking at aims towards education for a multi-cultural society, suggests that

> . . . any child growing up in present-day society, and certainly any coloured child, is bound to experience conflicts in the formation of his identity, and in the end he needs to be able to judge the behaviour and works of any human being on their own merits, irrespective of the race or cultural background of that human. So the use of teaching materials which present non-white people as interesting, brave, creative, wise human beings is essential in the education of all children and especially supportive to the self-confidence of ethnic-minority children.[16]

This emphasis means that the teacher should scrutinize all books and apparatus to ensure that they offer a positive view of different cultural groups.

The link with parents is again even more important for schools with a multi-racial catchment area. Immigrant parents are less likely than British parents to know about the British educational system and the ways in which young children learn.

> A research study where 700 immigrant and 400 British heads of households were asked about housing, education and employment suggests that immigrant parents are aspiring for their children. Because of their own lack of information these parents have to rely on what the teachers tell them about schooling and their children's progress.[17]

This places heavy responsibility on schools to work closely with these parents.

The practicalities of such work are not helped by many immigrant parents being involved in shift work and therefore not easily able to come to school. The report of the Committee of Enquiry into the Education of

Children from Ethnic Minority Groups recommends extended community provision for immigrant families. It urges schools

> . . . to 'reach out' to parents by, for example, more teachers under-taking home visiting and by making information on the school's policies more accessible to parents. . . . Other recommendations relate to the need for better co-ordination within local authorities or services for the under-fives, the conversion of former primary school premises for nursery use, the extension of the opening hours of nursery schools and units, the need for those who work with under-fives to be made aware of the particular difficulties faced by West Indian families and the need for there to be more nursery nurses and health visitors from ethnic minority groups.[18]

INDIVIDUAL NEEDS
Whilst parents regard their child as all important, the teacher considers individual needs within the context of the total class. It is impossible to respond to every child's idiosyncrasies but if certain principles are applied they will allow choices to be made, learning needs to be met and extended, and the children's responses to a learning programme to be considered in future planning.

Choice
Choice is not only a question of what children do, but what they do not do. It fosters self-awareness and intellectual self-control; it allows children to pause, consider and reflect. Choice also motivates.

The nursery and reception teacher will be aware that some children need guidance in making choices: again a knowledge of previous home experience is important in determining what level of decisions a child can make. The First School Survey indicates that a low expectation existed in many schools:

> Most of the schools gave the children some contributory role in the school community at least on routine monitorial duties such as milk distribution, tidying up, giving out materials. In a minority of schools the children were encouraged to take some responsibility for choosing an activity or pursuing a programme of work. It was unusual for the children to become self-reliant, or to take responsibility for their own behaviour and work without close supervision. . . . Children's capa-bilities were more likely to be under- rather than over-estimated.[7]

If children are to become both responsible and autonomous they need training and support from the earliest age and the priority the school places on this aspect of development will be reflected in its hidden curriculum.

Meeting and extending learning needs
Teachers recognize that children of the same chronological age may be at

different stages of development. Just as their previous rate of development has been influenced at least partly by environmental factors, so will it continue to be:

> . . . the intellectual development of the child is no clockwork sequence of events; it also responds to influences from the environment, notably the school environment. . . . Experience has shown that it is worth the effort to provide the growing child with problems that tempt him into the next stages of development.[5]

The onus is on the school to provide the best possible environment in which individual children can thrive. We interpret environment here in the broadest sense to include the materials which children use and considerations about how the children and adults use their time.

Sylva, Roy and Painter offer three suggestions for improving school practice:

1 Make the most of materials (activities with clear goal structure). With them, children can progress to complicated schemes in a self-initiated and self-sustaining manner.
2 Encourage children to work in pairs. Teachers do this already because they want children to acquire social skills. They might do it even more, however, as it has been shown to improve the intellectual level of children's play.
3 When staffing permits, encourage the subtle tutorial.[19]

Bruner looks more closely at the activities which are most likely to extend children:

> Those forms of activity which challenge children most have common attributes. They are activities in which there is a goal, a means of achieving that goal and where the child knows what he is doing and can get on without anyone else. He also knows he is making progress. Building, drawing, doing puzzles come into this category. The next category includes sand, dough, pretending, play with small toys. The third category, the least challenging, includes gross motor-play, informal games and general playing about. NB This hierarchy only relates to intellectual challenge, not language development or social play. . . . If we single out those activities most likely to produce high elaboration and concentration in play they are structured construction, art and music, and school readiness tasks.[5]

We do not suggest that the curriculum should consist solely of these activities. Individual children may also require help to compensate for experiences missed and this may include an emphasis on developing physical and social as well as cognitive skills. The child's emotional stability will of course be basic to the development of any of these skills.

Routines
Individual needs are reflected in the children's different responses to classroom routines. Bruner's findings indicate that teachers have over-estimated the child's need for a stable routine.

> Regularity of routine was roughly defined as the amount of repetition of activity at relatively fixed times from day to day – whatever activity constituted the regularity. Regularity might conceivably have a steadying effect on children and thereby increase the richness of their play. It seems, however, to have little or no effect on the children – possibly a slight aid for the younger ones in improving play, but of little magnitude.[5]

Some teachers will find this statement rather sweeping, particularly regarding children who lack stability in home life and who appear to settle under regular regime. However, it certainly suggests that teachers might take a further look at assumptions held about what young children can tolerate in their learning. The daily presence of one teacher is likely to be the most important element for a child starting school.

Starting where the child is
Despite the wealth of information available to parents about early learning and pre-school activities, many young children arrive at school without basic play experience. Some have no opportunity for messy play and development of large motor-skills in their homes. A number of children will have been offered second-hand experiences from television rather than encountering real situations for themselves. Where the teacher is aware that this is happening, every effort to compensate should be made in schools. (There is a danger that schools may be similarly at fault: 'In some schools radio and television were used so much that children's complementary direct experiences were curtailed.'[7]) Children's motivation through real situations should carefully be considered when planning a programme for the youngest age.

The teacher has a difficult task in regarding and providing for her children as individuals and the process requires time and close, rigorous observation. However, when she has assessed a child's needs she should hold fast to her professional judgments which are in the child's interests. This may involve the teacher justifying her decisions to parents: '. . . It has been pointed out to us, albeit with the best intentions, some parents can exert undesirable pressure on teachers to introduce written recording of mathematics, and especially sums, at too early a stage because they believe that the written record is a necessary sign of a child's progress.'[3]

In the main the child's predominantly egocentric stage of development should be recognized and catered for by having few compulsory large-group activities and by giving instructions individually when they first come to school. However, respect for the individual child must be balanced with development of his social awareness. Entry to school means encouragement in the beginning of collective responsibility.

What a child has to learn is frighteningly complicated – yet in large part he must learn it before he is seven. One has only to look at an ordinary infants' school admission class to realize how exceptional is the child who does not know how to behave, and by contrast how very much the rest have learned.[10]

THE CHILD AS A PERSON
Although the teacher's relationship with every child will differ, certain approaches will assist the development of self-esteem and confidence which are the springboard for sound development for all children.

Respecting the child's contribution
One ground rule is to respect the child's contribution rather than to impose an adult viewpoint or standard. Lesley Webb writes:

More subtly non-educative are the magnificent friezes and murals seen in some well-cared for schools. Many of these are quite blatantly teacher products – and 'products' is the only word to use. . . . The children's contributions are minimal in all such cases, but the displays are obviously regarded as a criterion of excellence in that parents are specially invited to see them. . . . What the educators need to ask, however, is what ends are gained by such display? Are the children learning anything worthwhile? Are the parents?[10]

Respect for children's contributions should go hand in hand with a sensitivity for their other personal needs. Dr Mia Kellmer Pringle, formerly Director of the National Children's Bureau, identifies four basic needs:

. . . the need for love and security: for new experiences: for praise and recognition and for responsibility. These needs have to be met from the very beginning of life and continue to require fulfilment to a greater or lesser extent – through adulthood.[20]

Margaret Donaldson suggests that security for a child means 'assessing his skills with sensitivity and accuracy, understanding the level of his confidence and energy and responding to his errors in helpful ways'. She also reminds us of the potency of the teacher's attitudes: 'If we do not genuinely respect and value children, I am afraid they will come to know'.[3]

Encouraging emotional independence
We have already considered the need for children to have new experiences

and to have the responsibility to make choices from an early age. Lesley Webb considers a further aspect of responsibility – the move towards emotional independence:

> This early formed ability to be emotionally independent over a fairly wide area of their lives is one many adults in our society find difficulty in accepting. Five-year-olds, after all, are still largely emotionally dependent on adults, and are certainly not functionally or socially independent. Confusion between their patent immaturity when compared with older children or adults and the very real maturity appropriate to being a well-adjusted five-year-old leads many parents and teachers to give less credit for autonomy to young children than they might. . . . Our guidance, explanations, help in complex situation or matters beyond their physical capacity, and informed intervention to extend their knowledge, can produce a degree of self-directedness among four- and five-year-olds, with decreasing dependence on adults, which may destroy the sentimental images of young children cherished by too many adults.[10]

Emotional independence involves the child being sufficiently confident to cope with his mistakes. We should bear in mind Margaret Donaldson's statement: 'it is also quite clear than an error can play a highly constructive role in the development of thinking'.[3] This approach will help both teacher and child to learn from situations which have 'gone wrong'.

Opportunities for success, praise and recognition
Although mistakes have their positive value, young children do need repeated experiences of success in order to boost their self-confidence.

Behaviour problems
The teacher will want to do what she can for all children but certain individuals pose specific problems from the time they enter school.

> There is much that frustrates, frightens and baffles the growing child just because of his inevitable lack of experience and power. . . . Nor does he know that his frequent feelings of uncertainty, his lack of confidence and his failure to understand adults' reactions, are shared by many, if not most, of his contemporaries. This awareness comes largely with maturity except for the fortunate minority whose parents and teachers have the gift of remembering these feelings and by using their memories, enable the young to cope with them more easily.
>   In one sense then, all children are vulnerable and likely to experience unhappiness and stress. In addition, certain groups are made doubly vulnerable because of the presence of specific, potentially detrimental personal, family or social circumstances. It is such children who should be regarded as being 'at risk'.[20]

Lesley Webb makes the important point that teachers should avoid jumping to conclusions about the reasons for 'difficult behaviour'.

> It is impossible to establish direct causal connections between adverse circumstances X and overt behaviour Y. We know a great deal of damage is done by separating babies and toddlers from their mother, for example, but we cannot say whether the experience will give rise to late aggression, withdrawal, placatory behaviour or pilfering. In some cases it seems to have no adverse effects at all. . . . Similarly, but conversely, it is unwise to assume that one symptom (e.g. pilfering) has always the same kind of cause.[21]

Margaret Wood suggests that 'What is important is that adults should try to adjust their behaviour according to an understanding assessment of the temperament, anxieties, desires, motivations and other characteristics of children'.[22]

This asks a great deal of teachers who have a class of thirty children. However, we return to the central importance of every teacher knowing her children as intimately as possible. This knowledge may prevent her from making glib assumptions and will at least heighten her awareness of the complex nature of the job.

REFERENCES

1 SMITH, T. (1980) *Parents and Pre-school* (Oxford Pre-school Research Project) Grant McIntyre
2 BRIERLEY, J. (1978) *Growing and Learning* Ward Lock Educational
3 DONALDSON, M. (1978) *Children's Minds* Fontana
4 BRUNER, J. (1977) *The Process of Education* Harvard University Press
5 BRUNER, J. (1980) *Under Five in Britain* Grant McIntyre
6 CLEAVE, S., JOWETT, S. and BATE, M. (1982) *And So to School* NFER/Nelson
7 DES (1982) *Education 5–9* (The First School Survey) HMSO
8 NEILL, S. (1982) Open plan or divided space in pre-school? *Education 3–13*, 10, autumn, p.46
9 BLATCHFORD, P., BATTLE, S. and MAYS, J. (1982) *The First Transition* NFER/Nelson
10 WEBB, L. (1974) *Purpose and Practice in Nursery Education* Blackwell
11 WEBB, L. (1976) *Making a Start on a Child-study* Blackwell
12 LLOYD, P. (1975) *Communication in pre-school children* Unpublished study, University of Edinburgh, quoted in 4 above.
13 HICKS, D. (1981) Teaching about other peoples: how biased are school books? *Education 3–13*, 9, autumn, p.14
14 JEFFCOAT, R. (1977) Children's racial ideas and feelings *English in Education* 11, 1, pp.32–46
15 DAVEY, A (1981) Pride and prejudice in the classroom *Education 3–13*, 19, autumn, p.4
16 JAMES, A. (1981) Education for a multi-cultural society: aims for primary and middle school *Education 3–13* 9, spring
17 REX, J. and TOMLINSON, S. (1979) *Colonial Immigrants in a British City* Routledge & Kegan Paul
18 COMMITTEE OF ENQUIRY INTO THE EDUCATION OF CHILDREN FROM ETHNIC MINORITY GROUPS *West Indian Children in Our Schools* (Interim Report) HMSO
19 SYLVA, K., ROY, C. and PAINTER, M. (1980) *Childwatching at Playgroup and Nursery Group* Grant McIntyre
20 KELLMER PRINGLE, M. (1974) *The Needs of Children* Hutchinson
21 WEBB, L. (1975) Children with problems in the infant school *Education 3–13* 3, 2, p.78
22 WOOD, M. (1973) *Children: The Development of Personality and Behaviour* Harrap

IN THE CLASSROOM

PRE-SCHOOL/SCHOOL LIAISON AND CONTINUITY

CATCHMENT AREA

The teacher could get to know the catchment area by taking short walks round it after school or at lunch time, especially if she lives some distance from the school herself. It will help her learn about the type of housing, and the playspace available – and generally find out about the child's environment outside of school.

HOME VISITS

These are controversial but supporters argue that they offer teachers the opportunity to gain real insights into the home environment and its effect on the child. The teacher may wish to announce her intention of making a home visit by means of a letter addressed to the child, prior to offering a place in the nursery or admitting him to the reception class. If she is friendly and flexible and keeps her visit brief she can be reasonably sure of a good reception from parents.

PRE-SCHOOL VISITS

There should be opportunities for the child to visit the school with his peers from the nursery or playgroup and with his parents. Teachers will find it useful to note the children's reactions to these visits.

WELCOME PARTIES

It is helpful to provide one session when parents are invited into school without their children. If it is a daytime visit, a short-term playgroup could perhaps be set up and manned by a group of parents. Evening functions do mean that fathers are more likely to attend. Such an occasion is a chance to offer verbal information to parents, to show them around the building and to include an informal discussion period to answer queries over coffee. The aim is to make the session a social and leisured occasion, with sufficient members of staff available to talk to parents individually, and encourage them to feel that the school is geared to meeting their particular needs. Childminders should be invited if the parents are unable to come. It is also helpful to have welcome occasions in school, such as family assemblies when other members of the family are particularly invited to look at the school and, perhaps, at a special project.

INVITATIONS TO SCHOOL EVENTS

Parents and pre-school children will appreciate an invitation to a special school assembly or Christmas play. The invitations can be written and decorated by older children or siblings in the school. Such events give a 'taste' of the school and are tremendously exciting for a youngster about to make his entry into school life. In rural areas transport may need to be arranged. Parents are generally happy to offer lifts if the school approaches them.

WRITTEN INFORMATION

Having met the requirements for offering written information to parents, it is as well to remember that nothing can take the place of the personal approach (see Chapter 6, p.239).

If circulars are sent to parents, be prepared for many of them not to be read: they need to backed up with identical information on a school noticeboard prominently sited for parents.

It often helps to have another member of staff read through any letter sent to parents just to check that the information offered is clear and unambiguous, and that the approach is friendly and helpful.

LIAISON WITH OTHER PERSONNEL

Health visitors, social workers and playgroup supervisors are all involved with pre-school children. If the information they have about children and families is offered and received in a truly professional spirit it can only be beneficial to all concerned. Regular contact – perhaps a monthly liaison meeting at the school over a cup of coffee – will help easy communication.

HEALTH

Back-up services

Liaison with the medical services and regular contact with health visitors in particular will help to alert the school to any problems before the child is admitted.

Children with special needs

These children must have an appropriate school placement. If a child suffers from a physical disability the school should ensure that there are sufficient resources to cope with his needs before accepting him, e.g. ancillary help, ramps for wheel chairs. If not the child may be forced to leave the school because subsequently the teacher finds that she cannot cope.

Information from parents

Parents sometimes find it difficult to be totally frank about their child's health problems for fear of stigmatization (this is so particularly where there is a history of enuresis or convulsions). Personal discussion can help, together with the knowledge that any information given is in total confidence. In a relaxed, leisurely conversation, parents and teacher will be able to talk frankly with the common aim of helping the child with any difficulties.

PREVIOUS EXPERIENCE

Discussions with parents
Individual discussions with parents should be useful for both parties. The teacher's questions will help parents to consider both positive and negative attributes of their child's development, and they may welcome advice on developing individual strengths and helping with weaknesses. A good relationship established with parents at this early stage will reap dividends for the future.

Teacher's visits to nurseries and playgroups
Personal contact or a telephone call to arrange such a visit helps to break the ice and make the initial visit friendly – but brief! Most groups will welcome such contact for the benefit of the children concerned.

Visits by playgroup and nursery personnel to school
Playgroup supervisors, matrons and nursery teachers could be invited to the school for a semi-social occasion – this could develop into a regular termly event. Aim for them to see the school in session, if possible, in order for them to identify different practices and see how their children have progressed. Once the relationship has been formed future liaison time can be taken up with discussion of specific issues. Discussion of individual children must of course be confidential.

In-service training for pre-school groups
The teacher may be able to offer the groups specific advice about the relevant educational activities for the children, for example how to extend play provision (see p.34). Organizational help may be welcomed too. Playgroup personnel sometimes do not appreciate their own important role in the child's learning; they may be trying to spread themselves amongst the whole group and need encouragement to focus on developing language with a small group of children. If such suggestions on provision and organization are made tactfully they will usually be well received!

RESOLVING DIFFICULTIES
1 It will be difficult for some teachers working in particularly demanding areas to remember the many and various requests made by parents about individual arrangements for their children. It helps to write down all messages and routines.
2 Flexible reception and dismissal times (e.g. staggered over fifteen minutes) allow a leisurely welcome and farewell to be offered to children.
3 There needs to be a clear school policy on administration of medicines. If children are to be given drugs in school it is helpful to have a set time of day for this (e.g. at the end of the morning). Other precautions are to accept only one day's dosage at a time, and insist that all medicines are named and labelled.

INFORMATION FOR PARENTS

Parents' and children's reception
Addressing the parents by name whenever possible will help make them feel individually welcome. Many parents are shy and may well have unhappy memories of 'school'. Some mothers may feel the separation from their child very keenly, particularly if it is the last well-loved child of a large family. So however rushed the teacher feels, she should try and present a calm, unhurried front. It helps to be in the classroom, well established, some little while before the first child and parent may be expected to arrive. Try not to allow one person to monopolize this time; talkative parents can distract the teacher from the children. Skill in handling parents at the beginning and end of the sessions grows with experience.

The environment
It is better for parents to see their child's classroom for the first time when it is empty. They can then wander round, get to know the room, and be shown the toilets, pegs and areas for the lunch boxes and drinks.

A personal introduction to the teacher
Parents like to meet their child's first teacher at an early opportunity. If she wears a name badge she can be easily identified and parents will see how to spell her name. If the teacher is meeting a group of new parents she may like to offer a little information about her background and interests. This helps parents to see her as a person, which can be reassuring.

Continuity in the classroom

SECURITY OF ORGANIZATION

Records
These should be kept in a prominent place for any supply teacher. Information required immediately will need to be brief and identify key points of daily organization. Particular notes should be kept of routines for enabling calm management of children and details of any children with special needs.

Routines
Any supply teacher is advised to keep the routines (not necessarily the activities) simple and straightforward to maintain security.

Names
Children's names should be learnt as quickly as possible. They can be written on stick-on labels and attached to a jumper or dress.

Staffing
It may be advisable to deploy an experienced member of staff to work in a

temporary capacity with the youngest children, even if this means having a supply teacher for her own class.

MAINTAINING GOOD PRACTICE

As parents see their child thriving as a member of his class their respect for the teacher will grow. The school needs to encourage as many occasions as possible for maintaining parent-teacher contact. The children will enjoy hosting their parents on many of these occasions.

There might be a school policy to remember special family occasions, e.g. a card for a new baby, a letter for a sick child, a card for father in hospital.

CONSISTENCY IN THE CURRICULUM

Observation

The teacher needs to observe the children very carefully, particularly at the point of entry to the school. All activity for developing further learning will be based in the child's past experiences and present capabilities. Observation of the child's play and level of language will help the teacher make the most appropriate provision.

Listening to children talk also helps a teacher to judge just what they are learning from the experiences that she has provided. She will also assess children's progress by observing their actions. The child's responses will indicate among other things just how much he has understood of requests and instructions given to him. Recent studies have shown that children under five often fail to undertake a task, not because they are unable to, but because they cannot understand the adult's use of language.[3] Michael made a beautiful Meccano construction on his first day at school. The teacher was thrilled. 'Oh that's lovely Michael,' she said, and chatted to him about it. It was time to pack up. 'Now, can you take it to pieces?' Michael looked puzzled. 'No,' he said. 'I don't know who she is.'

The role of language

The child's use of language is a major tool of learning. Joan Tough (1976) has ably demonstrated how the teacher's own language and questioning strategies will assist a child who, in his response, will take a further step in his language. The teacher's provision should include plenty of pretend play, arranged in pairs, preferably in a small, partly-enclosed place where there will be no interruptions. She can encourage children to work with her putting out the painting equipment, getting the room ready for a selected activity, or putting flowers in water so that there is a goal to be achieved together. Children also need to be able to work at a challenging activity without having their train of thought interrupted by speech. Such interruptions are not only discourteous, they are also counter-productive.

Active participation in children's play (for example, becoming the model at the hairdresser's) should occupy some part of the teacher's day. If she can organize her time and resources so that managerial tasks and the associated administrative speech (requests, commands) are limited, this will free her for genuine reciprocal conversations with children. Such conversations cannot always be provided by parents. She needs to see if children understand the meanings of words outside the context of stories, i.e. in other situations. The children will need plenty of environmental clues if they do not appear to understand. At the same time the teacher needs to see the spoken word from the child's point of view, grasp what it is they do not understand and show them ways of asking for more information. For example, when children bring the class register to the school office and stand with it in their hand looking a little lost, they need to be shown how to ask if they should wait or go straight back to the class.

Children need gentle correction when they make errors – e.g. 'I done it'. This approach needs to be discussed amongst the whole staff and a consensus reached. Constant correction is debilitating and unnecessary but reflecting on meanings of words, substituting words, even sharing jokes about words and their meanings (all of which are greatly enjoyed by young children) are ways of looking at language in a 'disembedded' way.

Continuity with the receiving teacher

EXCHANGE AGE-GROUPS

One of the most effective ways of getting to know about provision and approach for another age-group is to observe an experienced teacher in the classroom and then to work with that age-group oneself. It may be possible for infant and nursery teachers to exchange posts for a short time. Clearly this must be carefully organized so as to avoid upsetting the children, but the insights offered to both teachers as a result will be considerable.

EXCHANGE VISITING

Exchange visits between receiving teachers and playgroup leaders could focus on practical activities and routines. For example the teacher might sit in on a story-telling session at a playgroup and use a similar approach when the children first come to school.

SCHOOL POLICY

School staffs may find it useful to discuss a school policy on children's behaviour and provision of continuity in classroom routines (e.g. are children to wash their own paintbrushes after use or leave them in/by the pots?). Young children cannot be expected to adapt easily to wide variations in procedures imposed by different adults.

VISITS

By the time children move to another class they should be reasonably familiar with the geography of the building, and visits may be arranged to the new room. This can be on an individual basis (e.g. message carrying), on a group basis (to join a class story) or the whole class might visit to see a play.

ESTABLISHING RAPPORT

The receiving teacher needs to establish a rapid rapport with her new group of children. It will help greatly if, with the aid of visits to the previous class, discussions with the child's previous teacher and her own vigilant observations, she can compile a piece of personal information about each child in the class, e.g. their favourite activity, where they live, the name of their brother and sister. This personal link can reassure the child and help him to settle in and continue his pattern of learning without undue disruption.

Special provision for non-English speaking children and ethnic minorities

Teachers need to be sensitive to the diverse cultural needs of all children but certain points need to be considered when dealing with immigrant and minority groups.

ENCOURAGING POSITIVE SELF-IMAGE

The teacher's relationship with the child is all-important in developing his positive self-image. She needs to take care in pronouncing his name correctly, and to find out something of his home background and his interests, if possible before he starts school. The effective starting-point for learning is when the child reveals something of himself to the teacher.

Photographs on display of people from the child's ethnic group may be used for conversation, and books depicting family life in ethnic minority groups should be available.

USING OTHER PARENTS

On admission, mothers of children from the same ethnic group who have been at school for some time may act as hostesses and interpreters for new parents. These mothers may also be prepared to talk with small groups of staff about their lifestyle and cultural traditions in order to alert teachers to differing expectations.

SOCIAL ARRANGEMENTS

The teacher needs to ensure that children are familiar with arrangements for going to the lavatory and for undressing for PE and swimming. It is important that the child is at ease with these social arangements. Sensitive 'pairing' with another child who can help him may be useful but the teacher still needs to keep an eye on the newcomer.

DUAL LANGUAGE

Many multi-racial parents expect to communicate their own traditions and language to their children and young children generally adapt to learning two languages. In order to aid continuity, occasional school notices, letters and displays could be offered to parents in their own language. (Beware displays that include pigs and cows as these will be offensive to certain ethnic groups.)

CONTACT WITH PARENTS

Contact with parents is essential, particularly during the child's initial curriculum during the early years and this will need careful explanation and demonstration. Again it is helpful to use supportive parents of the same nationality to act as ambassadors for the school.

If the children are engaged in cooking activities they could compare their native dishes and invite parents in to help. Alternatively mothers may be persuaded to prepare national dishes to offer on a social occasion at school. A recognition of non-Christian festivals to which parents are invited may also prove a successful contact point.

THE ROLE OF OUTSIDE AGENCIES

The teacher will need to rely on co-workers in order to provide a framework of support and elicit co-operation from some new families. Community workers, pre-school liaison and a range of community activities encouraging parents to familiarize themselves with the school building and personnel will help to establish a good rapport.

THE ROLE OF THE TEACHER

The teacher herself needs to become acquainted with the lifestyle, expectations and values of the community in order to develop a positive relationship with children. She needs to know, for example, the expectations for boys and girls and differing hygiene and eating customs. Some authorities have exchange schemes for teachers: others arrange reasonably priced trips abroad.

INDIVIDUAL NEEDS

Choice

EQUIPMENT

All necessary apparatus and equipment will need to be easily accessible if the child is to select his resources for learning, e.g. low open shelves with apparatus colour-coded for easy identification.

CREATIVE ACTIVITIES

Creative activities should allow the child to make varying choices about the use and type of materials, e.g. collage work with a range of materials, painting paper in a range of sizes, shapes and colours.

PHYSICAL INDEPENDENCE

Physical independence is important. It is worth checking that the child can attach paper to an easel using clothes pegs, that he can fasten his own painting apron with strips of velcro, that he can hang his completed painting to dry over a low clothes-line.

CHOOSING ACTIVITIES

Plan the session to enable the child to make choices about his use of time and selection of activity. This needs to be done gradually if the child is not used to an enriched environment, e.g. he might start by choosing whether or not to join in music or story sessions.

SNACKS
If a mid-morning snack is provided on a self-service basis the children can pour the amount of milk or squash they wish to drink rather than be expected to consume a standard measure.

DISPLAYS
Children can be consulted about displays, e.g. which children's work is going to be pinned up on the wall and which backing paper will be used.

OTHER CHOICES
Children can help to decide what bulbs to buy for planting, where to go for a local walk, what food to have for a summer picnic or Christmas party. After a discussion a majority vote can be accepted.

PLAYTIME
If staff supervision allows, children can choose whether to stay indoors or to go outside at playtimes.

Meeting and extending learning needs

FOLLOW THE CHILD'S RESPONSES
Children are very adept at meeting what they believe to be the wishes of adults and this can be a problem when the teacher is trying to assess the child for herself. The chances of receiving a genuine response from a child are much greater if the teacher has established an environment which offers respect for all ideas and where time is given to individual children.

1 It is often useful for the teacher to check how children respond to her instructions or suggestions to make sure that they understand what was required of them. An alternative is to ask one child to tell another about the activity that the group are involved in; the teacher can then check if the child has grasped the situation.
2 Teachers' requests can be aimed at provoking thinking responses from children: for example, prayers can be varied by suggesting that a different child (or group) think of something to focus on each week.
3 Children sometimes throw red herrings during group stories or discussions. The teacher can sometimes see the child's logic, develop the point he is making and weave back to the original topic, if appropriate. Obviously there are times when these diversions have to be ignored in order to maintain group control and complete a teaching point, but the teacher may find the opportunity to refer to the interruption later and to talk privately with the boy or girl.
4 Home interests can be integrated with classroom learning. For

example, a child may be excited at the prospect of his dad buying a new car. He can be encouraged to collect pictures of various cars, sort and classify them, or give a list of criteria for purchasing a car.

PROBLEM-SOLVING
1 Very young children are capable of thinking through situations, and enjoy tackling questions like 'What would you do if you lost mummy in a shop?'; 'What can you do to help mummy if she is very busy at home?'
2 A small group of children can be encouraged to create their own stories, with the teacher's help.
3 The teacher will need to be sensitive to the child's level of questioning: if he does not know the answer, she and the child can investigate together.

FILL IN THE GAPS IN EXPERIENCE
1 Children who have had little experience of sedentary activities at home will take longer to adjust to them in school.
2 The teacher needs first to identify if a weakness is due to lack of ability or lack of experience. A broad range of materials should then provide for all levels of development. For example, a newly-admitted child may simply make coloured splodges on paper when painting, while another child of the same age may be able to handle a finer brush, paying attention to form, colour, and the spatial arrangements on the page.
3 It is not always possible to teach children individually when the teacher has a large group and the demands on her time and energies are heavy. However, a small group of children can cluster around one child's interest (say, spiders) and in this way the teacher can fulfil an individual child's demands while drawing in other children at the same time. If she notices a learning gap – perhaps a child who does not understand relative position and cannot grasp the idea of 'behind' – she can weave this into her storytime and drama using, for example, *The Tale of the Turnip*, again meeting individual needs while handling a larger group.

DEVELOP PLAY IN THE PLAYGROUND
1 The younger children benefit if they can have a separate playtime from the other children in school.
2 In some schools teachers may prefer to make their own arrangements for playtimes. If they accompany their own class outside as and when a natural break occurs in the session they are in a good position to observe the informal interactions in the playground. Consistent social groupings and 'loners' can be noted. Some play can be encouraged in pairs.

DEVELOP PLAY IN THE CLASSROOM
1 Fantasy play reveals a great deal about individual needs. A well-resourced imaginative play area needs to be made available to as many of the children as possible during the course of the day.
2 A student could observe play while the teacher is involved elsewhere. Only well-socialized children play cooperatively. Children should be

noted who regularly cause friction in the play area.

EXTEND THE CHILD PHYSICALLY

Depending on their stage of development and opportunities for practice, some four-year-olds are well-developed and physically co-ordinated. These children need challenging physical experiences both inside and outside: the climbing frame should be sufficiently high and complex; a varied obstacle race can be set up, and they need opportunities for constructing with large, heavy apparatus, e.g. large planks and bricks, milk crates and barrels.

EXTEND THE CHILD SOCIALLY

1 Small groups of children could be taken shopping. One or two of the more confident children can be encouraged to undertake a simple transaction in the local shop, e.g. buying sweets for the party, food for the hamster.

2 The underconfident child needs a stress-free situation in which he can relax and express himself, both in language and by other means. This does not necessarily involve a one-to-one relationship with an adult – some children are more likely to communicate when approached in a very small group and talk may be encouraged whilst they are engaged in some practical activity, e.g. clay, collage. A reticent child may respond to friendly conversation but retreat from straight questioning.

EXTEND THE CHILD INTELLECTUALLY

1 *Sensory experiences* Tasting, smelling, visual and tactile experiences should involve progression, e.g. increasingly fine distinctions in matching tactile cards, appreciation of the range of shades of one colour.

2 *Reading* There is no law about the age of five years being the time to start reading. Whilst any environment for young children will provide a range of pre-reading activities, often there are inhibitions about initiating a reading scheme. If individual learning needs are to be met, the chances are that some under-fives will be ready to embark on a reading book.

3 *Information* Children acquire a considerable amount of hard information through the media. Sustained and elaborate conversations may develop as a result of children sharing experiences of last night's television programme. Bearing in mind the children's increased knowledge, the teacher needs to look critically at her own approach to some curriculum content to note how much of it is quickly becoming outdated and inaccurate (e.g. farming techniques).

4 *Play* Further challenges may be offered by providing new materials or a change in organization, e.g. supply string, rubber bands and Plasticine for more adventurous brick building; put the bricks on an incline or split level.

STRUCTURE SITUATIONS FOR SPECIAL NEEDS

1 *Physical skills* PE sessions offer a chance to observe children's gross motor movements. Particular activities such as balancing, throwing and

catching, hopping, will need to be practised regularly by children with poor co-ordination.

2 *Communication skills* Some individuals require considerable time with one adult before communication can be established and their particular route to learning identified. An ancillary helper or parent, if briefed carefully, may be able to help here.

3 *Social skills* We need to distinguish between shy and withdrawn children. With shy children it may be just a question of waiting to approach a child at an appropriate moment and of maintaining contact, even if just a touch, or eye contact, and a smile.

Whilst it is unwise to 'jolly' a child into large group activities, it can be helpful to look for a practical way of making that child accepted by his peers. This may be done by giving him a special task in the class or requesting his help with a newcomer in the group.

4 *Aggressive children* These children always feel inadequate in some way and the secret is to develop their self-esteem so that their anti-social behaviour becomes unnecessary. Responsibility for specific tasks in school may help, together with as much personal attention as the teacher can manage. Again, skilled voluntary help may be able to assist. Apart from this, clear limits to behaviour tolerated need to be communicated to the child. The fewer rules the easier it is to be consistent.

Routines
Whilst most children thrive on a routine they will quickly become bored if there is not sufficient variety in the organization to provoke thought and challenge. It is wise to review the routine monthly, and note the effect of any change.

CURRICULUM
If possible a new item should be included at least once a week in sessions for jingles and rhymes, and a regular supply of new stories – to be read, told, sung, accompanied by visual aids and music.

TIME
Time is precious – it is wasted by lengthy daily routines when children are waiting for things to happen.

REGISTER
Formal register taking with very young children is unnecessary – a silent head-count after school has started is sufficient.

QUEUES
These can mean that a number of children waste time waiting for everyone to be ready. When possible children should be encouraged to move freely to the toilets, to the outside play area and to have their mid-morning snack when they choose.

STIMULUS
Visits to other colleagues' classrooms, both in the teacher's school and other schools, help to bring a fresh eye to routine.

Starting where the child is

MOTIVATE CHILDREN THROUGH 'REAL' SITUATIONS
1 Make use of natural resources, such as an approaching thunderstorm. draw the children's attention to the sky (colour, clouds); the stillness in the trees and bushes; the drop in the temperature.
2 Present children with complete experiences. When cooking, for example, they can buy ingredients, bake them and then eat them!
3 Offer them the chance to get to know something in depth: e.g. 'close your eyes and *feel* a shell. *Look* at it through a microscope. *Listen* to it.'
4 Make familar activities complex and varied.
Water play
Colour the water by
    using food dye
    immersing coloured tissue or crêpe paper in the water. How does this
    affect the water when compared with other forms of colouring?
Perfume the water.
Vary the temperature of the water, e.g. by providing warm water and letting the children add ice cubes to it.
Play situations with water
    Washing dolls and dolls' clothes.
    Fishing game, using coloured water, seaside shells and pebbles. Cut out fish from rigid plastic (or pieces of old hotwater bottle), attach paperclips, and make fishing rods complete with small magnets.
    Window cleaning or painting with water, using decorators' brushes and buckets of water.
    Sailing boats, a selection of home-made and commercial ones. Encourage the children to make their own and experiment to see how effective they are in the water.
Home corner
Turn the home corner into a hospital, dental surgery, shop, hairdresser's, office, post office. These adaptations are quickly made if 'instant kits' are kept with essential props. An office, for example, would need an old typewriter, stationery, carbon paper, paper clips, split pins, rubber stamper, sheets of home-made stamps (paper perforated by a sewing machine), in-tray, etc.

AVOID BEING PRESSURIZED
1 Parents need to understand the significance of all classroom activity. This will involve continuous dialogue and workshop activities run for the parents.
2 Young children do not always need to record with paper and pencil – paintings and constructions are just as valid.

3 The children may not want to record the same experience through various media – once they have had the experience, they will not necessarily want to paint or write about it.

GETTING TO KNOW EACH CHILD
1 The teacher should consciously think about each child (or half the class then the other half) each week/two weeks at a given time.
2 Unwelcome responses which spring from logical thought and contingent circumstances (e.g. Would you like to come for a story? No.) should be accepted. If the child does not accept his invitation, are alternative arrangements available?

PREPARING THE CHILD FOR COLLECTIVE RESPONSIBILITY
1 Collective responsibility can be developed by group enterprises, e.g. joint paintings and collages; group collaboration when making dough, mixing paints and clearing away; group puppet shows.
2 When the children act as host to their parents on a public occasion in school, they can be encouraged to show them class and group achievements.
3 Sometimes children feel distress or tenderness for their peers but need an adult to show them ways of translating this into action, e.g. 'Karen is crying. She has lost her shoe. Peter, you help her. Look in the porch first.'

THE CHILD AS A PERSON

Respecting the child's contribution
1 Respect for children's work will be conveyed by the teacher accepting their unaided contributions and using her skill to mount and display them attractively.
2 Constant correction is disheartening but the teacher needs to try to shape a child's response over a period of time.
3 Appreciation of genuine efforts at tidying up is more important for the child than a rigid adherence to a standard.
4 In cases where responses are totally unacceptable and other children are in danger of being influenced (e.g. violence towards other children) it is as well to talk about the problem frankly with the parent.
5 The children need to have someone who will listen to their questions carefully and provide a considered response.

LOVE AND SECURITY
1 It helps to have a child's name on his peg, together with a photograph, if possible.
2 The carpet area needs to be sufficient for all the group – every child should have enough space.
3 Heavy self-closing doors and crowded cloakrooms may alarm small children.
4 If the child has an accident he must feel sure of a quick, helpful response from his teacher (e.g. dry clothing if he has wet his pants).

5 Fixed points in the day offer security. A familiar beginning to a group story often helps to set the right atmosphere for young children, e.g. 'And now you shall hear my story'.

6 Each child needs time and the knowledge that his teacher has some time for him when his concerns are of prime importance.

7 Asking for and exchanging information, rather than a language examination, will develop a balanced conversation with a child.

8 Children need to be dressed appropriately for the weather so it is helpful to have a school stock of spare mackintoshes, boots etc.

Encouraging emotional independence

MISTAKES

1 The child needs forgiveness and understanding when he makes mistakes. This does not mean 'never mind'. If a child knocks over paint, he can be helped to clear up the mess, and to discuss why the accident happened and how it could best be avoided. If the same child paints in the next few days, and if all goes well, he deserves congratulations on managing his tools. If the accident has put him off painting, he may need to be gently encouraged to try again.

2 Mistakes in thinking or handling material can be turned into constructive opportunities. For example if a child puts too much water in the paint (a common complaint) the children can discuss the options: add more paint, pour away some of the water, use a bigger paint brush, share with someone else.

INDEPENDENT THINKING

1 Children need to be encouraged to have confidence in their own opinion rather than just offering the teacher the answer she wants. In turn the teacher needs to be aware of asking loaded questions.

Opportunities for success, praise and recognition

1 Initial careful observations should enable the teacher to assess the child's self-management skills. From this point it should be possible to teach him informally how to button his coat, put on his wellingtons etc. through a detailed breakdown of each skill. Aim for the child to achieve something new on a regular basis.

2 Children can acquire these skills by doing things with their teacher rather than having them done for them. So long as both the teacher and child are right/left handed it is best to help him from behind when fastening buttons, doing up zips etc.

3 A large cardboard shoe shape with lace holes and a long lace is good for tying practice.

4 The least able group of children in the class need to have at least one successful experience during the course of a week which is publicly recognized, e.g. tidying up, arranging flowers, taking a message, fetching a book.

Behaviour problems

Most behaviour problems arise because a child lacks self-esteem. The general preventative rule is to help each child feel more adequate as a person through personal attention, offering real responsibility and showing faith in that child's capabilities. However, this is not·a recipe for total success, and some setbacks are bound to arise.

AGGRESSION

Difficult though it might be the aggressive child desperately needs to receive consistent, calm treatment. Disapproval must be shown towards aggressive incidents, but once this is made clear the incident can be regarded as over and the child given a task to keep him well occupied, with the opportunity of receiving praise.

SHOUTING

A noisy home and the habit of shouting causes some children to shout when they are playing in school. It is a difficult problem, but some success can be achieved by periods of individual rather than group play; offering a special absorbing task with a definite conclusion (e.g. arranging items on a grid, ordering, jigsaws) and using every means available to break the habit, plus quiet praise after a quiet interlude.

WILD BEHAVIOUR

This can occur as a reaction to rigid or unfamiliar discipline, or if the limits of behaviour are not communicated clearly to the child. Expectations need to be made clear, but there also need to be plenty of opportunities for excess energy and aggression to be let loose legitimately.

PILFERING

Pilfering is not a moral issue with such young children. The teacher needs to be quite sure about what the child is pilfering and what he is doing with the pilfered articles, in order to deal with the situation. Let the children legitimately take school things home and, when appropriate, bring home things to school. There should be a school policy about toys, birthday presents and other items.

WITHDRAWN BEHAVIOUR

Some children are naturally quiet and retiring; others seem to put up a barrier against the world. The teacher needs to keep in touch with this type of child by eye contact, physical touch and casual comments. It is better to avoid trying to involve him directly, but instead be aware of any sign of his uneasy involvement in school life – his activity may indicate more than verbal communication could at this stage.

APPRAISAL QUESTIONS

PRE-SCHOOL/SCHOOL LIAISON AND CONTINUITY
What means do I have to become informed about relevant aspects of a child's past experiences?
Could I devise a better system for obtaining this information?
How do I use this information in my planning and provision for individual children?
Is there any evidence that provision for settling children into the nursery classroom is inadequate? If so, how could this provision be improved?
Is the receiving teacher sufficiently familiar with my children by the time they enter her class?
Is the receiving teacher sufficiently familiar with the approach in my class to enable her to build upon this?
How familiar am I with the approach in the receiving classroom?
How do I use this information when planning my own programme?

INDIVIDUAL NEEDS
What measures do I take to make each child's introduction to the nursery personal to him?
What provision have I made for the most able child in the nursery?
What provision have I made for the least able?
In planning my work have I made provision for other named children intellectually and/or socially?
What activity/regimes have I set up specifically to meet these needs? Are they successful?
Have I discussed individual children with colleagues and asked their advice?
Is there any child about whom I know very little?

THE CHILD AS A PERSON
How many tasks set out below have I tackled today that children could have tackled just as competently?
1 preparing and clearing up activities
2 curricula tasks, e.g. coping with cookery
3 sending and delivering messages
4 personal and social skills, e.g. buttoning coats.

What decisions are my children encouraged to make about
1 the activities they select
2 the materials they use
3 how they use their time
4 when they go to the lavatory

5 when they have a mid-morning snack
6 playing inside or outside?

What activities do I make compulsory for the children?
How do I justify these activities in terms of their value to individuals?

FURTHER RESOURCES

BOOKS

BASHAM, M. (1981) *Starting School* Longman
An excellent book for headteachers to offer parents.

BLATCHFORD P., BATTLE, S. and MAYS, J. (1982) *The First Transition* NFER/Nelson
Report of the research project *Transition from Home to Pre-school* undertaken by the NFER.

CLEAVE, S., JOWETT, S. and BATE, M. (1982) *And So to School* NFER/Nelson
Report of the research project for NFER which looked at the transition from home, nursery and playgroup to school.

CURTIS, A. and WIGNALL, M. (1981) *Early Learning* Macmillan
A ring-bound folder which provides a practical approach to assessing and fostering children's all-round development.

DONALDSON, M. (1978) *Children's Minds* Fontana
Essential reading for anyone concerned with how young children learn.

HICKS, D. W. (1981) *Minorities* Heinemann Educational
A teacher's resource book for the multi-ethnic curriculum.

SYLVA, K., ROY, C. and PAINTER, M. (1980) *Childwatching at Playgroup and Nursery School* Grant McIntyre
Part of the Oxford Pre-school Research Project, this book shows how the structure of pre-school time and setting affects how children benefit from the experience. It includes suggestions for applying research techniques to individual classes.

TIZARD, B., MORTIMER, J. and BURCHELL, B. (1981) *Involving Parents in Nursery and Infant Schools* Grant McIntyre
This book offers both an historical perspective on parental involvement and many practical examples of how to achieve it.

TOUGH, J. (1976) *Listening to Children Talking*; (1979) *Talking and Learning*; (1980) *Talk for Teaching and Learning*; (1981) *A Place for Talk* (Schools Council Communication Skills in Early Childhood Project) Ward Lock Educational
Research aiming to promote the teacher's role in developing language skills in young children. The books are more valuable than the videos.

WEBB, L. (1976) *Making a Start on a Child-study* Blackwell
Practical suggestions for observing children.

HOME/SCHOOL LINK SCHEMES

OPEN UNIVERSITY PARENTHOOD COURSES *The Pre-School Years: The Child 5−10 years*
Videos, cassettes and book for parents and workers involved with this age-group. These may be useful as a focus for discussion at parents' groups.

2

VIEWS OF THE CURRICULUM

INTRODUCTION

VIEWS OF THE CURRICULUM

The curriculum is central to the life and work of the school. It includes:

1 Formal learning (how to read, how to manipulate numbers, how to express ideas in language, how to throw and catch a ball, how to swim etc.). This is the content of the curriculum in terms of knowledge to be acquired. The content of the curriculum will vary, depending on the abilities of the children, the expertise of the teacher, the aspirations of the parents or the expectations of the education authority.
2 Intellectual skills (listening, observing, reflecting, making deductions, formulating and solving problems, testing hypotheses). This aspect of the curriculum is concerned with the presentation of the content, classroom methods, child development, and timing.
3 The 'hidden curriculum', i.e. the ethos of the school – sympathy, sensitivity, self-discipline, humour, tolerance can be nurtured or quashed by the unspoken but powerful messages conveyed by the 'hidden' curriculum.

These three areas are interrelated, but taken as a whole they are the bedrock on which all learning is based. Any worthwhile curriculum must include all of them.

First schools, because they are reasonably sized, examination free and group- rather then subject-based, with organizational patterns which can respond quickly and sensitively, are in a good position to plan curricula for children which really develop every aspect of growth. This is one of the strengths of the first school and the delight of teachers working in them.

However, no coherent curricular decisions can be made unless they are underpinned by a rationale for working. The Warnock Report offers an excellent example of a general statement of aims:

> First to enlarge a child's knowledge, experience and imaginative understanding, and thus his awareness of moral values and capacity for enjoyment: and secondly to enable him to enter the world after formal education is over as an active participant in society and a responsible contributor to it, capable of achieving as much independence as possible.[1]

All schools are now required to provide a general statement of aims, from which specific objectives arise. These objectives are thoughtfully put together by whole school staffs but there is a feeling of unease among first school teachers because the 'aims and objectives' model of the curriculum emphasizes the gap between theory and practice, when in fact it should be bringing the two aspects closer together: 'For many teachers aims are one thing and practice is quite another'.[2] Cockcroft advises: 'Because it is easy for long-term aims to become overlooked as a result of the day-to-day pressures of the classroom, all teachers need to review the aims of their teaching regularly in order to discover whether these aims are being fulfilled within the classroom or whether they are giving way to other more limited and unintended aims.'[3]

There are several reasons why this is so. First of all, aims, objectives, presentational techniques and resources are parts of a whole and need to be seen as such. The First School Survey states: 'Good guidelines contain basic aims and specific objectives, clearly defined indicators of progression and detailed suggestions as to how the work might be developed.'[4] Problems of organization or presentation cannot be referred back easily to aims so that the curriculum is made up of separate parts rather then interlinking sections. An interactive rather than a one-way linear design is appropriate for a first school because this reflects the nature of the work.

Secondly, the aims and objectives model does not go into fine detail.

In mathematics about two-thirds of the schools had guidelines that were not supportive, sometimes because of the general nature of the statement and its lack of detail in indicating sequential stages, progression to be sought, practical experiences to be included and resources available. Fewer than half of the guidelines for language indicated possible stages of progression and even when there was a reference to this it was confined to progress through the reading scheme.[4]

Thirdly, much of the work in a first school arises out of everyday occurrences. The skill of the teacher is shown in the way she can relate children's concerns and interests to an agreed curriculum. To do this she must either carry in her head an intelligent summary of what has been decided and consult the curriculum document from time to time as an *aide-mémoire*, or she must make her day-to-day planning an integral part of the curriculum. In practice she does both. Therefore the curriculum document needs to be written at varying levels: some concise statements the teacher can keep in her head, and some more detailed sections which she can refer to and annotate.

The First School Survey states categorically: 'There were many instances where guidelines were not used or were generally not supportive.'[4] Perhaps curriculum guidelines are not being used because the 'aims and objectives' curriculum model they refer to is not appropriate for first schools. We therefore suggest replacing it with a set of 'first principles' which should help teachers weld together intention and reality. We have drawn up the following list but school staffs may well want to add to it.

1 Acquiring knowledge is basic to the curriculum.
2 Acquiring knowledge involves growth in the learner.

3 Curriculum content needs to be matched to the pupil's stage of development.
4 Learning opportunities need to be matched to individual needs of the children and curriculum content.
5 Progress in all three areas of the curriculum – content, intellectual skills and affective learning – needs to be monitored and evaluated and written records kept.

1 ACQUIRING KNOWLEDGE IS BASIC TO THE CURRICULUM

In British infant schools the *content* of the curriculum, i.e. the actual *knowledge* to be acquired, is not dictated from a central source but is agreed upon by all the teachers in the school under the mature direction of the headteacher. Recent talk of a 'core curriculum' has alarmed some practitioners. Furthermore the progressive tradition, in which method is as important as content, is seen to be threatened by talk of accountability. Sharpening the content of the curriculum may be interpreted as a move away from good first school practice.

In fact there is no need for concern; quite the reverse. Knowledge is the *content* of the curriculum and must not be confused with method. The *content* should be centred around forms of knowledge, the *method* around children's needs. The content is universal, but the methods may be parochial. For example, children who live in high-rise flats have a good understanding of maps. Their teacher may well use this as a vehicle for teaching measurement, or extending reading, using the children's experience as a base for her method, but the content of the work will be the same as in any other school.

How can content be organized? We suggest that a useful framework for a first school might be

1 language, humanities and the expressive arts (i.e. reading, talking, dancing, worshipping, painting, singing)
2 science
3 mathematics

and that all three should have an equal share of time.

2 ACQUIRING KNOWLEDGE INVOLVES GROWTH IN THE LEARNER

Our second principle deals with the method by which children acquire knowledge and the growth of intellectual skills.

As we said earlier, the teacher's skill lies in translating the curriculum principles into stimulating classroom activities and experience: the curriculum is to be thought of in terms of activity and experience rather than knowledge to be acquired and facts to be stored; or as Mike Hill puts it: 'What is important to the growth of the primary child is not a particular fact or a particular group of ordered facts but the method or the process of acquiring them.'[5] In other words, this view of the curriculum sees it as a way of cultivating the intellect and nurturing the personality.

A child who was estimating the size of packages and tins was dismayed because when he checked his work he found he was wildly inaccurate, although he could measure competently. His teacher helped him to persevere and at the end of the session he was heard to·say, 'That's good, I didn't think I could do it but now I know I can.'

3 MATCHING CURRICULUM CONTENT TO THE PUPIL'S DEVELOPMENT

A group of five-year-old children were changing their shoes. Some had plimsolls on, some had buckled shoes, some had lace-up shoes. Because one child remarked about the 'different feet', the teacher sat on the floor and the children stood round her, counting and classifying. This activity was entirely verbal and short. On another day, a group of seven-year-olds were talking about shoes, following a child telling everyone that his had cost a lot. The teacher then counted the shoes, but this time recapitulated the multiplication table of twos, helped the children extrapolate, went easily into the table of fours and had great fun dealing with the table of threes which required some children to stand with their feet spaced apart. This activity was recorded. In both instances the children's interest was a starting-point, but the content and presentation were geared to the stage the children had reached, and the knowledge the teacher wished them to acquire.

A great deal of helpful material is available for teachers outlining the developmental stages of young school children. Philippe Muller[6] arranges his guides as developmental tasks; Margaret Donaldson[7] gives a comprehensive outline of Piaget's theory of intellectual development in the appendix of her book; and Brierley[8] provides information on the growth patterns of children. Some excellent fiction offers yet another dimension. *Mr God This is Anna*[9] provides a unique insight into children's development and thinking. Added to this, there are numerous concept hierarchy charts and texts which list goals to be reached ordered in development stages.

The fact remains that it is the classroom teacher who translates this information into practice: 'Teachers know, in their bones, the importance of the distinction between developmental and chronological age.'[10]

So, in practice, how can curriculum content be matched to each child? We suggest the skeleton of content, under forms of knowledge, in our first principle now needs to be expanded so that school staffs zoom into fine detail. Individual teachers need to become familiar with the ~ontent broken into small stages and at the same time make quite sure that they understand the content themselves.

4 MATCHING LEARNING OPPORTUNITIES TO INDIVIDUAL NEEDS AND CURRICULUM CONTENT

'The success of a nursery or infant school is rightly measured by how the teachers help their pupils to a wide and active experience of their world and what their pupils learn from this experience.'[10]

It is the teacher's job to provide young children with first hand experiences in an appropriate environment. These organized and structured experiences will be selected, extended and linked together to become progressively more demanding.

For example, most young children are offered domestic play in the Wendy House. This is an attractive mini-house full of domestic furniture with which children are usually already familiar. So the teacher is building naturally on the experiences the children already bring to school.

What kinds of learning are taking place in this situation? First of all, the children are learning the physical skills, for example, pouring, carrying, putting the tablecloth on, spreading things out, folding them up etc. These physical skills are important for learning because holding a pencil, counting beads, filling up test-tubes, using a pair of compasses all require good co-ordination. But, just as importantly, through handling shapes, sizes and textures children build up mental images of these *ideas* which, much later on, they will substitute for the real thing.

Besides physical skills they are learning the social skills of sharing, organizing, relating, making decisions and solving problems. They are acting out various family roles.

They are using language and either talking to themselves to order their thoughts ('Now I'm going to hoover up . . . .') or talking to one another, in a variety of ways.

But intellectually they are using *thinking* skills which will serve them in very good stead. The teacher may ask them 'Clear up now, please' and so everything has to be left tidy. This is the beginning of learning habits and study skills, organizing materials and space.

The quality of the provision directly affects the learning. Real water spills but 'pretend' water can be slopped all over the place. China cups break but plastic ones require less careful handling.

In such a situation, where an enormous amount of learning is already going on, the teacher can extend that learning and link it to an agreed curriculum. For example, she may suggest that the children invite some adults to tea, bake the cakes, write the invitations. This will involve weighing, measuring, writing. The children will need to count the plates, the chairs and anticipate all the things they will need. Later the 'home' may turn into a hairdresser's, or a fish and chip shop, or a travel agency.

Visits, trips, use of the outside environment, playground and garden, displays, centres of interest, things the children bring from home, local events, news items, family happenings, seasons and festivals are all rich sources of learning. These areas can be linked to book-based learning, and to children researching for themselves. 'With the younger children play was sometimes used by the teacher as a basis for more directed work and with children of all ages their current interests were capitalized upon when appropriate, to extend their learning.'[4]

There are other learning situations which are based on 'activities initiated by the teacher'[10] and these are usually closely related to the agreed curriculum. For example, place value, word-attack skills, new techniques in art, punctuation, need to be taught carefully at the right time to the right children. The children still require active, first-hand experience. The setting, (individual, small groups, class groups) needs to be considered. Is there opportunity for children to 'exercise initiative and raise questions? Is the pace of the work suitable for the children? Is there sufficient opportunity for them to practise newly acquired skills? Is the work presented in a variety of ways? Is there sufficient new learning? Is individual help available? The most professionally demanding questions may be questions of validity. Did the activity and materials match the learning to be acquired? How does the teacher assess understanding?

5 MONITORING AND RECORDING PROGRESS

Although teachers working in a school will become more and more intimate with the curriculum, nevertheless a working document is essential. The First School Survey rates as 'urgent' the need for guidelines in all parts of the curriculum and suggests that where the written document is well thought out the corresponding work in the school is usually of good quality.

But can a written document reflect the careful, planned work that goes on in every first school classroom and at the same time record the unpredicted situation that has yielded excellent learning? How can the teacher, through the model of the curriculum, be helped not only to offer systematic learning but also to harness spontaneous interests to an agreed programme of work?

There are ways of tackling this, and it soon becomes clear that several documents are needed, all linked together, but serving different purposes. The teacher needs an outline of content together with ways of presenting that content which can be amended in the light of experience. She may find it useful to have this in two 'layers' – one showing a skeleton of the work, and the other showing greater detail. She then needs to record (and draw conclusions from her recording) how individual children and groups of children have received what has been offered to them. In this way she will be directing her attention to content, intellectual skills and affective learning together. Moreover she will be constantly adjusting the curriculum from feedback of actual classroom work, both planned and spontaneous.

The written document, important though it is, will be a part of a *whole*, the other ingredients being discussions, visits to other schools, background reading, displays for teachers' use, a library of children's work, video recordings, in-service work, observation of the children as a year-group, class, individuals etc.

The written curriculum has two major functions: it is a guide for the teacher, a record for the child. However excellent the written

document may be, it can only record parts of the work. No child or
teacher, no classroom or school can be pinned on paper, nor would we be
wise to try.

WHAT THE THEORY SAYS

ACQUIRING KNOWLEDGE IS BASIC TO THE CURRICULUM

To enable children to acquire knowledge the teacher herself must know 'the very real objective differences that there are in forms of knowledge and therefore in our understanding of mental processes that are related to these'.[11] She must understand the structural patterning and mental approach of that form of knowledge, rather than just the content. In other words the teacher must think mathematically, think scientifically, and have an appreciation of the expressive arts.

Because young children are being introduced to different modes of thought for the first time, teachers themselves need an in-depth understanding of the disciplines. It is also why a workshop situation is ideal for in-service training. The teacher needs to share her specialism with colleagues and also learn from them, not only classroom ideas and content but the underlying structures of the disciplines: 'This type of transfer is at the heart of the educational process – the continual broadening and deepening of knowledge in terms of basic and general ideas.'[12] It is fundamental to Bruner's spiral curriculum, where the same ideas are returned to again and again but each time expanded further.

The whole argument is summed up clearly by Dearden when he writes:

> To take the case of science first: if all that is meant is a pottering about in which one may or may not notice that reflections in a spoon are distorted, what things look like when seen through coloured glass, that some objects float while others sink and so on, then no doubt this account is unexceptionable. With very young children especially there is an important place for this kind of learning, but such limited and undirected curiosity does not amount to science. All of this could and did and does go on where science has never been heard of. Such finding out does not even begin to resemble science until problems start to present themselves which cannot be solved without putting forward, and then testing experimentally, suggested solutions of a non-obvious kind. Even the perception of a scientific problem requires more than naive curiosity, and the concept of an experiment implies more than pushing and poking at things . . . .'[13]

Pushing and poking is a necessary stage, but a child will not be introduced to scientific thinking if left entirely to investigation. He needs the skilled intervention of a teacher who understands scientific method and can gently expose the child to this kind of enquiry.

Michael Oakeshott clarifies this beautifully. He talks of knowledge being composed of 'information' and 'judgment'. Information corresponds to Dearden's 'poking and pushing, floating and sinking' which is acquired fairly easily by the learner from the contingent world. Judgment is reliant on information, but is peculiar to a mode of thought.

Judgment, then, is that which, when united with information, generates knowledge or ability to do, to make, or to understand and explain. It is being able to think – not to think in no manner in particular, but to think with an appreciation of the considerations which belong to different modes of thought. This, of course, is something which must be learned; it does not belong to the pupil by the light of nature, and it is as much a part of our civilized experience as the information which is its counterpart.[13]

ENTHUSIASM

Children will acquire knowledge more easily and pleasurably if the teacher herself is enthusiastic. The teacher's enthusiasm springs from insights into the material she is teaching and her own competence within a discipline.

'In approximately half of the schools the teachers communicated their enjoyment of books to the children through the enthusiasm with which they shared their favourite poems and stories.'[4] This is just one example of the teacher's own understanding and delight being communicated to the children.

Michael Oakeshott suggests: 'Learning, then, is acquiring the ability to feel and to think and the pupil will never acquire these abilities unless he has learned to listen for them and to recognize them in the conduct and utterances of others.'[13]

THE STRUCTURE OF THE DISCIPLINE

'To know the structure of each discipline is to know the problems of teaching it.'[14] The teacher, for example, will need to understand the release of emotional energy in poetry and literature, be able to accept more than one solution as perfectly proper sometimes in mathematics, and be aware of the power of observation in science.

If the teacher understands the structure of the discipline she will also understand the revisionary and pluralistic nature of knowledge.

LINKS WITHIN A DISCIPLINE

A teacher who is familiar with correspondences within a form of knowledge can link bits of the discipline together. She will have many and varied ways of presenting that material so as to strengthen a child's understanding in a variety of situations.

LINKS ACROSS DISCIPLINES

If the teacher thoroughly understands the structure of the material she is using she will be able to teach across the curriculum. Both the Cockcroft Report and the First School Survey emphasize this as vital to promote understanding. HMI commented: 'It was no surprise that the school day was more likely to be divided according to activity than by subject, or that skills and knowledge acquired in one area of the curriculum were used in another.'[4]

PROVISION FOR VERY ABLE AND LESS ABLE CHILDREN

A grasp of content enables the teacher to cope with the very able or very slow child more successfully. Very able children may be more difficult to cater for:

. . . by the time they are eight or nine years old they may be insufficiently challenged and produce work, especially in reading and writing, which does not always match their ability . . . . Another reason why teachers find it more difficult to match the level of the work to the abler than to the slower children in their classes may be that these children are more demanding with regard to *subject content*.[15]

TEACHER LIMITATIONS

A professional teacher will know the limits of her own understanding and will not attempt anything unsuitable for the children or herself. Peters is unequivocal: 'To teach something in ignorance of it is not just difficult: it is logically impossible.'[16]

A teacher who knows very little about animal biology was once brought a dead mole and the child who brought it showed great interest in the little creature and wanted to know all about it: low-key investigation with a small group of children was all the teacher could manage.

ACQUIRING KNOWLEDGE INVOLVES GROWTH IN THE LEARNER

Values and attitudes

Values and attitudes are developed in children as part of a 'hidden' spiral curriculum. At first the child will comply through invitation with little understanding. At a second stage he begins to identify with the required values and attitudes, although not consistently. Finally his values are materialized and become part and parcel of his way of life.

The child learns to perceive himself as others perceive him in relation to the roles he performs. From parents and siblings he begins to acquire a conception of the role of the child and later, in school, the role of the pupil. The 'culture' of the school is initially bestowed on the child through the teachers and, later perhaps, his peer group.

David Hargreaves writes: 'The social psychological perspective on the "good teacher" is concerned with such factors as the overall relationship between teacher and pupils, their mutual attraction or hostility, the ways in which they perceive, evaluate and react to one another, the ways in which the teacher's behaviour creates, sustains and changes these relationships.'[17] Personal relationships are desirable in themselves, and are reciprocal. If the child has no opportunity to contribute, the relationship will be arid.

Motivation
Professor Vernon helps teachers understand the need for success when discussing 'achievement motivation'.

> At the age of three to three-and-a-half years the child begins to experience pleasure in his *personal* competence to perform a specific task, and regret and shame if he fails. He turns less frequently to adults for help and support and the experience of competence becomes its own reward. At four to five years some children, instead of trying to overcome failure by greater effort, may resort to avoidance of the situation, or denial or concealment of failure. Individual differences in achievement motivation begin to appear at five to six years in the degrees of difficulty of the tasks children seek to perform.[18]

Reality in the curriculum
The unnatural regimentation of young children which is a result of large numbers and the actual presentation of curriculum content (e.g. the use of cardboard money), can sometimes provoke a sense of bewilderment which is an affront to the child's logical reasoning and acts as a barrier not only to formal learning, but to the willing adoption of attitudes and values. (For example, a child asked, 'What country uses this *cardboard* money anyway?')

Intellectual growth
Solving problems, forming hypotheses, coming to decisions and making deductions are all part of a child's intellectual growth and can be nurtured or largely eliminated in the classroom.

> When young children first come to school, much of their mathematics is 'doing'. They explore the mathematical situations which they encounter . . . and come to their own conclusions. At this stage their mathematical thinking may reach a high level of independence. As they grow older this independent thinking needs to continue; it should not give way to a method of learning which is based wholly on the assimilation of received mathematical knowledge and whose test of truth is 'this is the way I was told to do it'.[3]

It is through the intellectual skills that the curriculum is largely knit together in the first school. Solving a problem depends on discussion, on social interaction, on content (i.e. knowledge) and sometimes on small motor control. It yields new learning and brings its own reward in the delight of accomplishment.

If we place priority on children thinking this may mean that we do not always have a tangible end-product but look to the process of education to enable the child to learn for himself.

Obviously thinking cannot be isolated from the whole process of learning but its central importance should be remembered when the curriculum and environment are being planned.

COGNITIVE STYLES

'New pedagogical procedures should acknowledge this interaction between the preferred strategy of the learner and the material to be acquired and tailor the presentation of materials to the psychological requirements of the task and the cognitive predisposition of the learner.'[19] This aptly summarizes the need for the teacher to allow different styles of learning to flourish in the classroom. Some children need physical movement but others can sit at a task for a longer period. Some children need to rectify mistakes immediately, while others will make a fair copy at the end. Some children need frequent bouts of reassurance, while others like to work in a fairly isolated place. Offering children opportunities to develop their own cognitive styles is a major management task for a first school teacher. Choice within the limits and individual control by the children of their own working space and materials is a beginning. How difficult this is to manage in a classroom with twenty-five or thirty children!

An atmosphere where children can express their emotions (laughter, anger, grief) and learn to control them can be incorporated into the school day through stories, music, drama, poetry or even scientific investigations. A class of five-year-olds had hilarious fun playing with balloons as part of the Christmas activities but calmed down when the activity ceased. How can children recognize and control their emotions if they are not given an opportunity to express them?

PROBLEM-SOLVING

A great discovery solves a great problem but there is a grain of discovery in the solution of any problem. Your problem may be modest; but if it challenges your curiosity and brings into play your inventive faculties, and if you solve it by your own means, you may experience the tension and enjoy the triumph of discovery. Such experiences at a susceptible age may create a taste for mental work and leave their imprint on mind and character for a lifetime.[20]

If the problem is challenging, if the children have the knowledge and skills to solve it, if the teacher genuinely requires the problem to be solved (rather than knowing the solution herself and passing on the problem as a disguised exercise), the level of curiosity and motivation will be high. The teacher's own awareness that challenging problems can be found in play, classroom routines, and ongoing learning situations will raise the incidence of them in the classroom, to the benefit of the children: 'One only has to listen to children who have been given freedom to discuss their intellectual problems to be convinced that the only way to develop a critical facility is by using it.'[21]

ROTE LEARNING
'Fluent performance is based on understanding of the routine which is carried out; mechanical performance is performance by rote in which the necessary understanding is not present.'[3] Teachers need to decide if sometimes rote learning is a suitable technique to use. They will understand that it is low-level cognitive activity, although to a layman the acquisition of facts can appear impressive. Whilst children enjoy rote learning the intellectual benefits are slight.

Language
Verbal communication is essential to the development of thought, and as such is an important skill. 'Almost without exception the teachers recognize the importance of spoken language as an essential foundation for learning to read and write and provided many opportunities for children to express themselves orally.'[4] This is the only area commented upon in the First School Survey where teachers were unanimous in their practice. This in itself reflects the enormous importance of fostering language skills, and successful classroom work has reinforced the need for further time and thought to be given to them. First school teachers have been convinced by their own observations and results of the value of oral language.

Skills
By 'skills' we mean here those learned habits which children need to acquire to work confidently, creatively and independently. These skills are to a certain extent dependent on the management of the classroom which will actively encourage and develop these habits.

In any random group of young children there will be those with poorly developed skills and those whose skills have been helped and nurtured at home. If handled sensitively dual standards and teacher expectations will present no problems to the children. For example, poor cutting-out from John might call for dismay from his teacher, but the same standard from Tina would receive encouragement and a smile and further help on another occasion.

DIFFERENT APPROACHES
Able children will learn a great deal incidentally and develop skills in leaps and bounds, for example such children may learn word-attack skills effortlessly. Slower learners require careful observation and planned teaching. For these children learning will need to be broken down into tiny components, each skill carefully and slowly presented, with the aim being for the child to succeed at, for example, cutting with scissors,

holding a pencil correctly, copying a simple shape. The children will need regular attention and checking – some of which can be done by a carefully-briefed voluntary helper.

Other children may require skill teaching to counteract a specific weakness which may sap confidence and produce behaviour problems. Having pin-pointed the difficulty (e.g. reversals of letters) the teacher will need to find a range of materials aimed at teaching this skill. Brief, daily practice with the materials will need to be planned and parents' cooperation enlisted to use some particularly interesting materials at home. The remedial service may be able to offer individual help for the child or loan specific remedial games.

PRACTICAL SKILLS
These include cutting, glueing, colouring, doing-up shoes, coats, ties, blowing noses, looking through a microscope, using a ruler etc.

SOCIAL SKILLS
These include eating, listening, sharing, accepting change and disappointment.

There is a hierarchy in acquiring social skills. For example, nursery children or rising-fives cannot usually share very happily. (Sharing equip-ment is an advanced social skill as anyone who has attended a practical evening class will know!) On the other hand, very young children are usually very sympathetic towards other children, sometimes much more so than eight-year-olds.

Sex-stereotyping

It is important that small children should be encouraged to express a wide range of emotions, at the same time learning to be gentle and sensitive to each other and aware of their rights. Boys will have had less opportunity to develop nurturing feelings, and to care for others. It is easy (and it will seem natural) for staff to encourage different modes of behaviour between girls and boys, to reward and punish them in different ways. It takes immense effort to become sensitive to this before it becomes possible to explore alternatives. The objective is to enable children to discover their own qualities and abilities irrespective of their sex and the sex-stereotyped constraints.[22]

MATCHING CURRICULUM CONTENT TO PUPILS' DEVELOPMENT

Matching

'Matching' is a technical term, which Wynne Harlem discusses in *Education for the 80s*:

What matching does mean, in simple terms, is finding out what children can already do and what ideas they have as a basis for providing experiences which will develop these skills and concepts. The keynote of matching is thus finding the right challenge for the child, the size of the step he can take by using but also extending existing ideas. There is as much mismatch if this step is too small, leading to boredom, as there is if it is too large, leading to failure.[23]

Continuity

The idea of continuity implies the existence of goals towards which teaching and learning are directed and of planning which gradually leads children to their attainment. . . . There is firstly a matter of identifying goals which can be broadly agreed. These need to be concerned with understanding and skills in different aspects of the curriculum, perhaps more than with its content, although the content is the raw material from which understanding, skill and the ability to use knowledge can be developed.[24]

Joan Dean points up for teachers the interaction between content and those intellectual and physical skills which were discussed earlier. In some areas of the curriculum (notably music, mathematics and beginning reading) continuity is vital if the children are to make maximum progress. Careful observation of the way a child tackles a task can give valuable clues as to whether he is understanding it and whether he should be helped towards the next stage. Continuity therefore has much to do with the *timing* of content.

Children are in an infant school for two or three years, in a first school for three, four or five and a junior or middle school for four years. However, it is rare for the school to plan so far ahead as this, looking at the way teacher knowledge and skill can be built up and planning developments sufficiently far ahead to build up resources.[24]

This is a sobering thought but it is within the capabilities of school staffs to do something about it, given sufficient resources.

Observation

This observation should be double-pronged. We have already mentioned observation of the child as an individual but it is useful also to observe children as a group.

Schools are built, organized and administered on the assumption of human homogeneity rather than human diversity. Children are placed in classes with materials, furniture and books thought to be appropriate to their age and stage of development; so how important for the education of the individual and for the individualizing of teaching is the teacher's knowledge of group behaviour?[21]

Observation of peer group behaviour can provide useful information for teachers when forming groups for discussion and activities.

MATCHING LEARNING OPPORTUNITIES TO INDIVIDUAL NEEDS AND CURRICULUM CONTENT

Most teachers in the survey schools used a range of teaching approaches which varied to take account of the characteristics of the children, the resources available and the teacher's personal inclinations. Most employed a variety of teaching methods during the course of the week to suit the work in hand.

To meet . . . challenges a teacher needs to be able to call on an extensive repertoire of teaching and learning methods. Crude descriptions of teaching as progressive or traditional, explanatory or didactic, fail to convey the variety and range of modes of teaching teachers have at their command.[4]

Teaching methods: stories

In isolated cases, legends, folk stories and Bible stories were used to develop an understanding of the past. The work for some children included stories of famous people. Work on the topic 'King Arthur' involved eight-year-olds in making a large pictorial map of Camelot showing the river, road, castle and travellers.[10]

The First School Survey contains warning notes:

Most children had the experience of listening in groups of different sizes but a great deal of listening took place within a class group. . . . Children were occasionally expected to listen for too long without responding and so became inattentive. . . . The children almost always heard stories as a class group, usually at the end of the afternoon session. Sometimes conditions and organization were not conducive to the enjoyment of the story, for example when classes were put together and the group was too large. Occasionally classes of younger and older children were combined and in such cases the story that was read was often not suited to all the children because either the content, the language, or both were too difficult or too simple for some.[4]

Games

Most children love playing games provided they understand the object of the game and the outcome (e.g. does the winner have least or most?) and they are active participants who do not have to wait ages for their turn. Games increase children's attention span, perseverance and motivation, offer skills practice and deepen concepts. Games also increase social interaction but need to be carefully overseen with some players! This is where knowledge of individual children is vital.

Investigations
HMI noted: 'Many teachers did not sufficiently encourage individual independent investigations.'[4]
The Cockcroft Report reiterates:

It is necessary to realize that much of the value of an investigation can be lost unless the outcome of the investigation is discussed. Such discussions should include consideration not only of the method which has been used and the results which have been offered but also of the false trails which have been made in the course of investigation.[3]

Discussion
Commenting on discussions HMI note:

While it is unlikely that every opportunity for extending language will be taken by teachers or children, in the liveliest schools oral language development occurs every day and throughout the curriculum. . . . One of the main purposes of the discussions was to plan work and consider future activities.[4]

Extension of play activities

. . . in general, there was little evidence of the development of imaginative and dramatic play; teachers rarely intervened or took part, and it was not unusual for teachers to be engaged in other activities, such as hearing children read, while such play was taking place.[4]

It is a temptation to take advantage of play as a self-maintaining activity but it can be used successfully to promote an agreed curriculum.

Displays
The First School Survey gives some fine examples of the use of displays in the classroom.

The displays in the seven-year-old classes indicated an extension of work on topics such as symmetry, spirals, tessellations, wheels and maps. In the classes of older children the displays reflected their widening interests and developing skills, and included material on a specific historical period and the dating of local houses, the metric packaging of goods, the making of magnetic needles, and the use of maps and tables giving the time of the tides as part of a project based on the sea shore.[4]

Teacher-directed learning
The fine balance between teacher-directed activities and self-sufficiency within the curriculum is highlighted by HMI:

> In 35 of the schools such satisfactory arrangements and methods were practised in one or more of these classes, but in other classes of these schools and in the classes of the remaining 29 schools the children's work was either over-directed to some degree or the children were given too little help in organizing their work.[4]

MONITORING PROGRESS AND KEEPING RECORDS

Start with the children
The Primary Survey reinforces the notion that children progress at different rates, learn in an uneven, sometimes erratic fashion and cannot be neatly categorized.

> It must, however, be recognized at the outset that there is no one standard which is appropriate to all children at a given age. Individual children vary in their capacities and abilities and some children perform moderately in one area of the curriculum and yet show good ability in another.[15]

It follows that the written curriculum must be sufficiently elastic to cater for different rates of progress and at the same time be presented in total.
Once again we are reminded of the two kinds of planning that are needed in the first school:

> Both the rigidly timetabled approach and the individual approach, which sometimes masked unplanned work, contained weaknesses. The former often gave rise to a series of isolated topics unrelated either to the children's current interests or to each other and were followed up inadequately. The latter frequently lacked the essential basic planning needed to ensure adequate content and continuity. . . . Both approaches might be made to work if a clearly prepared scheme was used . . . .[4]

The development document
Kirby has given an excellent account of classroom practice:

> Practice is the outcome of the sensitive understanding of children, of current ideas on education and the principles underlying them, and is unique to each situation and the teacher. . . . It means fluidity of approach and content, for there is no blueprint of method to be applied by all.[21]

We have already taken as a basic premise that classroom practice and curriculum design must go hand in hand. The teacher needs supportive documents, which are not only organic, frequently used, and sometimes amended or even thrown away, but are also part of the whole jigsaw of the school curriculum (see p.85).

Cooperation
The First School Survey

> . . . as did the survey of primary schools before it, shows the importance of good leadership in the school, not only from the head but also from other members of staff each taking responsibility for an aspect of the work. . . . If primary and first schools could ever have been operated by teachers working separately and pursuing their own inclinations, that day is past.[4]

Thus findings of national reports re-enforce the need for a team approach in schools (see Chapter 4, p.162).

Monitoring and assessment
The child himself, his work and play, and his progress record are the best evidence of successful teaching.

In summarizing assessment procedures the authors of *The Practical Curriculum* say:

> . . . we have tried to show both how hard it is to assess a school's procedures for deciding, planning, and monitoring its curriculum, and how some indicative evidence can be gathered. Success in achieving specific various kinds of experiences, introducing different forms of knowledge, using various modes of teaching and learning, developing values, attitudes, skills and the capacity for self-expression are all legitimate approaches to assessment. Comparing the school's policy with private reports and comments on the school is another.[10]

The First School Survey reported that 'in the majority of schools little use was made of assessment'.[4]

REFERENCES

1 DES (1978) *Special Educational Needs* (The Warnock Report) HMSO
2 ASHTON, P., KNEEN, P. and DAVIES, F. (1975) *Aims into Practice in the Primary School* Hodder and Stoughton
3 DES (1982) *Mathematics Counts* (The Cockcroft Report) HMSO
4 DES (1982) *Education 5 – 9* (The First School Survey) HMSO
5 HILL, M. (1980) 'The teacher's craft and basic skills' in C. Hill (ed.) *Primary Education* A. & C. Black
6 MULLER, P. (1969) *The Tasks of Childhood* Weidenfeld and Nicolson
7 DONALDSON, M. (1978) *Children's Minds* Fontana
8 BRIERLEY, J. (1978) *Growing and Learning* Ward Lock Educational
9 FYNN (1974) *Mister God This is Anna* Collins
10 SCHOOLS COUNCIL (1981) *The Practical Curriculum* (Schools Council Working Paper 70) Methuen Educational
11 HIRST, P. (1974) *Knowledge and the Curriculum* Routledge & Kegan Paul
12 BRUNER, J. S. (1977) *The Process of Education* Harvard University Press
13 Cited in PETERS, R. (ed.) (1967) *The Concept of Education* Routledge & Kegan Paul
14 FORD, G. W. and PUGNO, L. (1972) *The Structure of Knowledge and the Curriculum* Pergamon
15 DES (1978) *Primary Education in England: A Report by HM Inspectors of Schools* HMSO
16 PETERS, R. S. (1966) *Ethics and Education* Allen and Unwin
17 HARGREAVES, D. (1972) *Interpersonal Relations and Education* Routledge & Kegan Paul
18 VERNON, M. (1969) *Human Motivation* Cambridge University Press
19 KAGAN, J. (1971) in *Personality, Growth and Learning* Longman/Open University Press
20 POLYA, G. (1945) *How to Solve It* Princeton University Press
21 KIRBY, N. (1981) *Personal Values in Primary Education* Harper and Rowe
22 HANNON, V. (1980) *Ending Sex-Stereotyping in Schools* Equal Opportunities Commission
23 HARLEN, W. (1980) in C. Richards (ed.) *Primary Education: Issues for the Eighties* A. & C. Black
24 DEAN, J. in 23 above
25 BLATCHFORD, P., BATTLE, S. and MAYS, J. (1982) *The First Transition* NFER/Nelson

IN THE CLASSROOM

ACQUIRING KNOWLEDGE IS BASIC TO THE CURRICULUM

The structure of the disciplines

The first task is to decide together as a staff, with perhaps specialist help, the basic structures inherent in a discipline. This calls for inspired in-service training, sometimes with investigation at the teacher's own level. Some teachers shy away from a subject because they feel they are not equipped with its basic thought processes – they fear the *structure*, not the *content* which, at first school level, is usually easily learned.

The structure of the three forms of knowledge in the first school could be summarized as:

the expressive arts	experience and expressing that experience
science	observation and drawing conclusions
mathematics	finding relationships

These key phrases will only have emerged after energetic discussion but they can act as a focal point in the teacher's mind when she is dealing with many hands and voices in a busy classroom.

The children will show that they, too, are absorbing the structure of the discipline. For example, when the mothers had put out the bean bags, hoops and balls for the obstacle race on sports day, some children ran onto the track and rearranged the equipment so that the red hoops, balls, bean bags were together, all the green, all the yellow, and so on. A display of cotton-wool snowmen of different height and girth were jumbled up by the teacher every day after the children had gone home, but every morning they had been put in rank order.

The power of symbolism in mathematics could be investigated with teachers through an understanding of place value. By the insertion of one small mark 10^{43} (an enormous number) becomes 10^{-43}, a very small number indeed. It is only when the teacher herself has discovered the power of symbolism that she can help children begin to acquire the same understanding but in a manner appropriate to their age and abilities. She can, for example, from their earliest days help the children to represent action in symbols, even if those symbols are merely conkers representing one try in a game, or blobs on paper representing the members of a family.

A class of eight-year-old children were considering Mary Coleridge's poem, 'The Deserted House'. The teacher asked the children to find clues in the poem as to why the house was deserted. 'Because it was flooded', 'Because it was damaged' were some of the replies. Then one child posed the hypothesis that the poet herself didn't really know and had only written the poem to 'help herself find out'. Such responses are the result not only of careful organization of the learning situation but also of a clear perception of the structure of the discipline the teacher is offering the children.

If the teacher is able to differentiate between the the various disciplines in her own mind, she will be able to exploit the learning potential of any situation. For example, a child brought in a beautiful foxglove. The children observed it closely, handled, smelled and touched the flower and then made some detailed drawings, paintings and a collage. The teacher was a biologist herself and was able to sharpen the children's observations and give them appropriate further information, such as the fact that the foxglove is poisonous. The plant was tall and so the children were able to compare the length of the foxglove with other flowers. They had not yet understood formal measurement.

The word 'foxglove' itself gave rise to speculation – does a fox use it as a glove? The children thought of other flower names – bluebell, buttercup, dandelion. Some children wrote about the foxglove and the teacher selected some flower poems to enjoy.

The teacher's input was unobtrusive but because she viewed the fox-glove from three different points of view she was able to increase the children's awe, curiosity, intellectual advance, pleasure and attention.

EFFECT ON CONTENT

If content is seen as part of structure the teacher herself will be constantly enlightened. Children and teacher together can make observations, receive feedback from the actual material, and do some research. For example, the children had learned a poem about dandelions and were trying to find some in early June. They found ragwort instead and it was by applying the structure of scientific thought in careful observation that the teacher and children together found dandelions at various stages of growth. They subsequently reached conclusions by looking for the milky secretion of the dandelion and were able to classify the plants.

EFFECT ON THE CURRICULUM

The curriculum shrinks once the teacher understands the *nature* of a discipline. She will not need to cram all suggested material into her work, because she will be secure in the basic ideas: she can, in fact, become much more selective. For example, is it absolutely necessary to include work with magnets if the aim is to help children observe, and comment and hypothesize?

EFFECT ON METHOD

A teacher might arrange her poetry sessions in a quiet, comfortable environment, with the children grouped intimately and perhaps a 'do not disturb' notice on the door. The teacher will have chosen an appropriate time of day, and the material will be matched to the general experience and language of the children. Mysteries will be explored and laughter shared.

The children may respond with sighs, spontaneous clapping or there may be a 'quiet time' at the end for individual reflection.

In maths she may offer the same problem to individual children, e.g. 'continue the series 12, 24, 36, . . .'. John might offer 12, 24, 36, 48, 60; Diane 12, 24, 36, 72, 84; and a discussion can ensue.

She may allow the children to observe living creatures and accept their inaccurate observations, or crude observations as appropriate to the children, realizing that original observation is a scientific path of enquiry.

LINKS WITHIN A DISCIPLINE

An example might be the idea of growing, presented under the scientific umbrella. A display, as a basis for discussion, might include not only fast-growing plants such as sunflowers and nasturtiums, but the growth of fungi on cheese or fruit, the growth of the children from babyhood to the present, the growth of hair and finger nails, the growth of stick insects, the growth of crystals etc.

The deliberate search for many examples of the same idea can deepen the child's understanding. Including his own contributions adds point to displays and discussions and promotes healthy learning.

LINKS ACROSS THE DISCIPLINES

Taking the idea of 'beginning and end' the teacher could extend it across the curriculum. She might discuss a piece of music; she might tell a story and discuss several endings; she might ask the children how they feel at the beginning and end of playtime.

This useful technique leads down any number of fruitful investigative roads. It often arises naturally from children's responses, for example, the theme of secrets could be explored as follows:

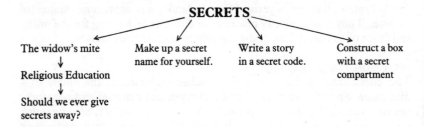

SECRETS

The widow's mite	Make up a secret	Write a story	Construct a box
↓	name for yourself.	in a secret code.	with a secret
Religious Education			compartment
↓			
Should we ever give			
secrets away?			

EFFECT ON CHANGE

A grasp of structure will enable the teacher to revise the content of her work without anxiety. The *revisionary* nature of knowledge means change in content, due perhaps to social pressures (e.g. metres instead of yards). *Pluralism* of knowledge means two views within a single framework: an example of this may be teaching children the letter names of the alphabet, the phonic names, or both, according to the professional decision of the teacher. Change put within the structure of the discipline loses much of its threat. Change in content can only be bewildering.

COPING WITH ABLE CHILDREN

If the teacher is thoroughly familiar with the discipline she is teaching she will be in a good position to stretch an able child in an impromptu way, perhaps purely verbally at first and then, on reflection, with planned and recorded activities. There is not much point in rushing to the guidelines or manual when a child has outpaced the work the teacher has prepared. For example, suppose a group of children are being taught the correct use of compasses and thereby properties of a circle. If a child is obviously very adept and able he can be helped to construct an equilateral triangle or hexagon to fit inside his circle.

ACCEPTING PERSONAL LIMITS

How many of the class tadpoles die before they become frogs? How musical does a teacher have to be before she teaches the recorder? Children's enthusiasm can be infectious but there is little point in attempting unrealistic projects.

Content of the disciplines

At this stage the school staff needs to identify, in brief general terms, the *content* of each area of work.

The *expressive arts* might include:

listening
speaking, including singing and making music
writing, including painting, drawing, model making
reading
movement, including drama
worship, appreciation of aesthetic forms and social awareness.

Science might include:

observing plants, insects and animals in my own environment
observing phenomena, such as weather
observing my body.

Mathematics might include:

spatial understanding
number
structures and mechanisms
logical thought and measurement.

This structure needs to be in the teacher's head. It is simple and therefore non-threatening; it is sound and therefore can be used as a reference for enquiry; but most important of all it has been *internalized* and therefore can be put to use in the classroom.

ACQUIRING KNOWLEDGE INVOLVES GROWTH IN THE LEARNER

Values and attitudes

POLICY
Joint staff policies need to be developed on approaches to various aspects of children's personal development. As with any policy making, the most valuable aspect is perhaps the discussion that takes place in an attempt to achieve some consensus. Topics which might be covered include: what attitudes staff consider worthwhile to foster, by what means; how to maintain continuity of approach. Examples of individual children are always helpful, as are attempts to monitor the personal development of certain children throughout the school.

A JOINT APPROACH
Although school plays an important role in this area the influence of home is strong and the benefits of having mutually agreed values and attitudes transmitted both at home and school are obvious. Teachers will need to communicate their intentions in this field to parents and invite frank responses. Contact with parents, in small groups, could be encouraged to discuss such areas as child management, discipline, and coping with such problems as lying and pilfering. Although such discussion groups require skilled handling, most parents will genuinely appreciate the opportunity to exchange views on matters which are controversial and give rise for concern. Perhaps the greatest benefit is for parents to learn that others share similar problems.

MESSAGES VIA THE 'HIDDEN CURRICULUM'

Respect for children
This can be shown by giving children time and attention; by displaying children's unaided art and craft work; by offering them an attractive and carefully planned room in which to work; by remembering personal details, e.g. Lucy's mum is in hospital, Joe doesn't like wearing his tie.

People are more important than property
Accidental damage to property can be regarded as a minor accident although individuals do need to clear up resulting mess. Vandalism should always be treated from the standpoint that *people* have been hurt.

Responsibility
Children respond to being trusted provided the demands are not unreasonable, e.g. infant children can only work quietly and purposefully without an adult for a very short period. Expectations can be extended as children mature and acquire more self-discipline.

'Do as I do'
The teacher's own attitudes and values will provide a model for the children. A caring, consistent, humorous approach will develop similar traits in children.

Teacher expectation
The teacher will need to offer positive reinforcement (well done, how kind of you, Sally) to encourage certain standards of behaviour until they become commonplace. If, for example, the teacher says goodbye individually to the children at the end of the afternoon session, gradually children will come to her with a morning greeting.

If a child does not behave in an acceptable way the teacher can make sure he is put in a position of trying again and becoming successful. For example, if he has been running along the corridor, he can go back and try again.

Are the children encouraged to appreciate the non-teaching staff? Are the dinner ladies supported by the headteacher so that they receive the same standards of courtesy and consideration as the teaching staff? Are the parents made welcome when they help in school? Is the lollipop lady invited to the Christmas party?

Reality in the curriculum
The children enjoy using real materials in real situations, e.g.
1 Children can write Christmas and birthday thank-you letters, invitations to school events, real postcards to write holiday messages to friends.
2 They could make a plan directing a friend from school to their home.
3 Art techniques could be used, e.g. tye and dye for soft-furnishing material, lino prints for covers of books.
4 Members of the community might be able to contribute to children's learning.
5 The locality can be used as a source of learning.

THE TEACHER HERSELF
Personal experience outside school can add to the life of the classroom (Chapter 4, p.215). Children are always intensely interested in 'their' teacher as a person in her own right. References to 'that morning when everything went wrong at home' or stories about the teacher's own childhood reinforces the idea of teacher as a person. Opening up the school to other adults, if managed wisely, can bring a breath of fresh air and ward off the ever-present threat of an 'unreal' ethos in a school. Cooperative teaching also helps.

Intellectual growth

THINKING SKILLS
The teacher's role in developing thinking skills is to provide challenging

situations and through questioning and clues lead the child a step further in his learning. Children need praise and encouragement in their attempts to think for themselves. Less confident children will need to be helped to avoid looking for an acceptable answer without thinking.

Use the classroom environment and classroom activities
1 Pictures can be labelled with questions; interesting scientific specimens can be displayed without labels or written information. This can be added later so that children can confirm their own thinking.
2 Varied exercises in sequencing will help children develop an orderly pattern of response.
3 Children need opportunities to respond individually or within small groups to the teacher's open-ended questions.
4 A programme which allows the class to be occupied with self-maintaining activities enables the teacher to discuss with a small group.
5 Class activities can extend thinking, e.g. oral cloze procedure exercises. Certain classroom management techniques will encourage
    reflecting: display a child's work (writing, model, painting) and ask him to talk about how he did it, why he chose a certain colour etc.
    observing: in the early spring put a tiny vase of snowdrops in an unobtrusive place and ask the children (perhaps in the cloakroom before they go home) if they have noticed them. Ask again the next day to make sure all the children have made an effort at remembering and observing.
    remembering: the teacher might ask: 'What dress did I wear yesterday. Who can tell what it was like?' The child who is not good at remembering messages can be given plenty of practice, taking with him a written message to be used only in an emergency!

Extended discussion
1 Cards with relevant text and pictures can be used with an adult and a small group of children or as a class activity to discuss, for example,
What sort of clothes are worn in winter? Why?
What sort of person is best suited to be a zoo-keeper? Why?
Recall What is the best thing that has ever happened to you?
Inventions A machine to make beds; new uses for old jamjars.
2 Making up codes for written messages – children can then exchange and decipher them in groups.

COGNITIVE STYLES
The teacher's role is to provide a variety of activities within a broad framework to help the children organize their learning and establish their own preferred route to understanding. For example, some young children need more movement than others. If the organization of the classroom is such that a child can circulate freely, he can, within limits, move about and then return to his work. Is the child who frequently asks to visit the toilet really just wanting to stretch his legs? Are the children allowed to work standing up, sitting down, or on the carpet? Can they

choose sometimes? Does another child need constant encouragement and has he a short attention span? Do all the children concentrate hardest in the morning, or are some of them 'afternoon' workers? Can the children choose whether to go out to play?

When reading to their teacher some children use up their intellectual energy quickly and can only sustain reading for a short while. Others gather confidence as they read, and improve with each page. This is not always determined by reading ability but by personality also.

Some children are impulsive, some reflective. Is there a deliberate 'time lag' to cater for the reflective child's response?

Children need to express their ideas in language so that they can be helped to disagree, put forward novel ideas and reflect their individuality in their thinking. Recorded work may often not reflect the quality of the thought behind it. For example, a child handling a marble egg remarked on the cold, smooth surface, the 'peppermint cream' colour of the egg, and the wiggly veins. He wrote 'I held the egg in my hand. It was cold.' Adding 18 and 9 in her head, a child thought: $18+9=18+10=28-1=27$. When doing the sum on paper she thought $8+9=17$, wrote down 7 and carried the 1, $1+1=2$, wrote down the 2; answer 27.

Variety in classroom technique helps the children find their preferred route to learning. For example, sometimes the teacher needs to make sure the children have all the equipment ready for an activity before they begin. Sometimes she needs to outline the activity and the children select and organize their own equipment.

PROBLEM-SOLVING

A child's school life is full of problems. He may lose his shoe in a deserted cloakroom, or be given a pencil with his name on which he is obliged to keep safe for a whole term. Sometimes teachers increase children's problems by well-meaning strategies. For example, a pair of children had made a puppet play out of a cardboard box and scraps of waste material. The teacher wrote a notice for them: 'Here is our puppet play'. The children were too polite to discard the notice although they found great difficulty in displaying it anywhere and finally they propped it on the window-sill and then carried on with the original task.

The role of the teacher

Only if the teacher herself is convinced of the value of problem-solving will she use it deliberately as a classroom technique, and seize every opportunity of turning learning situations into problem-solving activities. For example, a group of children were being introduced to division. The teacher devised a problem where three farmers (Mr Giles, Mr Brown and Mrs White) had come to an auction sale to buy sheep. Each farmer wanted to buy twenty sheep. There were only twenty sheep for sale altogether. What should the auctioneer do? Among the responses were:

'Oh! You've made a mistake. You mean there were 21 sheep.'
'Give the two men seven each and the lady can have six.'
'Send two sheep home.'
'You will never get fair, so shoo all the sheep into a field to hide and say go and then let the farmers find as many as they can.'
'Let one farmer have them for a year, the next farmer for a year and the last farmer for a year.'

The fruits of problem-solving are discovery, intellectual vitality, a high tolerance of frustration and a feeling of delight when the problem is solved. This is not to say that children do not on occasions need to be told facts, supplied with information or asked to practise skills. The teacher can train herself to pose problems across the curriculum. Sometimes the problems are physical ones: 'How will you get the last drops of water out of the water tray if it is too heavy to carry to the sink?' Sometimes they involve social and moral awareness. When asked 'How can we make sure the people at the back of the hall can see what is going on?' the children's replies included: 'Some children sit down in front, and some kneel up in the middle, and some stand up at the back'; 'If you are small and a big person is in front of you ask them nicely to let you go in front'. In all cases genuine discussion, responses received with dignity, the possibility of several solutions, and enough time are essential requirements.

Children need to have enough experience upon which to draw in order to solve problems so the teacher needs to be sensitive to the stage of development the children have reached, and be careful not to intervene. Every child knows when he has solved a problem: the teacher's function is to talk it through with him, and recapitulate the stages of thinking afterwards so that he can reflect on his own ideas. Suppose, for example, when playing with the bricks in a carpeted corridor the children constructed an incline to roll marbles down. The marbles pick up speed and roll all over the place. How do the children solve this problem? By reducing the gradient of the incline? By putting up a barrier? By using one of the group to catch the marbles?

Classroom climate

When the climate of the classroom encourages individual thought, children will begin to formulate their own problems. They will recognize problems in play and tell their teacher, 'We've got a problem here.' Older children can solve second-hand problems if they are linked to familiar situations and people. Discussion of problems may take up a great deal of time. It is easy to unleash an investigation rather carelessly, motivate the children and then not have the time or facilities to bring it to fruition. For example, a teacher asked a large group of children to look at summer grasses. When, the next day, they each brought a handful of grass into the school, she not only showed dismay at the unexpected response but was ill prepared to receive or identify the specimens.

Teachers can exploit opportunities to help children find reasons, evaluate their findings, and reach conclusions. For example, about the time of morning assembly, the children were asked, 'Shall we have it at 9.10 or 10.15, just before morning play?' Their reasons for choosing the later time were as follows:

Because it is a rush with the registers.
So that in winter the hall is warmed up.
If anyone is late they won't miss assembly.
So that chidren can talk about assembly in the playground.
Because the headteacher isn't so busy later in the morning.
So we have time to organize our work.
So that we don't have to walk down the corridor twice.
So that there are not two lots of sitting down together.

Provoking thought is one of a teacher's main jobs. It is quite different from asking children to follow her own thought processes.

Unexpected responses bring liveliness to a classroom. Given the opportunity to think constructively children will develop and maintain sturdy intellectual independence. The classroom teacher can nurture this by her presentation of activities, e.g. 'Once upon a time there was a school where the children were hard workers and kind to one another. Unfortunately, they were very noisy . . .' Gradually, through clues, the children realize the story is about them, their school and the noise problem.

Play

The teacher can also become involved in play, allocate time to observe play, and provide play equipment which will stimulate thinking. For example, in water play if the children are allowed to fill their own tray they must decide, 'We need more water' or 'We've got enough'. If the teacher has provided large, shallow containers, these are difficult to carry filled with water. Children may deduce that some containers are more suitable for transporting water than others or, 'I filled it too full' therefore 'I can't carry it'. Children form hypotheses: 'Bubbles burst when they hit something'.

Investigations

Joint investigations by children and teacher(s) together are another way of helping children towards good quality thought, particularly if there is more than one adult or teacher and each contribute their specialism. It is good for children to see adults actively learning together.

ROTE LEARNING

Rote learning unrelated to everyday situations and outside the children's experience is a waste of time, for example, learning lists of spellings selected by the teacher, which include words foreign to the child, for 'testing on Monday'. One child of six was required to learn *shout*, *about*, *stout*. When asked what 'stout' meant she said 'something on a tea pot'.

However, children enjoy learning poems, counting as far as they are able,[1] and generally measuring their own success.

Practice of skills independent of the task is sometimes necessary, for example, when using a roller or wash background for a picture, first-school children may need to practise first.

Individuals will develop their own techniques for learning facts. A group of children who were interested in the Royal Family learned the names of all the monarchs from William I to Elizabeth II. When asked how they did it, they replied:

'I kept on reading it through until I knew it.'

'I made up a little song and sang it to myself.'

'I learned lumps and then joined the lumps together.'

Language

There are many good books available in this field, including structured kits to develop vocabulary and the Joan Tough material on communication skills.

1 Relationships are all important. Children are more likely to converse freely if the emphasis is on sharing experiences with an adult rather than on 'instruction'.

2 Sometimes children arrive at school with gross language deficiencies and will need the individual attention of a skilled adult and specific teaching of words and structures. The learning will not necessarily take place through total reliance on exposure to an enriched environment, but will require evaluation of the difficulty and then appropriate action. A simple example is the use of a nod instead of a verbal answer, or the use of the teacher's surname without 'Miss' or 'Mrs'. Another is the response 'Yes' to a dual-choice question such as 'Would you like a ball or a bean-bag?' The teacher's own language and syntax is an important model for the children, and while it is not desirable to have a wide gap between the language of home and school, nevertheless the richness and variety of the teacher's spoken word is important.

3 Sometimes it is useful when planning activities for the teacher to choose half a dozen words or phrases which will extend the children's heard vocabulary.

4 A good time to have a language 'input' is when children are beginning to read widely and silently. Five minutes with a small, carefully-chosen group of four to six children is much more beneficial than half an hour with the whole class. 'Fantasy' conversations (Mahoon 1980) are good starting-points, e.g. 'If someone gave me a wish today . . .'.

Skills

Play activities offer interesting contexts for developing skills.

Collage How to apply adhesives, which adhesives are appropriate for certain materials.

Dressing up Selection and rejection of sizes, shapes, colours and materials;

development of small motor skills, imaginative role play.

DIFFERENT APPROACHES

It is sometimes helpful to set aside a short time for group activities such as paper folding, cutting, language skills. More able children can be encouraged to demonstrate skills and assist.

Skills are more likely to be taught successfully if the activity is exciting. Activities linked to current 'crazes' on TV may incorporate very routine skill practice yet prove popular, e.g. simple handwriting cards with messages from 'Dr Who'.

PRACTICAL SKILLS

Some children will have no idea of what is required and will need to be shown, for example, how to colour without going over the edge or leaving gaps. They may need to be given strategies to follow, for example, when cutting a shape out of a large piece of paper, cut it out roughly first, then accurately; when cutting along a fold, lay out the paper first and then cut from the bottom up.

SOCIAL SKILLS

Grouping the children in pairs and actively encouraging them to work together, e.g. card saying 'work for two children', is useful here. The task needs to be such that a division of labour is necessary and the children need to organize themselves. A class magazine or newspaper, drama in a small group, puppet plays, recording weather, drawing up a roster of helpers are all activities for encouraging children's social skills, provided help is given to start them off and is at hand if they encounter difficulties. On the other hand, passive listening to lengthy 'news times' does little to encourage social skills.

Orderliness

An orderly approach to work does not come easily to all and may need to be systematically taught, as it makes learning easier. Children will need time to prepare for work and to clear away at the end of a session.

Starting work

It helps to have regular introductory patterns to starting work, perhaps a brief checklist, e.g.

Have the children a clear idea of the task?

Have they access to all the necessary materials, e.g. sharpened pencils, work books?

Do they know what to do if they have difficulties?

Distractible children

This situation and task must be manageable for such children, e.g. the child can be seated away from others and given a signal (such as a small flag) to show that he does not wish to be disturbed. The work task will need to be brief (initially), carefully structured, enjoyable and offer the child the opportunity to succeed and be praised.

Dawdlers

The slow child will become progressively less motivated as he sees others forging ahead before he has even started his work. When setting the group a task the teacher can check after five minutes that every child has made a start. Such regular checks may help to prevent individuals from falling drastically behind. (A sand-timer may help the child to pace his work, if he knows that he has to complete the task by the time the sand has completely flowed through the timer.)

STRATEGIES FOR SUCCESS

The younger the child the more support he will need to achieve learning.

1 Every child will need room to spread out his things and write freely. Coloured Sellotape boundaries are sometimes useful. Papers, pieces of lino or felt can mark out working areas or floor spaces.

2 The length of task needs to match the time offered, or there should be opportunities to develop the work later.

3 *Appropriate materials* Good quality paper is essential – heavy pencil pressure on thin paper produces disastrous results. Tiny shapes to be coloured in with thick crayons is an example of asking the impossible.

Self-sufficiency

From the earliest age children can be taught to be responsible for their own learning (see Chapter 1, p.29).

1 The classroom should be planned as a resource work space with areas clearly identified and equipped for the different types of learning to be tackled, e.g. language and writing resources, art and craft materials with paper ready cut and boxes of different collage materials.

2 Children need to be systematically trained to retrieve materials, return them and keep the room in good order. This takes time and patience at the beginning of the year but benefits are reaped once children can cope for themselves, thus freeing the teacher to 'teach'.

3 In written language work the children could be helped, via imaginative approaches, to learn commonly used words (try *The First 200 Key Words to Literacy*). They can have their own sentence-makers and an envelope containing their own 'personal' words (these need to be kept to a manageable number). Colourful displays could focus on key words in a project. Children can select words for themselves (e.g. the word 'apples' could be fixed on a drawing of a tree, with Velcro). Displays could include suggestions for starting/ending stories.

4 Simple reference skills can be taught systematically from the earliest age, e.g. alphabetical order, use of a simple dictionary.

5 The children can learn to attempt all spellings for themselves before approaching the teacher.

Sex-stereotyping

This is an area where an individual teacher needs to sort out in her own mind the very real difference between traditional 'good manners' and sex-stereotyping. Having done that she can monitor the way she selects children for certain jobs (lifting, moving furniture; comforting other children), the way she handles children, and her presentation of male and female roles to the children through pictures, stories, visitors. (An excellent checklist is found in Valerie Hannon's source book for teachers.)

MATCHING CURRICULUM CONTENT TO PUPILS' DEVELOPMENT

Matching

Teachers could write down their present practice and then discuss as a whole staff, for example, what kinds of listening skills are appropriate for the children. A composite list will emerge which needs to be sifted into a lightly arranged rank order, bearing in mind that the teacher will return again and again to the same activity but in greater depth.

Teachers are individuals and need to use their ingenuity, experience and expertise. This method of organizing the content of the curriculum allows personal flexibility within an agreed framework. For example, the musician will probably enhance listening through music, the poet through words.

A 'home made' curriculum, to which all staff have contributed, and which is an organic workable model is better than the most beautifully-published commercial scheme. First efforts may be modest but teachers gain experience, new staff arrive, in-service work gathers strength and teachers report their classroom experience, the 'determined' curriculum (Musgrave's term for the curriculum 'as it is now') will become a major working tool.

Teachers are well aware of the pressure to 'get a child on to a reading book'. Many parents equate neat presentation with progress. Others set unrealistic goals. If the teacher has a curriculum content which is free of jargon and easy to explain to parents, she has a valuable asset.

Continuity of content

The model of the curriculum which we have suggested views content as a continuum along which teachers and children will travel, albeit at different rates. This continuum can flow into the receiving school. The content goals and presentation techniques should also overlap the next stage of education.

A teacher's intuition is built on training, experience and that sometimes despised 'sixth sense', which is made up of observation and sensitivity. Intuition will tell her when to rest the child or children at any point in the continuum of learning. The decision will also depend on the stage of the term, the school calendar, local events and her own emotional and physical resources. A teacher will vary the pace, introduction of new learning and general classroom arousal to fit her own rhythmic pattern as well as the children's. She would not, for instance, initiate some very demanding activity on the day she goes on a hefty after-school course.

Children sometimes make intellectual leaps. Out-of-school experience, or the cultural milieu of the classroom where children are encouraged to think for themselves, helps children form associations. For example, one child worked out for himself a method of calculating the area of a right-angled triangle. 'If it has equal sides, make it into a square and halve it. If it has different sides make it into a rectangle and halve it. There you are,' he said. Some children work out phonic rules for themselves. There is a danger of teaching children content they have already acquired.

A long-term content plan gives each teacher a bird's eye view of knowledge to be acquired. A new member of staff can assimilate her section first and gradually ease herself into the complete design. Change becomes easy – small pieces of content can be discarded or added without damage to the whole scheme.

The teacher needs to be quite certain in her own mind about two things: what is the content and why is it included? Every first-school teacher understands punctuation but a firm grip of symmetries and the reason for including it might not be so clear. At this stage the teacher herself needs material to explain carefully the basic content of the curriculum. Ideally, the background notes should cue into the content plan but references to the staff library (book and page), a set of tapes, or duplicated notes in a loose-leaf folder will serve. A few minutes with the consultant or head-teacher will probably be most economical and rewarding.

Observation

A useful technique is to offer the same problem to differing age-groups. The responses will remind teachers that children are developing human beings whose views of the world and sense of causality is very different from their own.

For example, the children had been to the beach and collected shells. They held them to their ears and heard 'the sound of the sea'. When asked why, the youngest children said, 'It's been in the sea for hundreds of centuries so it's right in it,' obviously thinking of sound as a property of the sea which had been transferred to the shell. The six-year-olds said, 'A little bit of water is in it so it's whirling round.' Another child said, 'You're not hearing the shell at all – you're hearing with the other ear.' As the children were in the hall at the time he was quickly nonplussed as some of them showed him the flaw in his logic. The older children gave written answers.

Hearing through a sea shell
I think that when you hear the sea through a sea shell you don't really hear it, it is just an illusion. It is the air trapped in the shell that is doing it and you can do the same if you put your hand to your ear having the tip of your fingers just above your ear and your palm hitting and bouncing off your ear.

MATCHING LEARNING OPPORTUNITIES TO INDIVIDUAL NEEDS AND CURRICULUM CONTENT

Teaching methods: stories

The story form can be used across the curriculum: to teach religious education; to introduce scientific topics – 'The boy who never cleaned his teeth'; for counting and understanding time (*The Twelve Dancing Princesses, Rumplestiltskin*); for understanding relative position (*The Three Billy Goats Gruff*). Stories can be used to foster imagination, create atmosphere, and enrich language. Myths, legends, true stories, humorous stories, stories with complicated plots and themes can be used to encourage anticipation and recall. Stories may be compared, e.g. *The Prodigal Son* and *The Lost Sheep* – what is the same/different about these two stories?

DRAMA
Sometimes stories arise out of drama. For example, children acted out the theme of going swimming. One child pretended to lose his sock and the other children made up stories to fit the situation.

SPELLING

Once upon a time there was a cat. He lived with an old lady and an old man. One day the old lady and man treated themselves to some steak for dinner. The old man said that he had some carrots and peas in the garden if his wife would help him pick them. So both the old lady and the old man went into the garden. When they came back there was just time to shell the peas and scrape the carrots and gently grill the steak. What a lovely dinner they were going to have! But, oh dear, when they came in the steak was gone! Only the paper was left on the table. What do you think . . . .

The children can then use words to describe the cat, drawing the cat on a piece of paper in front of them and writing the words (bad, thief, naughty etc.) round the edge. The teacher could then write these words on the board so that the children can correct their own. On the other side of the paper they could put key words from the story under the teacher's direction e.g. *bad, steak, peas*, and then write words with the same sound underneath:

bad	steak	peas
had	make	bees
lad	break	knees
sad	shake	keys
dad	rake	

READING
The story form can be used in all kinds of ways to promote reading: story

frieze; a story where each 'chapter' is uncovered on successive days; children can make a story into a puppet play.

CLASS MANAGEMENT

The management of the class (very quiet, equipment all ready beforehand, no equipment, length of story related to age and attention span of children, potential distracters on teacher's knee or by her side, children in seats or on carpet) will depend on the reason for the choice of the story in the first place. In other words the content and form must be as one and it is the teacher's role to ensure this. The content chart discussed on p.65 can now be annotated with suitable stories, giving details of where they can be found in the school. *The teacher will of course add to these herself* so the curriculum becomes not only agreed but also individual. It can be kept fresh if there are enough opportunities at staff meetings, working lunches, or after-school seminars for teachers to share successes with colleagues.

Care should be taken to ensure that children are not expected to listen for too long without responding, and that the group is not too large for children to be comfortable.

If a child finds it difficult to listen to a story the teacher may sit him close by her, or even on her knee, or simply encourage him with a smile or nod. If children lose interest and begin to distract others their attention can sometimes be regained without loss to the story or the audience by simply incorporating their name into the narrative, 'And then, *Darren* . . .'.

Games

TREASURE HUNT

On a wet day the children might enjoy a treasure hunt for pieces of a square (a tangram). A square (say 12 cm by 12 cm) can be drawn, photocopied and then divided into five different (but not so very different) shapes. There needs to be one square for each child taking part. If the school is a spacious one, 150 children could join in, because the only rule is that the children walk everywhere and take *one* piece at a time back to their place. Mothers or senior children from the secondary school could cut up the squares and put the pieces in various pots round the school. The children assemble their squares and when complete, tell their teacher. They then write their names on the board so there is a cumulative list of winners, in each class. Those who finished first can colour their pieces according to a code – the first piece is coloured red, the second green, etc. This idea can be adapted for spelling, reading, science etc. In a small school children could play in pairs, with an older child partnering a younger one.

GAMES FOR YOUNGER CHILDREN

Stepping stones

Very young children can play games which signal success and provide intellectual and physical progress. For example rising-fives can play at 'stepping stones games' with large paper shapes, making patterns, copying patterns, counting the shapes.

Balancing
Balancing games are good fun for the little ones particularly if the adults join in! A track, say 10 cm wide, is marked on the floor on paper or cardboard with a felt pen. The children take turns to tiptoe along it with a bean bag on their head without wobbling over the edge. For each successful try, one bead or conker is given. The first person with three conkers is the winner. The winner can wear the winner's badge or hat or just have a clap. Of course the teacher might decide to go on until everyone has three conkers in which case there is a 'first winner', 'second winner', 'third winner' etc.

COMMERCIAL GAMES
Board games, played singly, in pairs, groups or as a whole class (e.g. 'Bingo' type games) grow in complexity from simple counting games (e.g. plain grid-board, box of counters, the player throws the dice, and times how long it takes to fill up the board) to complicated chess strategies. There are some excellent commerical games on the market (who has not been tantalized by the Rubic Cube?), but perhaps the best kind of school game is the home-spun one, adapted by the teacher to fill a learning need.

One class could organize a 'games room' as a special occasion and invite other children on a rota basis to come and play.

If games are entered where appropriate on the content guide, are easy to find, well looked after and encourage progression, they can add much to the learning situation. Children themselves can invent games. Machine games (e.g. Data Man) need to be accepted by teachers as having a useful role in children's play, as do computer games.

Investigations
Children usually need quite a lot of help in the first school when carrying out investigations (i.e. finding out something they really want to know). Once again, this needs to be a progressive technique. Children can investigate in three ways – using another person, a book or recorded information, or the evidence of their own senses – or combine all three.

For example, some six-year-old boys had made a large tower and for some reason wanted to turn it into Big Ben. They knew from television that Big Ben had a clock but they weren't sure whether the clock had a face on each side of the tower, i.e. four faces. Their teacher did not know, so she sent them to the reference library, where there was no information on this subject. They asked another teacher but she was not sure. They asked their parents. No one knew. Finally the junior school lent them a book which provided the answer and they happily made three more clock faces. What surprised the teachers was the fact that the children's curiosity did not wane although they had to wait several days for the information.

'Please see if it is dry enough for us to go out to play' is a simple investigation but it has results. 'Have any of the tadpoles got big enough for us to put them in the pond?' is an investigation, once again with results. 'Where would you rather go for your outing -- the Zoological Gardens or the Museums?' The children now collect information, order it and read off results.

Investigation features largely in science. For example, furred anorak hoods seemed unsafe, so the children investigated (with the hoods in use) how sounds became muted at certain distances, and therefore whether it was safe to wear them.

Investigations need teacher support and this technique, although valuable, takes teacher time both in and out of school. Sometimes children have to realize that they cannot accomplish all they have set out to do. 'Please help me make a dome out of a piece of paper for my model' was, in the end, too difficult for both children and teacher. A young child, when playing with the bricks, asked a specialist adviser (who happened to be in the school) 'Can you make a spiral staircase?'. 'No, I'm sorry,' she said, 'I don't think I can.' Some investigations are unrealistic.

Discussion

Discussion arises naturally in the flow of work and is most fruitful when a teacher is involved. Children need to be helped to use discussion as a form of learning. Every first school teacher will know all too well that young children delight in giving her information – many of them at the same time as someone else!

Discussions can be 'set-up' as part of a learning situation. For example, a task, verbal or written, labelled 'work for two people' needs discussion before it can begin. The children will need first to discuss and plan the work and then feed back the results of their discussion to the teacher before they begin.

Plays involving two or three children require a great deal of ongoing discussion. It is almost always improved by the teacher enquiring from time to time about the children's progress.

It is possible to design curricula activities so that discussion will be pointed and significant. For example, two children were given 'a story' to read. They were asked to underline all the words and phrases in the text which told them something about the chief character and then see if they each had the same list, and if not, why not. Extended reading skills and critical analysis is a productive source of discussion, but the teacher needs to prepare the activity thoroughly and match it to the children.

Extension of play activities

Home corner play, sand play, water play, dramatic play with costumes and puppets, bricks, miniature world play (i.e. Lego, dolls' houses), shop play, are all fertile areas for matching the content of the curriculum with groups of children.

For example, by pricing the apples at four pence each, the oranges at seven pence each, the lemons at six pence each, the shopkeeper could make a 'ready reckoner', using his/her multiplication tables.

Making miniature gardens round miniature houses with a miniature family is a lovely introduction to measurement, promotes real discussion and gives aesthetic pleasure. This can be extended if a written invitation is given to a friend in another class to come and see it. A little guessing game can be introduced. The houses or gardens are unlabelled and visitors have to identify the models from written descriptions.

Special occasions

Peak times in the school calendar, providing they are meticulously arranged and not too frequent, can be the most satisfying learning experiences of all.

The school Christmas pudding: weighed, measured, mixed, cooked, tasted by each class. A letter can be sent home asking for one or two ingredients from a given list and an empty pudding basin. Names are attached to the basins with sticking plaster and the puddings are mixed. Each child has a pudding to take home and cook. (A good way of cooking Christmas puddings is to put them in pans of boiling water up to the neck of the basin and put them in a slow oven for eight hours.) This old-fashioned activity brings delight to every family and pleasure to mothers who haven't got time to cook! One little girl's father was so pleased with his six-year-old's efforts that he lit the brandy round it but was mis-understood by his daughter who thought he was burning her pudding and burst into tears.

RUMMAGE SALES

The children can manage these. They can write the appeals and sort the articles (obviously with help) – putting out the shoes means pairing them up, sorting boys' from girls', children's from adults'. They could draw up a rota for the day, perhaps starting at 8.30am and finishing at 4pm. They can decide who can do the early shift! Handling the money is first-hand real experience. As each child is only in the hall for half an hour, parents see this as a valuable addition to classroom work rather than a distraction.

Small classroom sales are very enjoyable when arranged entirely by the children.

A PARENTS' TEA

Children enjoy arranging and cooking the food, providing entertainment, sorting out the seating, making the invitations.

A PET SHOW

Again this can be organized by the children, but will need unsqueamish adults to oversee arrangements.

A 'SWAP A BOOK DAY'

Every child brings a book from home and swaps it with someone else for the weekend. If carefully planned this can involve a tremendous amount of reading, writing, discussion.

OTHER SUGGESTIONS

A school trip; the secondary school band or choir pay a visit; a dance team come to school etc.

Displays

If the children arrange their own objects, write the labels, and have time to talk about the artefacts, specimens or items, displays can be used by the teacher as learning situations. The way items are displayed can help or hinder the learning. For example, a small insect can be comfortable but displayed in a container with a magnifying lid. Children should discuss with teachers whether a violet or silver table would be more appropriate than red.

Children's interests, current events and festivals can all be matched to curriculum content. For example, a mother's day card for the little ones might be fairly large with a picture and caption. The oldest children could design a folded card, make an envelope for it and write a poem for the inside.

Sometimes teachers can seize on an incident which sweeps away that day's plans. Such spontaneous work, used sparingly and carefully, can bring freshness to writing and point to speech. For example, Zoë fell over and was most upset. The other children crowded round, commiserated, recounted their own misfortunes and suddenly the teacher realized that this was a common experience. By the end of the morning one corner of the classroom was filled with writing and drawings which were full of vitality and a display was set up of all the things needed for grazed knees, cut fingers etc.

Teacher-directed learning

Children do not stumble into skills and concepts unaided. Nor can the content of the curriculum be introduced, and extended entirely through immediacy. There is a need for the teacher consciously to plan learning experiences such as handwriting skills, a new technique in art or craft, word attack skills, mathematical ideas etc.

If the children are solving problems, engaged in good quality play, concentrating hard while painting, they need to be left alone. If children are practising skills they need to have quick feedback and knowledge of results.

MONITORING PROGRESS AND KEEPING RECORDS

Start with the children

AN INDIVIDUAL PROFILE

It is useful to have a record of the child as a person containing all the information that school staffs consider relevant and helpful – favourite forms of play, health records, pre-school experience, family occurrences – perhaps with a photograph attached. If it is written in a positive, constructive way, schools may feel able not only to show it to parents but also to ask them to contribute so that it becomes a joint venture.

For example, the child who is reluctant to leave his mother during the first days of school: 'He screamed for the first four days. They had to hang on to him. Then on the fifth day he waved "bye bye" like a big boy. I wasn't surprised at him being upset, we were terribly close. I feel upset . . . I felt terrible . . . like lost. I still do now and I know he's only over the road.'[25] How will this mother feel when her son goes to the junior or middle school, especially if it is some distance from the first school? Frank but sensitive profiles can be used in an intelligent way to help both children and their parents. 'Enjoyed being king in the nativity play' not only records his expertise but prevents him having the same part next year.

THE DEVELOPMENT DOCUMENT

This is a record of how a child has progressed through the whole curriculum over the entire time he has been in the first school. It is a kind of 'curriculum map'. When opened out it shows at a glance the way the child has received the agreed curriculum, and his particular successes and difficulties. It records all three areas of the curriculum on one piece of paper and complements the curriculum document which is in the teacher's possession.

How to draw it up

There are several ways: what follows is only one suggestion. First of all, the agreed curriculum needs to be set out along the top of the record from left to right, e.g. play, science, mathematics, the expressive arts. These main headings will stretch across two or three sheets of A4 paper Sellotaped together. (The Sellotape makes a convenient 'hinge' so that the document can be folded up for easy storage.)

Under these main headings, supplementary headings may be added, e.g. under 'mathematics' – spatial understanding, number, structure and mechanisms, logical thought and measurement; under 'expressive arts' – listening, speaking, singing, writing, reading, movement, worship, drama and RE.

Along the other axis (running from the top left-hand corner to the bottom left-hand corner) the child developmental stages need to be listed. A crude but adequate tabulation in a five-to-seven school might be: beginners, middles, tops; another might be: reception, lower, upper school; a third might be year-groups – in mixed-age classes this is still possible.

How to fill it in

The developmental stages and curriculum content are now recorded. The main body of the record can now be completed by the teacher.

For example, to make an entry about a six-year-old's reading, the teacher would find the place on the curriculum map by running her finger *down* the page under the heading 'reading' to where it says 'middles'. The entries here would be directly relevant to the agreed curriculum worked out by the staff and may, for instance, note 'word-attack skills poorly developed' or, 'reads fluently, anticipating from text and using context skilfully'. It might also say 'reads reluctantly' or 'tends to forget glasses – must be reminded'.

Advantages
What are the advantages of this type of record? First, and most important, systematic teaching can be logged side by side with fluid, spontaneous learning, project or theme work. If the teacher has her own image of the curriculum map, when presented with a rich source of learning, (e.g. Christmas) she will be able to draw out of the situation those ideas and skills which are appropriate for the stage the child has reached. Moreover she will be able to link areas of the curriculum together. If the record is made of headings along two axes and the remainder is blank, the teacher can enter not only the activity, but the success or otherwise, of the child.

Second, the ever-present danger of the child's record degenerating into a checklist, and teachers then teaching to the checklist, with the attendant difficulties of mis-matching, fragmentation, repetition and lack of true intellectual advance, will, hopefully, be avoided. Entries need to be spasmodic and pointed – i.e. recorded when relevant and immediate, not left to the end of the school term, or worse still, school year, when memories have faded. A teacher will then use the record as a diagnostic tool. For example, if a child of seven is reversing letters within words frequently (e.g. gril for girl, shcool for school) the teacher can make a note of it and then take appropriate action and record the result. In this way each child's curriculum map becomes a monitoring document not only for the child but for the teacher herself, of the curriculum as a whole, and the ways in which it is offered.

Other advantages include continuity and progression and the fact that a slow or able child can be catered for either by being rested or led into the next stage. Teachers will be able to view the work as a whole, work as part of a team and have an overall policy. Pieces of children's work can be filed with the development document.

Some schools will make a note on the individual child's curriculum map when he has reached a milestone. For example, if he is a beginner the teacher may wish to record, under the expressive arts, 'PE – can dress and undress by himself'. On the other hand some schools will record outstanding successes and failures only. These may be entered in colours – red for successes, blue for difficulties (e.g. in red, 'exceptional facility with spoken language' or, in blue, 'cannot remember messages yet'. These entries would assume the teacher is planning further activities for both these children. It is helpful sometimes to lay out all the development documents on the floor so as to get an overall view of success and difficulties. This will also tell the teacher something about herself. Are there more blue entries than red, or vice versa? When the child is a 'top' is he still having difficulty in undressing for PE?

For the teachers

TEACHER'S DOCUMENTS
It is in the teacher's personal file (one for home, one for school, one for free annotation) that activities, presentation techniques, and learning outcomes, together with location of appropriate resources, need to be identified. The individual child's record will reflect the agreed curriculum and the agreed curriculum will be in the possession of the teacher.

Format and content
Each discipline needs to be broken down into sections which relate to the stage of development of the child. For example, under writing (writing with a purpose as opposed to handwriting) one of the entries might be:

Beginners

Materials	Activity	Learning outcome
soft pencil	Copy starter card	Writing is easy if we get
paper	and find words to	our words organized.
starter card	finish sentence.	It is fun to read your
	Then read to teacher	writing to other people.
This is my	or friend.	
I can see		
I play		
(through discussion		
or display)		

The teacher will draw her long-term and short-term plans from her curriculum, but also relate it to projects, topics, themes and special situations.

Vague headings such as 'length' are useless, but the document should not become so bulky that it is overwhelming.

A large closely-written file is daunting. It is easy to go overboard and make the work unwieldy. Complicated diagrams linking subjects, detailed pie charts, and concept maps overlaid with suggestions for teaching are suspect because their true value is usually in the discussion of the original design. New teachers coming to a school fail to follow the original line of thought and sometimes cannot see the wood for the trees. It may even engender a feeling of inadequacy. A simple, easily followed set of papers need not be without rigour. Indeed it is harder to design a simple but comprehensive content chart than a more complicated one.

Staffs may wish to prepare a 'skeleton' of the whole curriculum content (as discussed on p.83) on a single page, and add the work in finer detail. These two 'layers' are useful for a busy teacher. The first 'layer' can be offered to governors and parents, or sent to candidates on invitation to interview.

Cooperation

Because the written curriculum is meant to become a personal working document, entries should allow teachers to add their own successful ideas and methods and, in consultation with colleagues, delete superfluous items.

In some areas, such as handwriting, the whole school needs to follow an agreed scheme. It is necessary for staffs to decide whether there are other areas where a team approach is beneficial to the children, e.g. use of pencils, lavatory routines, etc.

It is neither possible nor desirable to prescribe how detailed the sequences of learning ought to be. The headteacher and consultant teacher will judge when that fine balance between the written record and evidence of the agreed plan has been achieved throughout the school. Of course this will vary from teacher to teacher and at different times in the term. Tact will be needed if a teacher diverts too far from the agreed curriculum.

'Tips' need never be despised. They sometimes mark the difference between a happy successful session and fraught nerves! Any ideas to facilitate good management are welcome and should be shared and written down.

No content should be included that is not thoroughly understood by the teacher. In a relaxed, professionally-orientated school individual teachers will not be afraid to ask, colleagues will be pleased to assist and the headteacher will be ever vigilant to detect where help is needed.

Monitoring and assessment

Monitoring and evaluation are discussed in Chapter 3, p.133. Consultant 'chats', year-group meetings, staff meetings, visits to other schools, background reading and a library of children's work are all useful ways of monitoring classroom practice and the efficacy or otherwise of the agreed curriculum.

1 A library of children's work is only a substitute for visiting colleagues' classrooms, but it can be illuminating to browse through a collection of children's work, particularly if the categories are identical with the headings in the written documents.

2 A display mounted by a consultant on one topic, theme, idea or skill is useful for other busy practitioners and can help to clarify the consultant's own ideas.

3 Standardized tests have their place if the results are studied carefully and action is taken in the light of the findings.

APPRAISAL QUESTIONS

ACQUIRING KNOWLEDGE IS BASIC TO THE CURRICULUM

Have I got a clear idea of the content of the school curriculum?
Could I produce a skeleton of it in a few minutes?
Are there any parts of the curriculum which I do not totally understand myself?
Are there any able children in my class whom I suspect are not being challenged sufficiently? What am I doing about it?
How do I plan a project with reference to acquisition of knowledge?
Is there a better way of doing it?
Have I taken time for myself this week for pure intellectual pleasure and relaxation?
How many books of any kind did I read last month?

ACQUIRING KNOWLEDGE INVOLVES GROWTH IN THE LEARNER

What improvement have I noticed in the behaviour of individual children this term?
Is there a child in the class who causes me misgivings *re* attitude to other children? What positive steps have I taken to help him?
Have I timetabled myself to observe the children at different times – when starting a task, when playing a game? What use have I made of my observations?
Have I given the children opportunities to make mistakes and then correct them?
Have I deliberately fostered self-sufficiency in the children?
Have I made provisions for children to continue with an activity until they have reached their own finishing-point, even if this means cutting across playtime or other planned activities?
What evidence is there that the children are keen and actively involved in the curriculum activities offered them?

MATCHING CURRICULUM CONTENT TO PUPILS' DEVELOPMENT

Who is the most/least mature child in the class? On what do I base my judgment?
If a child experiences difficulty do I check on all the previous stages to see if there is a gap in understanding?
What criteria do I use for grouping the children?
Are the children in the same groups for writing activities and mathematics?
Do the able children have the same opportunity for play, painting, sand,

water play as the slower children?
Does the more highly socialized, voluble child have more share of my attention than the shy one?
Whom do I send on messages? Why?

MATCHING LEARNING OPPORTUNITIES TO INDIVIDUAL NEEDS AND CURRICULUM CONTENT
When did I last tell a story as an introduction to solving a problem?
How old are the oldest workcards in daily use in my classroom?
Is my day varied in pace, tone, ethos?
Is there an element of surprise sometimes in my classroom?
When did I last notice the children were not understanding something? What did I do about it then? The next day?
Is there a piece of equipment in the classroom that has been unused for six weeks? six months?
Have I made any innovations with equipment recently?
When did I last take the children outside as part of their learning environment?
How many times did I interrupt the children this morning for purely managerial reasons?
Does my forward planning include consciously adapting or introducing a new way of presenting the curriculum?
Do the children and I look at pictures together? listen to music together? enjoy poetry together? Do I enhance their understanding by my questions?

MONITORING PROGRESS AND KEEPING RECORDS
When did I last look at the children's records? Why?
Were the records from the previous teacher any help to me? Have I questioned her about them?
Is my assessment of any of the children at variance with her assessment?
Would I mind if the parents had open access to all the records kept concerning their child?
If I put all my professional work in rank order, does keeping adequate records of the children's progress come high, low or in the middle of my list?
Do I annotate the children's records while the school is in session or do I always do it at home? Do I let the children know what I am doing?
Do I sometimes select one child to write about, or is it always the whole class?
Do I feel vulnerable if I have not made many entries on the children's records? Why?
Have I learned any new piece of professional expertise from any colleague in the last three weeks?
Are there any areas of the agreed curriculum which I know I neglect or in which I know I am particularly skilled?
Is there any area in which I have had to compromise in order to show

professional generosity and play my part in the team?
Have I moved forward in my view of the curriculum in the last two years?
Can I think of a recent instance when I have been able to relate a current
interest of the children with the agreed content of my school's curriculum?
Do I want to influence the curriculum? In what way?

FURTHER RESOURCES

BOOKS

BREARLEY, M. (1969) (ed.) *Fundamentals in the First School* Blackwell

BRUNER, J. (1974) *Beyond the Information Given* Allen & Unwin

DE BONO, E. (1980) *Children Solve Problems* Penguin

CAVE, R. (1971) *An Introduction to Curriculum Development* Ward Lock Educational

EISNER and VALLENCE (1974) (eds.) *Conflicting Conceptions of Curriculum* McCutchan

FORD and PUGNO (1964) (eds.) The Structure of Knowledge and the Curriculum Rand McNally

GALTON, M. (1980) (ed.) *Curriculum Change: the Lessons of a Decade* Leicester University Press

GORDON and LAWTON (1978) *Curriculum Change in the Nineteenth and Twentieth Centuries* Hodder and Stoughton

HIRST, P. (1974) (ed.) *Knowledge and the Curriculum* Routledge & Kegan Paul

HOOPER, R. (1971) (ed.) *The Curriculum: Context, Design and Development* Oliver and Boyd

KING, B. (1966) (ed.) *The Curriculum and the Disciplines of Knowledge* Wiley

PERIODICALS

Educational Research News National Foundation for Educational Research in England and Wales (NFER)

Educational Research The journal of the NFER

Curriculum The journal of the Association for the Study of the Curriculum, Studies in Education Ltd, Nafferton, Driffield, N. Humberside, YO25 0JL

COURSES

CURRICULUM IN ACTION A pack of materials to assist teachers to acquire skills needed to systematically evaluate their work in the classroom. Open University INSET 1981

3

ORGANIZATION

INTRODUCTION

Since the development of first schools in the late sixties, following the recommendations in the Plowden Report, increased knowledge about how young children learn has inevitably meant an emphasis on more informal structures within the classroom. If the focus of attention is now on children acquiring the skills and concepts to develop their learning rather than the teacher drilling them in subject content, then the onus is on the teacher to enable every child to grow intellectually according to his own rate of development. Clearly this cannot be done by keeping a class of children seated all day long in rows and instructing them as one body. However, although the teacher may be well aware of what she *should* be doing to encourage learning, she is faced with her own practical situation, which she will need to consider carefully. The following headings may provide a useful starting-point.

TIME

Every teacher is aware of the speed with which a day, a term and year disappears and the difficulty of spending enough time with children to help develop their learning. So how children spend their time in school will be one of the major priorities: 'The heart of the matter is what each child takes away from school. For each of them what he or she takes away is the effective curriculum.'[1] Teachers, therefore, need to look closely at the experiences that they are offering children. If the experiences are inappropriate it could be that some children are spending their time in planning ways of avoiding work and are actively preventing other children from working by disrupting them.

How much time is actually spent learning? The Schools Council Project on Open Plan Schools notes that 'the most surprising find was the large amount of transition, which included time spent in changing activities or changing location [which] took up about a fifth of the school week in infant units'. The authors do concede, however, that some of this time could be used to develop skills with young children:

> For example, a secondary teacher would not expect to have to tie pupils' shoelaces and would probably consider such a task to be unconnected with teaching. An infant teacher on the other hand might regard this as a legitimate teaching activity. The latter view is accepted, although it is still maintained that such time is non-curricular.[2]

Teachers do perhaps need to look at their programme and note just how much time the children spend moving around the school waiting for something to happen or clearing away.

Teacher time is probably the most precious resource in the school and as such should be deployed with care. The skilled teacher manages to set up an environment where some children are learning by pursuing various activities, leaving her free to teach others. What sort of tasks need teacher time? They include dealing with individual children's resource needs and assembling materials for work, as well as individual and group teaching. She can then isolate those tasks that could be avoided by meticulous prior preparation. These will include regular checking of all classroom equipment (from sharpened pencils to complete sets of apparatus); organizing the labelling and grading of materials which can then be available for children to use independently; planning meaningful second tasks for children who have completed their main activity. In the Schools Council Project *Extending Beginning Reading*[3] it was found that teachers of first- and second-year juniors were quite frequently involved for a whole hour in helping individual children to spell words they needed for written work. Clearly this is an example of poor use of a precious commodity. An attempt to reduce this drain on teacher's time could help to release some of it for diagnosis, teaching and guidance. One way to do this is by using hardware and/or ancillary or voluntary assistance. In order to make maximum use of this help the teacher will need to be able to delegate responsibility and work with confidence with other adults either in or out of the classroom.

In addition to class responsibility the teacher needs to spend time on her subject or pastoral responsibility. Much of this work will be done after school, by taking a lead at staff meetings, or during lunch hours, when the year leader might hold regular meetings with her team. However, the Primary Survey[4] stresses that consultant teachers do need some non-contact time during the school day in order to have the maximum effect on colleagues. Moreover teachers also need time to attend courses and consult with colleagues to further their own professional development. This will take place through school staff meetings and within the wider context of local and regional courses. Whilst some of these sessions may take place during the school day, increasingly in-service meetings occur after school has finished. Such sessions, to be effective, need to be sensitively organized to meet teachers' needs: 'Course members respond well to sessions which are varied in rhythm and have a range of activity – this seems to be particularly important when teachers come, rather tired, straight from a full working day at school.'[5]

CURRICULUM

Decisions about how the curriculum is to be offered to children will be governed by basic principles. Evidence points to young children benefiting from a continuous programme of learning, based on experience with concrete materials. But whilst the basic principles will determine the philosophy for working, the decisions about content and progression will need to be laid down according to recommendations in *Education 5 – 9*: 'Good guidelines contain basic aims and specific objectives, clearly-defined indicators of progression and detailed suggestions as to how the work might be developed.'[6] The Schools Council's study[2] makes the distinction between curriculum allocation, i.e. the opportunity that teachers provide for pupils to study a given curriculum context, and pupil involvement, i.e. what pupils choose to make of that opportunity.

On average junior-age children were allocated to curriculum activities for 66.4 per cent of their time and infant children for 61 per cent. The remaining time was spent in administration and transition activities. When looking at the proportion of time that children were actually *involved* in curriculum activity the figures of 76 per cent and 79 per cent for infants are substantially higher because they include administration and transition time. When looking at specific curriculum activities the highest proportion of time was allocated to language and maths, and yet these activities showed the lowest involvement levels from children: '. . . perhaps a better indicator of balance is to be gained from what pupils do rather than what teachers allocate'.[2] So the teacher needs to look at how her programme is received by children during the course of a day and over a longer period of time.

TEACHING AND LEARNING
Having decided on the appropriate programme the teacher must then consider how to group the children. These decisions will be affected by the wider forms of organization used within the school: the teacher may work in one classroom with one age-group, or she may be working continually with a team of colleagues, sharing a mixed age-group, and using a shared teaching space.

> The heart of the problem is how to match language, content, method and process to the pupils' differing ages and stages of development. Each teacher has to try to cater for levels in different attainment, speed of learning and emergent interests. Nor do pupils necessarily learn the various stages of development in the same order or at the same speed.[2]

Every teacher then is faced with the question of what form of organization she must adopt to enable each child in her class to spend his time in the most worthwhile manner.

The Plowden Report made a case for giving attention to the individual child: 'any class, however homogeneous it seems, must always be treated as a body of children needing individual and different attention'.[7] Unfortunately large classes militate against the individual child receiving regular attention. A study of teacher-pupil contacts in five junior class-rooms revealed that, over a six-day observation period, two specific groups of children received the majority of the teacher's time: the group of hardworking children who approached the teacher themselves and the disruptive group who required disciplining. The authors conclude: 'If teacher contact is desired then being average and passive . . . is not the way to obtain it.'[8]

Teachers who emphasize the importance of working with individual children need to match their perceptions with what actually happens. Deanne Boydell's small study[9] was of six junior teachers in the classroom, all of whom relied heavily on teaching through offering individual attention. On average the teachers spent three-quarters of their time involved in work-orientated conversation and only a quarter on routine and discipline matters. On further investigation, however, it was observed that the children were mainly aware of comments on the latter. Thus although these teachers were making an estimated 100-plus contacts with children every hour, of which the majority were individual and work-orientated, Boydell states that, paradoxically, 'Children's experience of the teacher will be that she leaves them totally alone for long stretches of time and periodically talks to them as a class, sometimes about work, but almost as often about classroom organization or behaviour.'[10]

Plowden also advocated the benefits of small groups of children working together when they 'learn to get along together, to help one another and realize their own strengths and weaknesses'.[7] However this form of organization requires planning and training so that the children know just what is required of them. Galton, Simon and Croll stress that the teachers they observed teaching eight- to ten-year-olds made very little use of group situations:

> In essence it seems most teachers concentrate on individualization both of work and of attention, as Plowden prescribed. While grouping exists, both spatially (geographically) and to some extent notionally, in reality the pupil works on his own.[11]

One of their main conclusions is that 'the whole issue of the purpose and organization of group work in the primary school classroom requires a great deal more attention than it has had to date'.[11] Whilst some group and individual teaching remains essential if children's various learning needs are to be met, the Bullock Report indicates a sensible compromise:

> We, therefore, consider the best method of organization (reading) to be one where the teacher varies the experience between individual, group, and class situations according to the purpose in hand.[12]

THE ENVIRONMENT
Each teacher needs to look critically at how the school building, the design and space in her classroom, the apparatus and equipment, can best meet the needs of the children. The aim should be to produce an environment which is exciting and attractive for adults and children.

Few situations can be said to be ideal. The design of buildings and outside areas will inevitably encourage or constrain different ways of organizing and teaching the children. However, if teachers are firm in their philosophy, such physical features can be adapted, and decisions about organization will reflect the teacher's priorities.

Some buildings require a particularly imaginative and sensitive staff to change them into a comfortable place in which to live and learn, rather than an institution. Display will play a large part in this change. It is an aspect of work which can be very time consuming, and so it is all the more important that the point and purpose of display is considered to find the most efficient ways of creating the best effects and to make it an effective means of learning. The Plowden Report justifies such work on aesthetic grounds:

> It should be the object of every school to do all in its power to add to the beauty of its equipment and environment, in exactly the same way as a householder with a sensitive eye for beauty will make such constant additions, improvements and adaptations, as his means allow, to the house and garden in which he lives.[7]

John Dewey described organization as 'nothing but getting things into connection with one another so that they work easily, flexibly and fully'. Good organization should enable the most effective use of resources within a school. Primary consideration must be given to decisions about what to teach, but organizational decisions will focus on the 'how, when and where' questions relating to the children, adults, curriculum and building. As such it is a key ingredient to maximizing learning opportunities for children, teacher's job satisfaction and professionalism.

WHAT THE THEORY SAYS

TIME

Organization of the child's time

AVOIDING WASTING TIME

All teachers are well aware of the short span of time that the child is exposed to learning in school. In *Extending Beginning Reading* the researchers note:

> The actual total time devoted to reading and writing activities was considerably less than most teachers might imagine it to be. The main reason for this . . . arose from alterations to school routines, interruptions by people coming into the classroom and interruptions by children within the class. Consequently a period which the teacher might regard as thirty minutes or one hour devoted to reading and writing activities could be whittled away by perhaps a quarter or a third. As a result, the teacher's objectives for the term which they had written out in advance may not have been fully implemented because of these curtailments to anticipated time.[3]

The teacher needs to bear this in mind when planning her programme.

The danger of paying too much attention to children individually is noted in this same report:

> The high work output of teachers was not always mirrored by high task-orientation in their pupils. In fact, in certain lessons, particularly when the teacher was engaged in listening to individual children's oral reading or helping them individually with spelling in a writing lesson, there were indications that with certain children an obverse effect took over: higher teacher output was then related to low pupil output.[3]

Clearly an 'overview' of the class on a regular basis is necessary as is careful attention to children who are known to have a low concentration span.

TRANSITION TIME

Young children do need considerable time to learn self-management skills (i.e. dressing and undressing themselves) and how to prepare and clear away activities. However teachers do need to look closely at the amount of school time taken up with non-curricular activity.

The Schools Council Project on Open Plan Schools indicates that some of this time is taken up with children changing their teaching space or activity.

> On average, pupils (of infant age) spend between 4 and 9 per cent of the school day during periods of transition, waiting for signals from the teacher before changing activity and/or location. For example, teachers signal the end of an activity and this is followed by a flurry of movement as pupils clear away and possibly obtain materials for the next activity. If a change of location is required, pupils form queues adjacent to traffic-flow areas. There they can wait until the last pupil is ready and a further signal is received from the teacher which allows them to proceed to their next destination.[2]

CHOICE IN THE USE OF TIME

A 'child-centred' approach to education implies that learning starts by developing the child's interests rather than predetermining what is to be learned. Many teachers are interested in children as individuals, and encourage them to develop as autonomous learners.[13] This will only be possible if children are allowed some choice in how they use their time.

Organization of the teacher's time

TIME WITH CHILDREN

Any teacher in charge of a large class of young children needs to be clear-sighted about what she is doing, well-organized and capable of maintaining good classroom control. In his sociological study of infant classrooms Ronald King observes:

> Teachers who were most content with the effectiveness of their control had two characteristics. First, they made their expectations and rules quite explicit. This refers to both work tasks and behaviour. Secondly, they used a great deal of approval and praise when the expectations were met and rules kept. Their rare use of disapproval was more effective than the disapproval of those teachers who used it much in sanctioning the failure to meet expectations and for breaking rules.[14]

In addition the teacher needs to be sufficiently informed about her children to know when and where her intervention is necessary and most desirable. Wynne Harlen's work[15] identifies how children's progress can be monitored through their daily action and responses and helps teachers to observe and act on this in a systematic way. Joan Tough's work on communication skills[16] looks at how the teacher's language affects children's learning. Both these studies provide practical assistance in devising checklists to help the teacher identify how she can use time with children most profitably.

USE OF CLASSROOM AIDS

In order to provide a range of activity in her classroom the teacher will need to make sensible use of learning resources that profitably occupy some children, thus freeing her to give attention to others. Such aids may include a range of commercial and home-made workcards, audio-visual equipment such as language masters, cassette recorders and overhead projectors, as well as radio and television. These resources, if used imaginatively and in moderation, can enhance a classroom; but they cannot take the place of the teacher's own contact with children and her sensitive response to their individual and immediate needs.

Workcards

Galton, Simon and Croll express their misgivings about workcards: 'The use of workcards as substitutes for teacher contact has obvious dangers. Many of the observers' descriptive accounts emphasized that the work the pupils were doing often appeared repetitive and that many children seemed to be bored.'[11] The authors explain that a main cause of this boredom lies in graded workcards which require children to solve increasingly complex problems related to a particular skill or topic rather than explain alternatives if the child experiences difficulty:

> In some cases moreover the observers' accounts indicate that such pupils have their books marked silently and then return to their place to work through the same problems yet again until they have completed a correct set of answers. Then the pupil will be back for a new workcard with more difficult examples of the same thing. It is not surprising if, under these circumstances, some pupils prefer to talk to their neighbour about other things rather than getting on with their work.[11]

If this type of situation is to be avoided and workcards used to reinforce first-hand experiences and meet individual and group needs the teacher needs to plan carefully to include them in her teaching strategy and regularly monitor their effect.

Technological aids

The Bullock Report voiced concern about teachers' unrealistic ideas as to what technological aids could achieve in the classroom. However, it continues:

> . . . these reservations made, we have no doubt that aids of this kind have a considerable contribution to make with regard to language development and the teaching of reading. They give the teacher extended opportunities at various levels of activity from individual tuition to full-class involvement.[12]

Furthermore, Bullock does not underestimate the skills required if these aids are to be used properly:

> In his continuous assessment of each child's progress and needs he (the teacher) should see technical aids as another resource available to him to prescribe for a particular situation. And that means knowing the child, knowing the strengths and limitations of various pieces of equipment and knowing whether any one of them is appropriate for that child on that occasion.[12]

To sum up, in Bullock's words: 'We must again emphasize the importance of the teacher's control over the media. They must serve his curriculum planning, not dictate to it.'

USE OF ANCILLARY AND VOLUNTARY HELP

However organized the teacher, there are many occasions in the day when extra assistance is badly required. The younger the age-group, the greater the need for another adult to meet the social and physical needs of children as they are learning to dress and undress, to move from one area to another, and to learn in a group setting. Paid ancillary help is available for some teachers but usually only on a part-time basis. Thought and planning must enable this time to be used to the best effect.

The Schools Council Project on Open Plan Schools noted that in their study ancillary assistance considerably increased learning opportunities:

> The smooth running of organization is based on teaming, indeed most organizations appeared in initial visits to schools to be dependent on the amount of ancillary help available in the unit. In fact some organizations depended quite clearly on the presence of an ancillary in specified spaces, e.g. stationed in a practical area, where the visibility from the practical area to the teaching area was poor. This allowed teachers to send groups of children into these areas knowing that materials would be supplied and supervision given.[2]

Parents as voluntary helpers

Using parents as voluntary ancillary helpers is still a delicate matter in some schools. There is concern about relationships with paid ancillary helpers, whether the right sort of parent will volunteer, and questions about parents' status at breaktimes – should they be accepted as full members of staff into the staffroom?

Sometimes staff views differ on the use of parents. One headteacher in the Open Plan Study reflected a common policy adopted: 'Involvement of parents in classroom activities was left to the discretion of staff. "They take groups for cookery, sewing, play a number game or just talk to the children."' However, in schools where there is a general keen commitment to encouraging parents' assistance, the benefits are obvious. The same study reports one example:

Parents are welcomed into school and encouraged to go along regularly and work under the guidance of the staff. Parents can be seen teaching cookery, pottery, sewing, woodwork, telling stories and hearing competent readers. The purposes and key teaching-points in the parent's work, e.g. the measuring processes in cookery, are clearly identified by the teacher in prior discussion with parents.[2]

Here we see teachers actively delegating responsibility, at the same time using their skills to counsel parents about maximizing on the learning involved in each situation. This surely is beneficial to all concerned.

Involvement with classroom activity is only one aspect of parent/ school relationships which is discussed more fully in Chapter 5. Here we are looking at the benefits to the curriculum and school organization of parental help. Whilst these can be considerable, the school should be aware of parental attitudes. In a study of parental preferences for home/ school contact parents expressed little enthusiasm to help in the class-room. The study concludes:

The poor response seems to result from the fact that although reasonably common in schools very few parents are actually involved. In discussion some parents said that they were suspicious of the motives of other parents in offering help and many thought that parents in the classroom would provide an additional distraction to the children. There was also some mis-understanding on the part of some of the parents of what exactly parents did in the classroom. They expressed the opinion that it is the job of the teacher to teach, and not of the parents.[17]

However, we are aware of the opposing argument as articulated by Bruner (see Chapter 1, p.9).

THE CONSULTANT TEACHER

Holding a post of responsibility in a school means extra finance and status, in return for which the teacher is expected to tackle tasks additional to her classroom work. The responsibility may be for a year-group or for an area of the curriculum. Both require a close look at children's work and at existing practices in the school with an eye to any change which may be necessary.

The Primary Survey stressed that where there was evidence of curri-culum development in a school it was usually due to the involvement of a curriculum consultant. It also stressed that 'Teachers holding posts of responsibility require time to perform their duties, some of which must be carried out while the school is in session. . . . They also need to keep up to date with current knowledge and practices elsewhere and this may take time outside normal school hours.'[4]

CURRICULUM ORGANIZATION

The Practical Curriculum states that teachers find it as difficult to know *how* to teach something as to know *what* to teach. Having decided on content the question remains of how it is to be presented to children and how the activities are to be balanced. These decisions must be based on the child's requirements: his ability to learn through concrete experiences, his concentration span and physical need for movement.

The pattern of the day

Brown and Precious, writing about the integrated day, described it as a 'school day which is combined into a whole and has the minimum of timetabling. Within this day there is time and opportunity in a planned educative environment for the social, emotional, physical and aesthetic growth of the child at his own rate of development.'[18] In practice, as shown by Peter Moran's survey in 1971,

. . . there are varying interpretations of this idea which include different ways of integrating curriculum activities: different ways of grouping children: operation of activities in varying sequences by groups, individuals and the whole class: opportunity for children to choose their own sequence of activity: timing of activities or freedom to complete them by the end of the session or the day.[19]

Dearden assumes some notion of integration when he discusses open schools. He suggests that such schools

. . . would wish to be open about what children learn rather than being bound by rigidly divided artificially compartmentalized subjects. . . . They want children to have open to them the opportunity to carry on with an interesting activity, rather than to be bound by set timetables. In terms of space they want to open out from the classroom and spill over into the rest of the school and out into the neighbourhood beyond. . . . they want the organization of the school to be so open that children can be variously grouped and can go to a variety of teachers or other adults drawn from the community.[20]

Undoubtedly a number of first schools function in this open manner. Others, though, retain a more traditional timetable. The Open Plan study found that 'responses relating to curriculum organization show that it is dominated, particularly at junior level, by the split-day approach whereby basics are covered in the morning and other activities in the afternoon'.[2]

We need to question whether such a heavy measure of 3R work is appropriate to the learning needs of children under nine years, and indeed whether the teacher is being fair to herself in trying to meet the demands of all of the children involved in this type of work at the same time.

However Moran's study and other recent research has shown the difficulties of attaching labels to teaching styles and programmes. In reality the matter is complex. Bealing's study of organization in junior classrooms indicated that a variety of styles operate within a relatively informal classroom layout. She concluded that 'there is a strong case for an analysis and conceptualization of observed classroom variability which stretches far beyond widely-used labels such as the integrated day and dichotomies such as traditional-progressive and formal-informal'.[21]

Teachers need to adopt a programme which they can manage and in which they can be effective. Whilst some forms of organization appear to be better suited to children, if they cannot work for the teacher they are best forgotten.

Whatever programme is worked the teacher needs to be sure that it is a balanced one. The Schools Council project found that with all age-groups there was a marked variation in time allocated to different curriculum areas. They conclude: 'Clearly there is no such thing as the primary school curriculum, but an enormous number of primary school curricula each achieving a different balance.'[2] The Project Report stresses that they are not putting forward a model of curriculum balance but clearly the amount of time allocated to particular activities will be affected by teachers' beliefs about how children learn. We should remember that the Primary Survey indicated that the children who achieved the highest standards were offered a broad-based curriculum.

Balance

A balance needs to be struck between activity and sedentary work. This is perhaps easier to achieve where children are actively pursuing their own learning, which will involve movement around the teaching area as well as sustained recording work. The teacher who invites a passive approach from children and uses mainly book-based materials may have to look critically at her programme to ensure that sedentary work is interspersed with opportunities for movement.

The Schools Council Project mentioned earlier noted both the time allotted to curriculum and the amount of time that pupils were involved in learning. Although sustained activity and concentration may well be a healthy sign of good curriculum organization it is not necessarily so. The Project makes a further point about the difficulties of identifying the nature of this involvement: 'There is little point in keeping pupils involved on tasks or activities unless they are comprehensive and worthwhile.'[2]

An audience for work

PROVIDING A VARIED AUDIENCE

Reference has been made earlier to the need for making learning in school realistic for children (see Chapter 1, p.52). If children are able to see the sense and usefulness of an activity they will approach the work with more enthusiasm and have a sense of achievement in its completion. The Bullock Report states:

> By far the largest amount of writing done in schools is explicitly or implicitly directed at the teacher. The remaining small proportion is divided between writing for self and writing for other pupils. . . . We welcome the development to encourage writing outside of the classroom, where certain constraints and criteria offer additional challenges.[12]

In the first school this extended audience can be used for all areas of the curriculum as a means of heightening the child's motivation.

DISPLAY
Display is an important feature of first school work. It serves several purposes.
1 The first purpose is usually to make the working environment attractive:

> What we see around us each day in a classroom ought to be there by personal choice like the decorations and objects in our homes. We may not be able to control the seasons or the weather, or even to do much about the structure of the building, but we can still do a great deal to make our working environment artistically useful.[22]

2 When children's work is displayed it can be shared with a wide audience. This serves as an added stimulus for good presentation. On occasions the display may be made available to other schools or members of the public.
3 The importance of developing a visually pleasing setting should be seen as a central part of curriculum planning. Display can be used to assist learning, if the children are involved in the process and the provision (of both children's and adults' work) is used to develop teaching points. The children gain self-confidence by having their own work presented, and are inspired by professional, adult work to see what can be achieved.

Monitoring the curriculum
One aspect of the concern about standards in education and increasing accountability has been the focus on what is actually happening to children as a result of their programme. As with most aspects of education there is no one satisfactory approach to monitoring. Central government has responded in the form of the Assessment of Performance Unit at the DES. Their sampling procedures are intended to reflect a standard for teachers to aim towards:

> If the educational process is monitored according to criteria which

reflect the best current practices in encouraging pupils' development in language, maths, science, moral and aesthetic sensibility and physical expression and dexterity, then the general level of these may rise towards that of the best. This is why it is so vital that the criteria used should both reflect the best practice and be reasonably comprehensive.[23]

However, although many teachers recognize that external moderation can be helpful, essentially they need to develop their own perceptive responses to classroom activity. The experienced teacher constantly moderates as she interacts with groups, looks at an individual's reaction to his work, involves a class in discussion, in short gathers evidence to judge her own effectiveness.

Possibilities for monitoring can be extended if the teacher has some professional assistance. Dr Jean Rudduck's project 'Teachers in Partnership' involved four studies focusing on collaborative in-service work. Two of these studies looked at the possibilities of the teacher observing her classroom with a partner – either someone outside the school or a teacher colleague.

> The teachers alternate the role of 'observer' and 'teacher': the teacher who is to act as 'observer' is invited into the classroom of the colleague to comment on issues designated by the teacher as a source of concern in his or her teaching: the partners meet after the observation to discuss the 'observer's' comments: the observer shapes observation and commentary to the agreed focus (i.e. the problem or topic nominated by the teacher): the teachers agree not to discuss their observations outside the partnership.[24]

Whilst this approach has much to offer the confident teacher, the study emphasized the problem of releasing teachers from the classroom in order to do such work, and also stressed that choice of partner is crucial – friendship proved to be the strongest bond.

Assessment

Information about children's progress is important if the teacher is to assess her provision.

> Teachers are more used to assessing the performance, progress and potential of individual pupils. They use these assessments to inform parents and to inform prospective employers and colleges of further and higher education. But the information they gather for these reports could also help in assessing the school's performance, reporting to governors and the local authority and reviewing the school's terms of reference, aims and methods.[1]

The approaches to and use of measurement in first schools is a sensitive issue. When describing the NFER material for assessment in nursery education, Maureen Shields stresses that the material should be a *resource* rather than a target at which to aim:

> It is a recognized danger that assessment, instead of producing useful information about children's development and performance, may come to determine what is taught. A central purpose has been to serve the needs of teachers, not to impose external standards on them.[25]

This comment applies equally to first school assessments.

Appropriate procedures need to be adapted for different areas of development, bearing in mind that part of a child's growth and development is intangible and difficult to measure.

STRUCTURED OBSERVATIONS

Many aspects of development will be noted through the teacher's own observations. These observations will be of more value if they are structured and set within a framework, otherwise there is a danger of subjectivity and exaggerated perceptions of a child's general strengths and weaknesses.

The Schools Council Project on Record Keeping in Primary Schools offers advice to teachers wanting to improve their observations of children:

1 Determine in advance what to observe but be alert for unusual behaviour.
2 Observe and record enough of the situation to make the behaviour meaningful.
3 Make a record of the incident as soon after the observation as possible.
4 Limit each anecdote to a brief description of a single incident.
5 Keep the factual description of the incident and your interpretation of it separate. Use only non-judgmental words in the description.
6 Record both negative and positive behavioural incidents.
7 Collect a number of anecdotes on a pupil before drawing inferences concerning typical behaviour.[26]

Rating scales and checklists

In order to direct observations even more, rating scales and checklists may be used (see p.135). However, the actual use of checklists needs to be considered. The Schools Council Project noted that whilst teachers found checklists were a useful way of focusing attention on the pupil, they were more doubtful about their use in communicating information to other teachers. It concludes: 'It appears, therefore, that checklists are more successful in communicating the work and topics which a pupil has attempted than in providing assessment data about achievements.'[26]

OBJECTIVE STANDARDIZED TESTS

Even structured observations have subjective elements. Occasionally, children's abilities need to be compared with a national standard or a learning problem identified through diagnosis; this may be done through objective tests. Such tests are not a substitute for the teacher's observations, but may provide valuable evidence to confirm professional judgment or offer another perspective.

However, the dangers of relying on tests as a way of measuring young children's progress need to be emphasized. The uneven rate and pace of a first school child's development makes it difficult to design a teaching programme based on one standardized or diagnostic test. Moreover in *Record Keeping in the Primary School* the authors note:

> Many teachers met during the project used standardized tests in order to obtain data which were reliable and seemingly objective, frequently without considering whether data of this kind were helpful to them making decisions about pupils' future learning. Tests made by teachers themselves were often seen to be much more relevant to this latter purpose.[26]

But devising tests is a skilled process and teachers must be aware of the language they use, the length of the test, and arrangement and appropriate match of tasks.

MARKING

This serves to check children's progress, provide an occasion for developing a teaching point and generally provide encouragement. For example, when marking spelling, Bullock suggests that 'the most important step the teacher can take is to improve the pupil's confidence in his own capacity'.[12] If the child spells 'made' wrongly the teacher can recap on the 'magic e' and show the child that he is capable of spelling a range of words ending with 'e'. The aim should be to provide a dialogue between the child and the teacher and for the marking to take the child on one step further in his learning.

It is neither possible nor desirable for the teacher to mark everything in an assignment, but children should be clear about what is being marked, whether it is quality of presentation, original ideas or mastery of a concept.

Records

A form of record keeping provides evidence of assessment. Teachers in the Schools Council Project on Record Keeping in Primary Schools identified various purposes for keeping records:

1 For purposes of continuity in teaching and learning.
2 To provide teachers with evidence about the success or failure of teaching methods.
3 For diagnostic purposes.

4 As evidence of the child's strengths and weaknesses if there is need to refer to other agencies.
5 As a defence against accusations of falling standards.
6 To keep a curriculum balance.
7 In order for the headteacher to control classroom curriculum.

The purpose of the Schools Council Project was to help teachers in primary schools 'to keep better records of the progress and development of the children in their care'. The main recommendations of this work focused on the importance of design, including clear layout and sufficient space for items. Content should be sequential, relevant and should differentiate between experiences offered and attainments measured.

They suggest that record content should also clearly present assessment information, including derivation of norms when grading or rating; use of criteria when assessing competence; details of all testing techniques used and names of standardized tests; and that tests devised by teachers should be presented in a standardized form.

The Report also recommended that decisions about records should be made jointly by all staff in a school and that the consultation should be extended to those receiving records in other schools. Clearly unless the information passed on is seen as relevant and is used by the next school the exercise is a waste of valuable time.

The final recommendation of the Report was that teachers need 'to be freed of many of the non-teaching and supervisory activities commonly a part of primary-school life'.[26] This must be a debatable point in the first school where it has been seen that many of the activities deemed 'non-curricular' are in fact an important aspect of aiding the young child's development (cf. Bennett, *Open Plan Primary Schools*).

Record keeping is seen as important but the emphasis is on a convenient way of noting down the evidence required which fits into the busy teacher's day and does not detract from the rest of her work.

The form of the curriculum

As the first school is concerned with educating the whole child it is impossible to formulate an inclusive written curriculum. *Education 5 – 9* looked at school work and concluded that 'a substantial part of the work could not be neatly categorized under discrete subject headings'. Whilst some aspects of the learning programme are clear and sequential, others are intangible and untidy, e.g. aesthetic appreciation, role play. However, the Survey stresses that 'What children learn from activities such as these provides the essential foundations for the study of separate subjects which begin to be more easily identifiable in the later years of their first school education.'[6]

All curriculum areas are important and all must be planned. However, the teacher will not always be able to include all that she wants within a week, term or a school year. We have already mentioned that a clear grasp of what different disciplines offer the child will help prevent anxiety about overcrowding a curriculum. Moreover, one teacher's planning should be in the light of a global view of what experiences are offered to the child at different stages of development throughout his first-school career. This assumes that a school staff constantly share experiences and work as a team to plan, execute, appraise and make any necessary changes in their programme.

DECIDING THE CURRICULUM

Whilst the Government urges a move towards a national consensus about the core curriculum, decisions as to how this curriculum is to be handled and the form in which it is to be offered to children remain in the hands of the school. The headteacher will remain responsible for the decisions made, but to ensure that every teacher understands and is committed to her workload, all staff should participate in making decisions.

THE ROLE OF THE CURRICULUM CONSULTANT

Although ultimately responsible, no headteacher can expect to have all the curriculum expertise required within a school. Whilst all teachers will participate in curricular decisions, the subject consultant within a school should take the lead.

> Teachers in posts of special responsibility need to keep up-to-date in their knowledge of their subject: to be familiar with its main concepts, with the sub-divisions of the subject material and how they relate to one another. . . . Additionally these teachers should learn how to lead groups of teachers and to help others to teach material which is appropriate to the abilities of the children.[4]

PRESENTATION

The form in which a school presents its curriculum is important for both practical reasons and good public relations. Essentially teachers require a 'working document' which arises as a result of staff collaboration. Governors and parents should receive a 'formal statement' – a clear and concise explanation of what is offered to children during their career at that particular school. The local authority will require both statements.

The working document

Experienced teachers in an established staff team will assimilate the agreed school curriculum and require little as an *aide-mémoire*. Inexperienced and less confident teachers will need something they can refer to, if only as an initial prop. It is also important to have some recorded statement of intention both as a guard against differing subjective interpretations of what was initially agreed and as something tangible to present to new teachers.

The 'formal statement'

This needs to be designed to provide information for the interested layman.

Maintaining the practice
Having agreed what is to be taught, staff need reassurance that they are working along the right lines. Teachers should always be encouraged to share concerns and turn to colleagues for advice without this being seen in any way as professional weakness.

Evaluation
The curriculum is dynamic and needs to be adapted in the light of practical experience, changing needs and increased knowledge. Evaluation is a way of testing the worth of what is being offered. It may be the result of the teacher looking closely at her own practice; a joint venture with the teacher's observations being moderated by a colleague; or an external exercise by governors, inspectors or advisers. Whilst there is a place for all three approaches the crucial factor is to help teachers to be more self-appraising, thus increasing their professionalism.

Change
As a result of evaluation it may be decided to change part of the curriculum, thus completing the circuit of decision-making – implementation – evaluation. The process of change is a delicate one and again teachers must be fully involved in it if they are to be committed to making it work. However, the initial impetus may come from one individual, be it the head or the curriculum consultant.

TEACHING AND LEARNING
The mode of teaching and learning within the school will be determined by the curriculum principles, the needs of the children and the preferred style of the teacher. HMI stress the need for these matters to be discussed amongst staff to enable some continuity of approach for children.

> In 13 of the schools the teachers followed a common policy within which they had some freedom to choose their own classroom and teaching arrangements. However, in 45 schools there was either no explicit policy or it was believed that each teacher should determine his or her own classroom organization and approaches to teaching. Some decisions should properly be in the hands of individual teachers, but complete freedom of choice can be counterproductive. Extreme changes of practice from one teacher to the next are, at best, temporarily disconcerting for children and it is wise to adopt a framework of common practice. For example there should be common expectations about the ways children use learning resources and shared facilities and there should be an agreed system of record keeping.[6]

Deployment of teachers

CLASS TEACHING
Traditionally first school teachers are deployed to work with a class of children and this has the advantage of offering continuity and security.

> As the class teachers were teaching the children throughout most of the day, they had the opportunity (which nearly all took) to integrate the work and make links between the various areas of learning. To the extent that this occurred, fragmentation of the curriculum was avoided and the children were helped to make sense of the work. The class teachers generally knew the individual children well and understood the stage they had reached in their personal development and learning.[6]

This is generally supported by the Primary Survey but here a note of caution is raised:

> They [the advantages of the class teacher] are not overriding advantages in all cases. When a teacher is unable to deal satisfactorily with an important aspect of the curriculum, other ways of making this provision have to be found. If a teacher is only a little unsure, advice and guidance from a specialist, probably another member of staff, may be enough.[6]

COOPERATIVE TEACHING
Teachers may derive support from one another if they teach cooperatively. This may occur when teachers are in separate classrooms with their own children, but they collaborate about their work. This is desirable both horizontally to ensure that children of the same age have parallel experiences and vertically to promote continuity.

TEAM TEACHING
An extension of this approach is team teaching which may operate in varying ways. Derek Waters describes it essentially as 'children brought together in larger numbers than in a traditional class, with the total responsibility for their education shared by two, three or even more teachers working in a team, usually with a defined leader'.[27]

The project on Open Plan Schools gives some indication of the variety of practices that can operate under this heading:

> Team size varied from two to four teachers, some with a floating teacher and others with substantial ancillary assistance. . . . Responsibility for curriculum areas shared a widely differing time scale, from one day to one week to one term. In some the work was structured with a workwheel, whereas another gave free pupil choice from the activities on offer. Pupil groupings also differed.[2]

The various advantages of team teaching are: flexibility in teaching and learning; a sharing of teacher strengths (an inexperienced teacher may learn from colleagues); children have the security of one teacher to whom they relate at the beginning and end of the day, but at other times their work and personalities are monitored by a variety of adults. On the other hand any form of team teaching demands frequent and meticulous planning by the teachers involved; compatible personalities; and a building which allows for some flexible grouping of children. Above all the teachers involved need a clear-sighted approach to what they hope to achieve by working in this way. This implies a thorough introduction to team teaching both in initial training and through in-service training.

Grouping for learning

CLASS

Some teaching of the class as a whole took place in every survey school. The teacher brought the class together when he or she wished to give information, to tell or read a story or to read poetry, to share views and knowledge of events in 'news' or discussion times or to listen to music. When the children's interest was aroused and their imagination captured, the class experience offered a valuable means of learning, especially when supplemented by individual or group work.[4]

Class teaching can enable the teacher to use her own time most effectively and also give the class a feeling of group unity. However, the same report notes the problems in attempting to provide for a range of ability when class teaching.

The most common result, particularly in a small group of these schools where class teaching predominated, was that the more able children were doing work that was too easy for them, but there were also a few examples of less able, especially eight- or nine-year-olds, taught by teachers whose main experience had been with older children, trying to do work that was beyond them.[4]

Clearly then the teacher must bear in mind that class teaching will not necessarily mean an appropriate match of work for all children.

One of the main strategies for promoting children's learning is through teacher questioning. If questions are sustained and probing they should take the child on a step further in his thinking. Plowden supported this form of teaching and suggested that it could only be done successfully with individuals and small groups of children. However, recently this view has been challenged by the ORACLE research group who looked into teacher-pupil interactions in junior classes and how they relate to teaching organization:

Our conclusion then is that, given contemporary class sizes, the Plowden 'progressive' ideology, based essentially on individualization, is impractical. Far from utilizing probing, higher-order type questions and statements with individuals, teachers in practice utilize this approach largely in the whole-class teaching situation. . . . In this situation the teacher does not have to concentrate her mind and her activity on the management of thirty individualized tasks, but on one only, the subject matter under discussion, on which she aims to focus the attention of the class as a whole.[11]

GROUPS

Whilst Plowden promoted an individual approach to learning as ideal, it recognized that the teacher would be using her time more economically if she taught small groups of children. The criteria for grouping are seen to be flexible – occasionally ability groups can be formed but this will change according to work tackled. However, group organization in classrooms is undoubtedly complex:

In particular no serious attention appears to have been given, even in relation to the teaching of science and mathematics, to the key issue as to how the teacher, responsible for the work of a whole class (perhaps split into four, five or more groups), is to ensure that each group engaged on cooperative tasks involving discussion and the use of materials and apparatus is effectively and meaningfully occupied.[11]

The authors continue to identify some of the detail required of successful group work:

To think out, provide materials for, and set up a series of group tasks having the characteristics just described (i.e. cooperative tasks involving discussion with children effectively and meaningfully occupied) in the different subject areas which comprise a modern curriculum would in itself clearly be a major undertaking, even if use is made of relevant curriculum development projects. To monitor subsequent group activities: to be nearby and able to intervene in the work of each group when this is educationally necessary or desirable: this would clearly be a major undertaking for the teacher, requiring as a first condition a high degree of involvement by the pupils in their tasks and so a high level of responsible behaviour. For the pupils to gain from such work also certainly requires the development of a number of social as well as cognitive skills: a degree of tolerance and mutual understanding: the ability to articulate a point of view, to engage in discussion, reassessing, probing and questioning. Such skills are not in themselves innate: they have to be learnt and so taught.[11]

Whilst the term 'group work' is commonly used in schools it is suggested that the intricacies of organizing work, and the potential to be gained from this approach, are not generally recognized. These aspects should form a focus for school-based in-service training.

INDIVIDUAL
Although Plowden advocated the merits of individual teaching and learning the practicalities of large classes do make it difficult for teachers to apply this in a meaningful way. Earlier in this section we mentioned that the teacher's and the child's perceptions of individual attention were very different (see p.95). The First School Survey notes misgivings: 'Individual work, when overdone, allows the teacher little time to discuss the difficulties with the children in more than a superficial way and provides too few opportunities for the children to learn from each other.'[4] Thus this approach is neither practical nor desirable when used for all children. However, where one child's needs are very particular, he will require an individualized programme for at least part of the day. There are also occasions when a brief period of individual attention from the teacher will succeed in establishing a teaching point, re-establish a child's confidence and enable him to rejoin a particular ability group.

WITHDRAWAL OF GROUPS
With large classes, and sometimes mixed age-groups, teachers are aware that they cannot always cope with the needs of the ability range. Occasionally an extra member of staff may be deployed to withdraw groups of children who have particular needs. *Education 5−9* notes: 'A variety of arrangements was adopted to help the less able children, the most common being the withdrawal of individuals or groups of children to work together with another teacher.'[6] But the Survey adds that more able pupils were rarely withdrawn from the class for this purpose.

It may be argued that the more able children are more confident and flexible and therefore more likely to cope with the change from the classroom and adapt to a different adult. Children with learning difficulties possibly benefit from stability from their classroom teacher, who is already well aware of their learning needs.

Admission, accommodation and transfer of children

ADMISSION
The central aim when children first come to school is to make it a happy and easy experience. This implies establishing firm links with the home and the child's pre-school group to ensure a continuity of approach (see Chapter 1, pp.22–5).

The child's readiness to adapt to and exploit the opportunities offered on admission to school will depend very much on him as a person and his past experiences. The reception teacher is unique in being asked to accept children into her class who have not shared a common fund of experience. Her role is a very skilled one in diagnosing individual needs and providing appropriate learning programmes whilst at the same time settling these new children into the pattern of school life.

The First School Survey confirms the belief of most reception teachers that it is best to admit children into the classroom gradually. During these early days both the new children and parents need time and re-assurance from the teacher, particularly if despite a carefully placed entry into school the child is unhappy.

> The impression the teacher gives to parents at this early stage is important. The parent needs to feel confident that her child will not be allowed to cry for long, and that she will be consulted if the teacher has any problems with him. It helps if the teacher can say something positive about the child when the parents come to collect them, because most parents are anxious to know how their child has 'behaved' at school.[28]

HMI also stress the need to consider part-time provision initially for children under statutory school age.

> Part-time schooling is as much as some of these children can reasonably manage at first. They need almost the kind of education they would get in a nursery class and that is not easy for a teacher to provide if there are 25–35 children in a class, a good many of whom are under five.[6]

Certainly reception teachers must be aware of how tiring a few hours in school can be for children who have had no previous experience of being in a group with a range of activities. This fatigue can build up throughout the week and should be considered when the teacher is planning her programme. The NFER Study *Continuity from Pre-school to Infant School* indicates that the areas where there may be differences for the child are in the school setting, the curriculum and the people. Amongst the differences mentioned are the daily programme with the strange routines and introduction of compulsory playtimes and set activities such as PE and assemblies. The physical size of the building and constraints on the child moving around the school may pose problems and the fact of an adult being less available to the child: 'Although children at pre-school spend much of their time in group situations, the groups tend to be smaller than those encountered at school: some children failed to respond when directions were given to the whole class.'[29]

The NFER Study also stresses other new things to be learnt such as different terminology, new sights and sounds, 'work tasks' which have to be completed. The authors conclude that each child's transition to school must be unique but they identify three essential factors which will help reduce shock to a minimum:

1 Changes and the introduction of new experiences must be gradual rather than sudden.

2 People, places and things must be to some extent familiar rather than totally strange.

3 The child must have a sense of security rather than instability.[29]

ACCOMMODATION

The way in which children are accommodated in school may reflect the philosophy for learning but will also be affected by expediency. Children do not always enter school in neat group sizes: teaching space sometimes varies considerably in area. In these cases an even distribution of children with one teacher in charge of an age-group may not be possible.

Mixed age-groups or vertical groupings are a feature of all very small schools. Village schools have always existed with two or three teachers working with a wide age-group of children. Recently falling rolls in first schools have meant that some teachers have met this form of organization for the first time. Both the Primary Survey and the First School Survey state their reservations about mixed age-groups. Whilst the Primary Survey[4] did not look at five- and six-year-olds, it found 'When match assessments were compared for single-age and 'mixed-age' classes, it was found that for seven- and eleven-year-olds the single-age classes showed a definite superiority in relating the difficulty of the work to children's capabilities in all ability levels.'

The First Schools Survey similarly expresses misgivings about teachers dealing adequately with the needs of all children within an extended age-range.[6] Whilst undoubtedly the weak and inexperienced teacher will find an extended age-group an additional complication, there are some benefits to be considered. Where children move into the area the school can accommodate them in more than one class if there are parallel groups. Children enter an established class and learn from those who are already familiar with classroom routines. They will also have the continuity of being with one teacher for two or three years.

It is possible to plan a form of mixed age-grouping to secure these benefits whilst being aware of possible problems. Many teachers can cope with a span of two years and will group the reception and second-year infant children together in order to offer new children a reasonable length of time in their first class. Other groups may be in traditional chronological age-groups. Alternatively if a mixed age-range has to be accommodated in another part of the school because of uneven group numbers, this may be balanced with a small class size. If at all possible the combinations of large class-size and age-span should be avoided.

TRANSITION AND TRANSFER

For the child moving from one provision to another, a smooth transition requires that the change is sufficient to be stimulating but not so drastic as to cause shock. . . . Some children appear to settle into school easily with no apparent problems, but the majority do experience difficulty to a greater or lesser extent. Symptoms may appear before, on or after transition. . . . The potential sources of shock are the discontinuities in the child's experience.[29]

Although these statements refer to the child's initial transition into school they apply equally to all changes that children undergo when passing through the school system.

For convenience the term 'transition' is used to describe the movement of a pupil upwards either within the first school or from first to middle school. The term 'transfer' refers to the child's movement across from one school to another, usually because of family mobility.

Transition
Where the transition is internal, school staff working closely together can plan to offer continuity of experience. The aim should be for the child to move throughout the school as smoothly as possible, with a different class and teaching setting providing sufficient stimulus to add impetus to his learning rather than detracting from it. If this is to be achieved, information about children must be passed on from one teacher to another thoroughly and sensitively and teachers must be sufficiently familiar with their colleagues' routines, methods and curriculum content to use this as a starting-point with their new class.

The transition is more complex when children move up to the middle school. The Schools Council study on Record Keeping in Primary Schools noted: 'the setting up of a liaison network between a comprehensive school and its feeder primary schools has in some cases encouraged secondary teachers to visit primary schools on a regular basis and vice versa'. This applies equally to first and middle schools as do the potential problems which may arise.

The problems of primary-secondary transition, as seen by the secondary school heads and teachers, seem to stem from the variety of curricula followed in primary schools. For example, it was alleged that it was often difficult to relate the stage reached by one pupil in a school where scheme x was in use, with that reached by a pupil where scheme y was used. Where secondary teachers wished to compare pupils from different primary schools for the purpose of 'setting' or ensuring a mixed-ability grouping they found that the subjective assessments of primary teachers varied from school to school. . . . If the liaison procedure is not to be solely a banner-waving exercise for the secondary heads of first year, a realistic amount of time must be allotted to it on both sides of the transition.[26]

Transfer

Information about a child transferring from one school to another is largely dependent upon what is included in the official LEA record card. This varies very much according to each authority. Teachers involved in the study of Record Keeping in Primary Schools considered that the following type of information was essential:

(a) pupils' names, date of birth, home address;
(b) vital information required for a child's well-being;
(c) person(s) to contact in an emergency;
(d) details of any handicaps, physical or social-emotional, which may affect progress in school;
(e) details of any learning disabilities, including spoken language;
(f) details of referrals to psychologists, reports from social workers, school medical officers, etc.;
(g) details of prescribed remedial treatment;
(h) stages reached on reading, language and mathematics schemes;
(i) details of screening or other tests carried out;
(j) other medical, academic and personal information.

They also recommended a common policy both within and between LEAs for transferring individual records, and suggested that essential information could be sent with the child on the first day of term so that the most relevant provision could be made immediately.

ORGANIZING THE ENVIRONMENT

The building

Education 5 – 9 comments positively on buildings:

> The premises, which if not purpose-built housed a primary school prior to reorganization, are well maintained. Teachers make them attractive and interesting and they contain displays of children's work, pictures and charts, natural objects, plants and flowers.[26]

Young children react positively to a pleasant environment which includes bright display and comfortable working areas. Teachers can take this even further and look closely at how every part of their school building and grounds can be exploited to offer children opportunities for learning.

First school buildings vary considerably in design. It is a mistake, however, to assume that certain practices occur in certain types of buildings. Although the building may offer (or constrain) opportunities for teaching and learning the willingness to use such opportunities must be there. Whatever the case it is important to determine the principles for learning and then to base practice on them, using the school building in the most imaginative way.

Circulation

Circulation of children during the school day can be a major problem in badly-designed buildings. Clearly all schools will need to look at their pattern of movement at certain times of the day, but where the curriculum approach is active children are likely to be moving around a great deal. Movement is perhaps easier in an open plan school, as the teacher may have oversight of a wider teaching area. However, this movement should be planned in order to cause the minimum of disruption. Where circulation is difficult teachers will need to adapt their organization accordingly.

Teaching space

Most teachers would agree that the vital areas in the school are those where most of the teaching and learning takes place. Such areas may be enclosed within four walls of a self-contained classroom, or they may be a bay which is largely open and leads directly onto practical and circulation spaces. Whatever the design, such an area acts as a home base where children will at least start and finish their day, and in some cases will spend most of a school year. As such this area should be planned with great care to provide for living and working.

Practical spaces

If the teaching area has an adjoining practical space this should offer extended opportunities for children. The Open Plan study suggests: 'In siting practical areas, visibility from the general teaching spaces, circulation and access are the key factors.'[2] Bearing these in mind it might be possible for teachers to develop their own practical spaces by 'spilling out' of traditional classrooms into wide corridors.

Outdoor spaces

Education 5–9 makes several references to school sites. When talking generally about first schools they noted that outdoor activity was well catered for in a majority of schools:

> The outdoor areas in about three-quarters of the schools offered good facilities for physical education and included both hard and grassed area. In addition the outdoor provisions sometimes included such things as fixed climbing apparatus, an adventure playground, a brick wall for ball practice, games pitches, playground markings and a swimming pool.[6]

However, in the preceding paragraph HMI state that:

> . . . apart from games, not much physical education took place out of doors. In some schools outside work was confined to the summer term and in other schools it was not part of the programme. . . . The school grounds offered further opportunities for studying living and growing things, but good positive educational use was made of them

in very few schools and schools with particularly rich or exciting surroundings were not making any more use of them than schools in less favoured areas. . . . The outdoor areas were being used positively to help foster aesthetic awareness in only twenty schools.[6]

Whilst it is recognized that the Survey only looked at eighty schools, and some first schools' outside premises are very limited, it is still important for them to be developed imaginatively and to the full. They can then be used for a variety of activities, including maths and language.

Safety
A safe environment is vital, and the younger the age-group the more important this is.

Material resources.
Financial constraints in recent years have meant that very careful consideration has to be given to ordering and buying materials. There is so much available on the market that teachers need to be well-informed about the relative merits of different apparatus before committing precious funds.

The Primary Survey makes the point that larger schools are generally likely to be better equipped than smaller schools but concludes: 'The small advantages in the levels of resources of large schools did not appear to improve the performance of their pupils other than marginally in art and music.'[4]

Education 5 – 9 stresses more strongly the lack of books:

In about a third of the schools the number and quality of the books were poor. In rather less than half of the schools there was a satisfactory provision of books for different areas of the curriculum. The deficiencies in twelve schools were considered to be serious. In these schools the lack of variety of books of quality and the narrow range of books containing information curtailed the children's reading for pleasure and inhibited their learning in more of the curriculum.[6]

Schools, particularly small schools, may increasingly have to rely on fund-raising from parents to supplement their captitation allowance for resources.

Having obtained resources, their storage and retrieval should enable teachers to use them easily and to the best effect. Whilst sharing resources can be both practical and economic *Education 5 – 9* adds a note of caution when looking at mathematics equipment:

In a few schools a resource area shared by two or more classes contained material that could be borrowed by individual classes. . . . The resource areas usually contained a wider range of equipment than could be provided in one class but lack of careful planning sometimes meant that the equipment was underused.[6]

If material resources are plentiful and well-organized, teachers are in a stronger position to attend appropriately to the learning needs of the children.

REFERENCES

1 SCHOOLS COUNCIL (1981) *The Practical Curriculum* (Schools Council Working Paper 70) Methuen Educational
2 BENNETT, S. N., ANDREAE, J., HEGARTY, P. and WADE, B. (1980) *Open Plan Schools* NFER/Schools Council
3 SOUTHGATE-BOOTH, V. (1981) *Extending Beginning Reading* Heinemann Educational/Schools Council
4 DES (1978) *Primary Education in England: A Survey by HM Inspectors of Schools* HMSO
5 RUDDUCK, J. (1981) *Making the Most of the Short In-service Course* Methuen Educational
6 DES (1982) *Education 5 – 9* HMSO
7 MINISTRY OF EDUCATION (1967) *Children and Their Primary Schools* (The Plowden Report) HMSO
8 GARNER, J. and BING, M. (1973) Inequalities of teacher-pupil contacts *British Journal of Educational Psychology* 43, 5, 234-5
9 BOYDELL, D. (1974) Teacher-pupil contact in junior classrooms *British Journal of Educational Psychology* 44, pp.313–18
10 BOYDELL, D. (1975) Individual attention: a child's eye view *Education 3 – 13*, 3, 1
11 GALTON, M., SIMON, B. and CROLL, P. (1980) *Inside the Primary Classroom* Routledge & Kegan Paul
12 DES (1975) *A Language for Life* (The Bullock Report) HMSO
13 ASHTON, P., KNEEN, P., DAVIES, F. and HOLLEY, B. J. (1975) *The Aims of Primary Education: A Study of Teachers' Opinions* Schools Council
14 KING, R. (1978) *All Things Bright and Beautiful* Wiley
15 HARLEN, W. (1977) *Progress in Learning Science* Schools Council
16 TOUGH, J. (1976/79/80/81) *Listening to Children Talking; Talking and Learning; Talk for Teaching and Learning; A Place for Talk* (Schools Council Communication Skills in Early Childhood Project) Ward Lock Educational
17 WEBB, D. (1979) Home and school: parental views *Education 3 – 13*, 7, 2
18 BROWN, M. and PRECIOUS, N. (1968) *The Integrated Day in the Primary School* Ward Lock Educational
19 MORAN, P. (1971) The integrated day *Educational Research* 14, 1
20 DEARDEN, R. (1974) How open can schools be? *Education 3 – 13* 2,2
21 BEALING, D. (1972) The organization of junior school classrooms *Educational Research* 14, 231–5
22 JARMAN, C. (1976) *Display and Presentation in Schools* A & C Black
23 KAY, B. (1976) The Assessment of Performance Unit: its task and rationale *Education 3 – 13* 4, 2, 108–12

24 RUDDUCK, J. (1982) Teachers in partnership *Journal of NAIEA*, 16, spring
25 SHIELDS, P., WEINER, G. and WILSON, E. (1981) *Record Keeping in Primary Schools* (Schools Council Research Studies) Macmillan
26 CLIFT, P., WEINER, G. and WILSON, E. (1981) *Record Keeping in Primary Schools* (Schools Council Research Studies) Macmillan
27 WATERS, D. (1979) *Management and Headship in the Primary School* Ward Lock Educational
28 TIZARD, B., MORTIMORE, J. and BURCHELL, B. (1981) *Involving Parents in Nursery and Infant Schools* Grant McIntyre
29 CLEAVE, S., JOWETT, S. and BATE, M. (1982) *And So to School* NFER/Nelson

IN THE CLASSROOM

TIME

Organization of the child's time

AVOIDING WASTING TIME

1 The classroom needs to be organized so that children do not have to wait for the teacher when they need support with their work.

2 Word banks, charts, classroom books and dictionaries all encourage children so search for words when writing. Young children find it difficult to select a word from a list on the wall: they need to be able to detach the word and take it with them to copy. Words may be attached to a magnetic board, or stuck on with Blutack. Colour-coded apparatus allows ability groups to select appropriate materials.

3 The children need an imaginative and progressive range of materials and activities (colour coded) to tackle when they have completed their main task. These can include: aids to develop handwriting, e.g. card with one lower-case letter mounted in sandpaper with arrows indicating correct formation; dot to dot patterns; writing patterns; tracing cards; simple handwriting practice cards with 'motivating' material, e.g. jokes, riddles, crossword puzzles; magic number squares.

4 Children need to be encouraged to be self-sufficient in using material resources within the classroom and, when they are older, around the school. Notices and discussion can specify the number of children allowed to work in various activity areas in the room, e.g. 'two at the weighing table'. A well-organized and equipped classroom will help teach children to leave every activity area neat and tidy, as will equipment that makes it possible for children to care for their possessions, e.g. containers with lids that fit easily.

5 Suitable activity can be provided immediately outside the classroom, where they can still be overseen by the teacher, e.g. story-book cassettes and headphones in the book area (using them could be a privilege). Children could search for information books and change library books in the central library area, perhaps accompanied by a parent at first.

6 Carefully matched pairs of children could tackle tasks in the playground, or, armed with an observation sheet, go on a discovery journey to note sounds, colours and shapes around the school.

7 Work needs to be appropriate for the child. Is the group of children busily and quietly occupied on workcards always the same group? The work may be too easy for them.

TRANSITION TIME

1 The youngest children should have to cope with the least movement in

school. Where the hall is some distance from the classroom, perhaps the classroom itself could be adapted for drama and movement.

2 Pre-recorded TV and radio programmes avoid time wasted waiting for the programme.

3 Clearing away times can provide learning opportunities, e.g. matching colour-coded apparatus and areas; matching shapes of bricks and wood-work tools to outlines, categorizing and sorting pieces of equipment (with teacher's help); half the class watch a group clear away and offer constructive comments on their success.

ALLOW CHOICE IN THE USE OF TIME

1 Older children could plan their daily programme after receiving the appropriate assignments.

2 Flexible playtimes allow children to continue work if they wish.

3 If playtimes and lunch hours are fixed, children can choose to go outside or work in school:

  a rota of staff or parent helpers could provide a voluntary storytime during the lunch hour;

  a variety of lunch-hour clubs may be provided;

  the central library area may be kept open and manned for quiet reading.

Organization of the teacher's time

TIME WITH CHILDREN

1 *Management techniques for social control of the class:* Disruptive children may need to sit near the teacher's table and near to the teacher when in a group. If a child is particularly disruptive the teacher may need to observe his behaviour and decide on particular rewards and sanctions to help improve it. This will need to be explained to the child and the approach should be consistently applied over a period of time, together with full praise, both privately and in front of the class, when improvements are noted.

2 *Noise:* A quiet voice helps prevent a noisy class. If the class are over-stimulated and 'high', the offer of a quiet story or poem may encourage calmness. A noisy group needs to be approached individually rather than across the room.

3 *Routines:* The classroom programme should be planned to ensure that children have interesting tasks to occupy them constantly whilst the teacher is involved in other teaching matters. This programme can be adapted in favour of a spontaneous activity but it always needs to be there as a backcloth.

Children will adapt more easily to familiar requirements and routines, e.g. staff may all agree to adapt a similar colour-coding for apparatus in their classroom.

Time is well spent sorting out initial difficulties before the class settles to activity (e.g. I've lost my pencil!)

A last minute check that children are clear about their work can take the form of a representative of each group summarizing the task in hand.

A recognized sign can be used when the teacher does not wish to be disturbed by children, e.g. the teacher sits in a certain area of the room, puts up a sign.

When teaching a group, if the teacher is centrally positioned she can have an overview of all of the children and if necessary, physical contact with certain children in other groups.

4 *Materials:* Classroom materials need to be well maintained and clearly labelled. A simple retrieval system will enable children to gather their own apparatus, e.g. colour- or symbol-coding with a large key for reference displayed in the classroom. Children need to be trained systematically in the use and storage of materials. With young children this will take some time and might well be a priority for the first half-term in their new class, when a regular time each day could be spend identifying apparatus. Young children will need plenty of time to gather and put away apparatus.

5 *Beginning the session:* Careful planning should enable the teacher to devote her time entirely to the children during contact hours.

She may like to greet them in the cloakroom as they enter school or be available in the classroom.

A prepared environment with activities laid out on tables means that children can be trained to settle to the task in hand immediately they enter the classroom.

With older children the teacher may like to leave appropriate instructions on each table to encourage groups to gather their own materials for work, e.g.

Blue Group Shopping sums
You need   1   shopping sum-cards – blue
            2   money
            3   pencils
            4   maths books

The children may immediately gather on the carpet when they enter the classroom. In this case the teacher needs to be based there already and the time can be used to develop activities and conversation whilst waiting for the total group to gather.

6 *Ending the session:* Children need to know when the session is coming to an end -- it is a good idea to remind them five minutes in advance. The last few minutes of the session should allow time to: finish the immediate activity, clear up; gather as a group, and for the teacher to give a brief summary of the tasks tackled – one child may be asked to read his story or a group to recount their discoveries from a science experiment. However hard the session, if possible the day should end on a positive note! Children appreciate and respond to a smile and friendly comment from the teacher that she has enjoyed the day and looks forward to seeing them tomorrow.

7 *Identifying where time should be spent:* The first priority is for the teacher to know the children. It helps to make a practice of selecting a

child at random in the register and for the teacher to ask herself: what do I know about John (a) as a person, (b) his educational development?

Two child studies a term can be a useful target – more if there is a student in the class.

Records should help to build up a picture of the child's general development as well as act as a curriculum *aide-mémoire*.

8 *Awareness of the effect of teaching style:* The teacher can become aware of how she uses language either by means of a personal checklist or by using a cassette recorder: how much language is used for general class management? how much learning is stifled by teacher dominance? A check on how thinly time is spread can be made either by using a list (or observer) to note the ways the teacher is involved with children during the course of a session. On analysis, could some of this involvement be managed by using other adults, or by children coping more for themselves?

USE OF CLASSROOM AIDS

Workcards
1 *Workcards to promote discussion:* Workcards can be designed for use by 'pairs' of children, e.g.

What is your favourite story book? Talk about it with your partner.
Write to your neighbour telling him why you like the book.
Perhaps he will want to read the book now.

2 *Workcards to practise skills*
Structured handwriting cards attractively mounted and using interesting content such as short excerpts from favourite books, rhymes, and TV.

Older children may have workcards encouraging them to develop library skills such as use of classification systems, location of information in reference books through use of index and contents page, e.g.

Football (use appropriate picture)
Would you like to know more about football?
1 Go to the library – look for the section of books on football.
2 Choose one book.
3 Look at the *contents page* and *index* to find out about these things:
   football training; a football match; football on television.
4 Talk with your partner about these things.
5 Tell the class what you have learned.

(It is important for the teacher to try out the activity for herself first.)
3 *Workcards for initiating practical work:* After demonstrating a particular art technique (e.g. printing or marbling) workcards can provide suggestions for small groups to develop this technique, e.g.

Use marbling for a background.
Paint and cut out figures of children playing.
Stick them onto the background.

A check needs to be kept of how capable the children are of following sequential instructions and how they cooperate in an activity out of the classroom. (If the teacher cannot spend time observing, a parent or student may be asked to observe unobtrusively, only offering help if necessary.)

4 *Readability:* Young infants require few words and pictorial representation or numbers. Simple sorting, matching and counting activity might take place with the teacher and the group may then continue practising the skill or reinforcing the concept in varying ways, e.g.

Pattern making with beads

Make this –ooooo–

This may be developed by giving the children beads and the following card written in three colours:

Make a pattern   2 red beads   2 blue beads   2 yellow beads.

Children can show their pattern to others in the group for an immediate check. If there are sufficient threading strings available the pattern can then be kept with the cards for the teacher to check.

5 *Workcards as backup:* The teacher may like to discuss a task at some length with a group of children and then leave them with brief instructions on a workcard as a reminder.

6 *Layout and presentation:* It is best to use good quality card, of a standard size, which will fit into a holder on the classroom wall. (Cards need to be clear, simple and uncluttered (except for 'special effects'), see below).

Laminated cards last longer.

An indexed stock of picture postcards and eye-catching pictures can be used for illustrating workcards.

'Special effect' workcards add variety, e.g. questions and problems on shadows can be written in white ink on black shadow-shape cards; reflection questions can be written in mirror writing; workcards requesting spell recipes may be presented on marbled paper in 'spidery writing'.

7 *Children's workcards:* Each child in the group is given two plain cards (one for practice) and asked to make up a workcard for his/her neighbour. (Depending on age and ability, the teacher may need to identify the curriculum area and provide many examples.) On completion the children exchange cards and attempt the task set out. They can then decide on whether it was a good workcard, and why.

Technological aids

1 The teacher with responsibility for resources needs to provide every teacher with a list of what hardware is available, ensure that equipment is readily available to staff, is kept in good order, and to be notified of any defect in equipment.

2 INSET sessions should encourage all staff to become fully informed about the working of equipment and give specific suggestions for using the equipment in helpful and imaginative ways in the classroom.

A language master can be used for simple numeracy exercises, or as a class dictionary for children to use when writing.

An overhead projector can be used for a memory game with a group, or children could cut out silhouettes and captions and 'perform' a story.

A cassette recorder could be used for making a classroom radio programme, provide recordings to enhance an interest table – a display on growing things may be accompanied by a child's recording of an experiment to see what happens to plants if they cannot get enough water, a joint art project could have a cassette recording of children describing what part they played in its execution and what materials/techniques they used.

3 Sample materials can be made for joint use in the school and to spark off further ideas, e.g. transparencies showing different shapes on the overhead projector, cassette stories recorded to encourage children to predict, recorded sounds to provide a stimulus for discussion and writing.

USE OF ANCILLARY AND VOLUNTARY HELP

The paid ancillary helper

1 A list will help identify classroom activities that require an extra adult with occasional teacher supervision, e.g. oversight of a painting area, manning a listening corner equipped with headphones and cassettes, manning a library area to organize exchange of books, sand and water supervision.

2 The ancillary helper's talents should be used to the full: is she at ease with groups of children? can she use enabling strategies to develop children's language? is she sensitive to the needs of 'difficult' children?

3 An established working routine will help to ensure that the ancillary helper is tackling a job which offers satisfaction and responsibility by giving the chance to initiate and carry a job through.

4 Sessions when the ancillary is in the classroom can be used to develop activities which require more complex organization, e.g. small groups for science experiments, children using the outside area for environmental work.

5 Brief but regular meetings with the ancillary can spell out her worth in the classroom and give the chance to discuss proposed areas of work. She may need to be reassured that she is a second member of a team which can be enhanced by voluntary helpers.

6 The ancillary helper might like to attend appropriate courses in the county. Some school-based sessions could be used both for school ancillaries and a group from neighbouring schools.

Voluntary helpers

1 When children are first admitted to school, a note can be made of parents willing to be voluntary helpers, and of their particular interests/talents, on a card-index file.

2 The staff as a whole should discuss appropriate ways of using volunteers, e.g. the possible problems of two adults working in the

classroom – is there sufficient space? is it better for the volunteer to be accommodated in a withdrawal area which cannot be manned by the teacher?

3 There needs to be a policy about parent volunteers being admitted to the staffroom. If a number of staff are very against this, a comfortable parents room should be made available and helpers joined there for coffee.

4 Some form of informal induction of volunteers is helpful, especially at the beginning of the term when several helpers are new. Two or three short meetings over a cup of tea after school will serve to introduce some of the apparatus, together with its purpose and method of use. Child management and the value of a one-to-one relationship with certain children, the need for discretion about information acquired in school are other topics which will need to be covered. Volunteers like to be reassured of the value of the work they are doing and will enjoy occasional meetings to review progress. A brief handout which reinforces some of these points may be appropriate. Above all, volunteers need to feel they are part of a team working within a total structure organized by the teacher.

5 There needs to be a good match between helpers and tasks. Some people really are better at dealing with things rather than children and as such will be happier checking and organizing apparatus: others may have a talent for gardening, sewing or woodwork. Children can gain from these interests but the level of activity needs to be appropriate for the age and ability of the group.

6 A cheese and wine or tea party at the end of the year is a welcome thank you for volunteers working in school. Alternatively the class might like to give the helpers a small thank you gift.

THE CONSULTANT TEACHER

Staff meetings
1 Staff meetings need a definite purpose. Organizational matters can be discussed during the lunch hour: curriculum and year-group meetings are better held after school when teachers are not under such pressure of time.
2 Regular dates should be fixed for meetings and a time limit kept.
3 The consultant teacher will save herself time at a meeting if she has thoroughly prepared the area under discussion. She also needs a clear idea of what she wants achieved.
4 A discussion paper circulated in advance will ensure that everyone is similarly informed.

Working with teachers,
1 The consultant may have an informal, hour long, advice and support 'surgery' in her classroom after school once a week.
2 The consultant needs a clear idea of how the staff feel she can be of most help to them. If she is released from her class she can work alongside another teacher. Some staff may not welcome a colleague working in the

same classroom; in this case a small group of children may be withdrawn from the class for a lesson. However the planning and follow-up for the work tackled should be jointly discussed with the teacher. The consultant's task is to guide and help colleagues develop rather than just assist.

CURRICULUM ORGANIZATION

The pattern of the day

1 Are set play times necessary? A trial period, when an ancillary either relieves each member of staff in turn to collect coffee or brings coffee to the teacher's classroom, will help to decide what effect this change of organization has on the children's concentration.

2 Fixed points in the day, e.g. use of hall, use of radio and TV programmes, need to be identified. Pre-recording will help flexibility.

3 Class-based activities, e.g. storytime, PE, music, need to be identified. The rest of the day can be planned to encourage continuity.

4 During class-based activities the concentration span of different children can be noted. If two teachers are working closely together it may be possible to share children occasionally for a story to provide a more appropriate timespan and content for less able and more able children.

5 Children need to learn gradually to complete two activities within a given period of time. Some children will need considerable time to complete a task to their satisfaction. Occasionally other work can be waived if one assignment is completed properly.

6 Children need to be encouraged to develop an assignment over a period of time, e.g. writing a serial story, making a series of observational drawings of a growing plant.

7 Older children could have a trial period during which they and the teacher plan the day as a joint venture. The rest of the class could offer constructive criticism of their suggestions.

8 Children sometimes find it difficult to settle immediately to the day. A group time to provide the setting for work is helpful. This may include a formalized signal such as a morning song, completion of certain routines such as adjusting the calendar and weather chart, or the teacher playing a short piece of music.

9 Individual teachers could describe the pattern of their day in a series of staff meetings. Perhaps visits to other classrooms during the day to see colleagues in action could be arranged. An observer (head/colleague/adviser) might observe the daily pattern and give an objective account of its effect on the children.

Balance

1 Regular points in the day can be interspersed with occasional unexpected events – a measure of unpredictability lifts the level of interest.

2 Output needs to be balanced with input – the children must have something to write about.

3 Occasionally it is worth concentrating on one aspect of the curriculum to the detriment of other areas, e.g. a 'maths fair' held for a week throughout the school.

4 Limited space may make it difficult to accommodate the range of concrete experiences in a classroom. So long as the teacher plans to introduce these activities over the course of the year this does not matter.

5 The means of recording to which children have access – e.g. writing, maths, movement, painting, craft, music, drama – may be unbalanced. A redress of balance may be necessary if one of these forms is over-dominant.

An audience for work

PROVIDING A VARIED AUDIENCE

1 Older children could write and illustrate short stories to take and read to the nursery group.

2 Children could design and make their own display notices for the school fête/sale/concert.

3 Children could write some of their own Christmas 'thank you' letters from school.

4 Schools may be 'paired' so that children can write monthly letters to their 'partner' in the other school. It is best if the schools are in different environments; but the children do need to be paired roughly according to ability. Photographs and postcards can all be included.

DISPLAY

Presentation

A standard mount for all 2D work provides design consistency. Margin proportions may be 25 mm on three sides and 40 mm at the bottom. If the picture is placed in the centre of the mount with the same space all around it will appear to be nearer the bottom of the mount rather than central.

A collection of fabrics will provide for a variety of backgrounds. These will need to be ironed before use.

Boxes and stands can be used to provide display at different levels. This will add interest to 3D objects of a similar height.

Display boards can be covered with cork tiles or neutral hessian or felt. This will add warmth to the area and provide a pleasing background even with minimum display. Labels are an integral part of the display and the lettering used should be a good example to children. Layout and spacing should be considered. A practical INSET session on how to use stencils and different pens will help here.

Criteria for display

During the course of a term every child should have had something displayed. Teaching objectives may be strengthened if the children are clear as to what the teacher is looking for when deciding whose work to display, e.g. best presentation, those who have tried hardest, the funniest poem etc.

Using display

1 Children can bring items to add to a display. One item from a child can be used to stimulate and develop display.

2 Thoughtful questions can be attached to displays, e.g. classifications – how many can you see? sequence and process questions – how do you think this wheel was made? (This can be used to develop group discussion later.)

3 An attractive range of junk items could be displayed, with an invitation to 'make a machine using these things'. Some of the ideas could be demonstrated practically by the children.

4 A completed display of work might help recap on a teaching point or identify a gap. For example, the teacher may say that written work should be neat, well presented, and should include some good describing words. Children's work can then be displayed and groups asked to look at the display to identify which of the three required elements is missing or is the weakest.

5 Older children can develop display skills for themselves, using a special corner of the classroom. The class can provide constructive criticism and advice about the display.

6 Children love to find their classroom transformed by display. If this is done after school by the teacher they can return next morning to a changed environment.

Monitoring the curriculum

SELF-MONITORING

1 The teacher can pick out five areas that give cause for concern or about which she has little information, e.g. what use is made of constructional toys in the classroom, and then decide on a systematic approach to monitor these areas during a term. Different aspects in the classroom can be monitored in different ways, e.g. a wallchart with coloured pegs might identify curriculum areas, a list of children enables the teacher to keep a crude check on the occasions she sees them for different curricular activities, a cassette recorder may give some indication of use of language in one area of the classroom.

2 The children can provide evidence about what happens in the classroom, for example, at the end of a morning the class could say who had been approached by the teacher, or the children might identify their favourite lesson and give reasons for their choice.

3 Children need to be observed both in and out of the classroom, e.g. how do they spend time in the playground and how does this prepare them for a working session afterwards? do some groups need a quiet settling-in period after a very active playtime? how do children make the

transition from work to play? how do they go home at the end of the day? – children bursting out into the playground may be one sign of their reaction to an overtight school regime.

SHARING OBSERVATIONS

1 Teachers will need to get used to working with other adults in the same teaching area before adopting this approach. A start can be made by leaving classroom doors open, working with a student or parent nearby, asking the headteacher to visit the classroom regularly. The teacher, colleagues and the headteacher can discuss developing a partnership and the choice of a partner – it needs to be someone with a similar educational philosophy.

2 Ways of releasing one partner from classroom contact will have to be settled. The headteacher may take the class, or occasionally children could 'double up'. If classroom release is not possible, the observations will have to be limited to after school hours when classroom layout and environment can be seen and commented on.

3 The 'observer' will need to provide an objective, written observation to provide evidence for possible future action. The situation being observed will need to be able to be identified within a limited period of time, e.g. focusing on one area of the room to identify circulation problems, watching one distractible child for two sessions to note how he settles to work, observing the quality of the children's talk when working in groups.

Monitoring is hard work. It needs to be done sparingly and systematically and the results should be used!

Assessment

At the beginning of each term the teacher can decide what needs to be measured and the best way of doing this. For example, a child's emotional development cannot be *tested*, but it can be closely noted and appropriate situations devised to ascertain whether he is maturing. A child's spatial abilities may be tested diagnostically to identify the weaknesses and a range of activities may then be provided to strengthen these areas, and a check made to note progression or otherwise.

STRUCTURED OBSERVATIONS

1 The situation should be as normal as possible. Children may react to different conditions, e.g. the teacher operating in a different role.

2 Disruptive behaviour can be measured by observing the child for a number of sessions over a period of time. The havoc caused to the class may lead the teacher to assume that the incidents had occurred more frequently than the evidence shows.

3 Observing a child's play will help assess his understanding. For example, sustained repetitive play in the water tray (repeatedly pouring water through a sieve) may be the child testing a hypothesis.

4 A child's development needs to be checked in more than one area of

the curriculum – a confident child with good oral language may produce poor written results.

5 *Checklists and rating scales:* Together staff can draw up a set of statements to use for a rating scale. A 'concentration' scale might be:

1 Very distractible in all activities.
2 Concentrates occasionally on a one-to-one basis.
3 Concentrates for those activities that interest him – otherwise distractible.
4 Generally good concentration.
5 Sustained concentration in all activities, regardless of the behaviour of other children.

Staff can devise their own checklists for different areas of the curriculum, which can then be used in turn in the classroom, and the main strengths of each identified.

STANDARDIZED TESTS

1 A standardized test needs to be looked at carefully in the light of what it tests, the practicalities of administration, scoring and interpretation, its appropriateness for the group of children.
2 A range of tests will need to be appraised and the appropriate diagnostic tests selected for use with children giving cause for concern. The educational psychologist and colleagues in other schools who are already using the test can offer advice.
3 The test must be scrupulously administered, using the same teacher for all the children. It is helpful to meet with colleagues to discuss the disparity between objective test results and the teacher's own observations. Considerable disparity, e.g. poor test performance by a child considered able by the teacher, needs investigation. Is it due to an inappropriate test or is the teacher making false assumptions about the child's achievements?

MARKING

1 Most of the work needs to be marked with the child (this is very important with five- to seven-year-olds). Where this is not possible, the work needs to be marked the same day and the child offered some positive comments as well as criticisms.
2 The order in which groups are marked should be rotated – the first group to be seen is likely to have more attention.
3 Imaginative symbols – e.g. a smiling face for good work, a sad face for poor quality work – can help communication.
4 Marking can help to identify a group for teaching purposes. A red circle on all work where certain phonic rules need to be learnt can lead to this group being collected together at a later stage in the day.
5 Comments made when marking should be followed up with the children. Different symbols to identify different weaknesses (poor handwriting/layout/insufficient length of work) can be used as above to identify a group of children with a common problem. At the end of the

week this group can be checked to see if there has been an improvement.
6 The child might like to give *his* opinion of his assignment – this is a useful way to develop self-criticism.
7 Older children can occasionally mark each other's work. They will need help to identify very clearly the one aspect they should be looking for (e.g. good use of words/an interesting story). Each child could comment on his neighbour's work but should be prepared to justify his comments to the teacher.
8 Good efforts deserve praise and public recognition, particularly when the child lacks self-confidence. There might be a 'special effort' display board; the child could read his own work to class, take it home to show parents or to a neighbouring teacher.

Records

1 Parents may be asked to offer information about their child prior to school entry which could then form the basis of a pre-school profile. This 'information' might be, for example, one of the child's paintings from playgroup.
2 The same records are not required for every child. Whilst a broad check on develpment will need to be kept for all children, more detailed records will note any deviation from the norm, for example, where a child is not progressing to word recognition a check on mastery of all the subskills needs to be made (e.g. Tansley's screening check in *Reading and Remedial Reading*).
3 The record format needs to be easy to keep and easy to interpret. Various formats can include checklists, flowcharts, graphs, teacher statements.
4 *Class records* should help the teacher note progression and assist continuity if a supply teacher has to take the class (record books should be clearly marked with a brief note for use directed at the supply teacher). The most useful records for this purpose are diagnostic reading records, level of maths work, and list of children in ability groups.
5 *Transition and transfer records* need to be formulated with the receiving school or teacher and the agreed format should ensure that minimal essential information is passed on about all children.
6 Within a school there should be critical appraisal of any records kept. The receiving teacher can be asked to look at the records of a sample of children she is due to take next year and check what they tell her about: the child as an individual; the programme of work she should be planning for him; any information that she could not find out for herself during the first contact with the child.
7 Most record keeping should take place daily and reflect the ongoing developments of children, e.g. the teacher will need to note a child's reading difficulties or mastery of a maths concept when it happens. A brief time can be spent at the end of each day to complete any observations on personal records.
8 Examples of children's work, dated and kept over a period of time, will

provide evidence of progression. However, this form of record keeping is bulky and cannot be maintained for all children, but it can form a basis for long-term assessment if the child has learning difficulties. Teachers need to agree criteria for selecting samples of work, e.g. at random, only the best work, child's or teacher's selection.

9 Teachers need to decide whether their records can be used to improve the quality of teaching and learning, and provide parents with sufficient information about the child (e.g. if there is a policy of 'open' records within the authority the 'sensitive' information should be omitted).

Curriculum form

Each area of the curriculum can be looked at in turn to decide how it can best be expressed, e.g. children's emotional development may best be understood by discussion of a series of case studies; development in art and craft by studying samples of children's work and looking at progression. Where the curriculum is written down it should be in a form that is useful to the teacher and which encourages regular discussion and review of any document. With more intangible curriculum areas it may be useful to see how this relates to the curriculum at a later stage: e.g. role play – expressive language and movement, easy communication, ease of recording, development of initiative, development of self-confidence and willingness to participate in problem-solving.

DECIDING THE CURRICULUM

1 The responsibility for decision-making needs to be clearly outlined to all new members of staff by the headteacher or a designated teacher.

Staff meetings can be divided into those where purely administrative matters are dealt with and those for considering professional issues. The latter should be held after school when there is time to discuss at leisure.

3 In a large school, regular year-group meetings may provide a more intimate and effective forum for active participation by less outgoing members of staff. Alternatively they may prefer to send written proposals to a full staff meeting.

4 In schools where there has previously been no requirement for joint decision-making, teachers may initially find it difficult to take an active part. A skilled chairman will gently persuade such teachers to contribute at their own level and ensure that their views are respected. This may take a considerable time and will require patience on the part of the head and the curriculum consultants.

THE ROLE OF THE CURRICULUM CONSULTANT

1 The consultant will rely heavily on her own professional excellence, combined with sound personal relationships and qualities of leadership, to enable her to help other teachers grow professionally.

2 One of her priorities should be to be available to teachers during lunch hours and immediately after school, and once a week her expertise may be used for specific school-based in-service training.

3 Small schools may find it difficult to cover the curriculum with very few teachers. Cooperative ventures may enable one specialist in a small school to exchange for one day a fortnight with a specialist in another school; two schools may have joint staff meetings with a contribution from one curriculum specialist; a consultant teacher, offering a particular specialism, may be appointed to work in three schools.

THE WORKING DOCUMENT
Forms of recording can be varied to suit the staff.
1 Every teacher may have her own school file, containing curricular documents as well as other professional papers and personal work notes.
2 A card index system is quick to refer to and can be adapted easily.
3 An abridged version of the agreed curriculum might be kept as a record for each child.
4 A tape cassette can be taken home. It can be used at staff meetings in place of a written statement.

THE FORMAL STATEMENT
This may be included with the school brochure which will also offer other information about the school.

Maintaining the practice
1 Staff discussions – both as a total group and within year-groups – need to be regular.
2 Children's written work may be viewed and discussed, to make sure that children of similar age are having similar experiences and that the match of work is appropriate.
3 Whilst the headteacher will have an overview of school practice, the curriculum consultant may occasionally be able to be released from her class to visit colleagues and offer support.

Evaluation
1 The teacher needs to test her skills of evaluation in a limited way initially, i.e. in one aspect of the curriculum.
2 Different forms of monitoring should have supplied evidence to judge effectiveness: e.g. questioning of young children in groups and individually, observation of class and individual activity, quality of written work, standardized tests for older children. Full use can be made of professional visitors, e.g. advisers, inspectors, who may offer objective evidence about an aspect of classroom activity.
3 Evaluation needs to be regular and systematic in order for it to become a natural part of the teaching process. The head will wish to focus teachers' attention on particular aspects (e.g. the quality of problem-solving in the classroom) so that findings can be shared and discussed.
4 The aim of school evaluation should be for teachers to be so conscious of their strengths and weaknesses that any external inspection should present few surprises.

Change

The pace of change needs to be judged carefully and teachers will need help to cope with innovation, e.g. classroom visits by the headteacher or curriculum consultant to reassure and support teaching and learning; appropriate in-service training; opportunity to visit schools where change is working successfully; adequate materials.

TEACHING AND LEARNING

A series of staff meetings might look at teaching organization. Each member of staff could give a short talk, based in her own classroom, about the way in which she organizes her work. The staff could identify which teachers encourage an active mode of learning – i.e. children moving around the room, actively involved – and which stress the passive mode, with children receiving their learning solely from the teacher. The strengths and weaknesses of both forms of organization could be discussed and an attempt made to establish at least some common practices. For example, the teachers of the active learners might initiate some set sedentary activities and teacher-directed tasks, such as learning poetry; the teachers of passive learners could be encouraged to make the children more self-sufficient.

Ideally, whilst no teacher should be made to feel inadequate, all should be prepared to adjust their practice to meet agreed school priorities.

Deployment of teachers

CLASS TEACHING

The strengths of being a class teacher should be exploited.
1 The teacher needs to make an effort to get to know as much as possible about each child in her group, perhaps by selecting a child at random from the register and checking what information is immediately available about his personality, home background and learning.
2 There needs to be a sound relationship with every child in the class. A strong personality clash between the teacher and a particular child might be discussed with the headteacher and the child's parents, and the child allowed to transfer to another class.
3 Special occasions, e.g. birthdays, could be celebrated with a card.
4 Children are people in their own right. They enjoy discussions which allow them to offer their point of view, for example about current TV programmes, new developments in the area.
5 The classroom is lived in by teacher and children. The layout could be planned jointly to some extent, with the children giving their opinions about placement of furniture and displays.
6 The teacher needs to identify her own strengths and weaknesses and seek help where necessary. For example, if she is underconfident in maths, the best practitioner (probably the consultant) could help.

COOPERATIVE TEACHING
1 In schools with only one class in a year-group, teachers may develop

cooperative work with a similarly placed colleague in a neighbouring school. Regular meetings could lead to matching of standards of children's work, sharing resources, assessment of each other's classrooms, making home-made apparatus, possibly even exchange teaching sessions.

2 Vertical cooperation. When discussing a child's work it can be useful to look at what he achieved with his former teacher.

3 A look at other classrooms which cater for the younger and older age-groups can pinpoint similarities in provision and reveal if there is sufficient additional challenge for children as they graduate to the next class.

TEAM TEACHING

Team teaching needs careful preparation. It is a good idea to visit schools which use team teaching in varying ways, listen to their evaluation of each approach, and decide which best suits the children, adults and building in question.

The team leader will need a clear philosophy of the approach to be used. Time will be needed for daily consultations for planning and evaluation. The proposed day will have to be scrutinized on paper to identify where staff will be deployed at different times of the day, and to look at the day from the child's point of view – e.g. where can he get help if he needs it?

A pilot scheme using team teaching for a limited period a week can be used to assess the teachers and the children.

Some basic questions will have to be answered:

Who will be responsible for record keeping?
Is it preferable for one teacher to be responsible for the reading progress of a group of children (this could be the registration teacher)?
How much direct teaching will take place?
How much will the teacher be generally available to a group of children?
Is it to be a split or integrated programme?
Who will be responsible for general display areas?
How much choice will the children have in planning their work programme?

Although organizational reasons may contribute to the start of team teaching (e.g. uneven groups of children, the design of the building) the implementation should mean increased opportunities for learning. As ever the crucial question is: What are the children gaining from this way of working?

Grouping for learning

CLASS

The following activities might be taught on a class basis.

1 *Stories, poetry, listening to music* There might be a set weekly time when a new poem is heard. Visitors could come to recite a poem/use cassette

recordings. A little introduction whets the appetite before delivering the poem – children might like to share their favourite poem with the class.

2 *Drama* Various means can be used to heighten effects of a story later to be acted out by the children, e.g. darkened classroom lit by one candle; background music; simple props for the storyteller such as cloak or hat; dramatic use of voice.

3 *Discussions* Topics suitable for mixed ability are needed (e.g. where there are no 'right' answers such as cloze procedures, suggestions for creating imaginary names, nonsense words, aspects of social and moral development).

4 Children can share their discoveries with the class, e.g. science activities could be investigated by a group which might then demonstrate its findings to the class and be prepared to answer questions from the class.

5 *Variety of teaching styles* Class teaching does not necessarily involve an authoritarian style. During discussions the teacher may adopt the role of chairman, introduce the topic and then keep a low profile, only coming in to chair responses from individuals. She may be a spectator, when a group of children perform a short play or give a series of talks to the class. The less dominant the teacher the more the children will grow in autonomy.

6 *Timing* The beginning and end of the day might be used for class teaching. Young children gain security from feeling part of a total group with their teacher at these times of the day. They can be used for planning and reviewing the day's work and for small groups and individuals to share experiences with the class group. The beginning of the day is a good time to introduce a new topic to the class. The children can be shown stimulus materials before they are put on display in the class. The teacher might bring in a range of articles linked with 'When I was a little girl' and talk about personal experiences.

GROUPS
Different criteria are used for grouping children and such groups may be changed according to the activity and developing abilities of children.

1 *Interest groups* may emerge where children are working together on a common interest, possibly in creative work or project work. This group is likely to last for the duration of a specific piece of work and may promote good discussion.

2 *Friendship groups* Unless this grouping is positively disruptive for the rest of the class it can enable children to work in a relaxed and sociable way. If the children are of mixed ability additional benefits can be derived from the more able children assisting less able friends.

3 *Ability groups* If children are working at a similar level in a certain area the teacher may use her time economically by developing a teaching point with such a group.

4 *Collaborative learning* Children need to be trained systematically to know what is expected of them in the way of group collaboration and discussion, e.g. before writing children might
   discuss with a neighbour the proposed content of their story;

discuss, in pairs, relevant 'describing' words for written work and then report to the full class.

5 *Group tasks to promote collaboration*

Four children could be given materials to create a model of a house and each child made responsible for one aspect of the model. (Older children may allocate the tasks themselves.)

Pairs of children could write a story, after discussing the plot together and deciding how to write it jointly.

Two children may be given an experiment to tackle, e.g. measuring how many times different balls may be bounced within a given period of time. One child could have the stopwatch and record findings by means of a simple graph using 'ball' symbols.

If the class listen to a story and are left in suspense before the end, groups of children could discuss a possible outcome for five minutes and then report to the class.

Small groups of children might produce a display and talk about a common interest they share, e.g. stamp collecting, pop music.

STARTING GROUPS OFF

Within a class of five groups, three groups could be allocated tasks which will keep them occupied immediately, e.g.

Group One – handwriting practice with a selection of cards to choose from.

Group Two – continuation of a creative activity such as developing a model village from small junk equipment.

Group Three – practising a new phonic rule which has been previously introduced.

Group Four will be basically a self-maintaining group but will require a few minutes of teacher time to remind them of the activity, e.g. shopping cards which have been introduced the previous day. The teacher discusses with the group how they will organize this activity and where they will find their materials.

Group Five – During this time Group Five have been requested to collect materials for a new maths game and see if they can work out how it should be played.

1 *Sequence of activity* The teacher talks to the whole class identifying the activity for each group. She spends a few minutes with Group Four, and then checks that Groups One, Two and Three have all their equipment and have started their tasks. She is now able to teach Group Five the new maths game.

2 *Dealing with different rates of finishing the activity* The children will need a second activity when their main task is completed. The type of task will depend on the teacher's intention for the child. For example, after sedentary recording work, a choice of activity-based tasks may be offered such as constructional kits, painting or imaginative play. Relaxation may be offered from a selection of games from a games trolley – these might include individual puzzles as well as games to play with a partner. The

second activity may be aimed to develop an aspect of the curriculum work, e.g. reading games. Where appropriate second activities can be colour coded to ensure that the children have choice, within limits.

INDIVIDUAL

Some children in the class will require *individualized tasks*, e.g. extra practice in a particular skill such as letter formation, or applying a number concept, or extension of task – e.g. problem-solving for more able children. These tasks may be set when other group work is being allocated. Some children will require individual attention from the teacher, e.g. immature children or very young children who cannot learn in a group. When the rest of the class are settled (perhaps ten minutes after being allocated to group activities) the teacher can use this time to work with individual children on a rota basis.

Occasionally other children may find individual attention from an adult too intensive. They may develop better working with a child of similar ability or within a small group.

LISTENING TO CHILDREN READ

1 Younger first-school children need regular periods of individual attention from the teacher to develop reading whilst they are still at the decoding stage. This can take place when the remainder of the class are occupied with group work. The period of time and quality of attention from the teacher should enable appropriate response to the child's miscues, and brief questioning about the content of the text.
2 Children who have reached the level of reading independently at a simple level may only require individual attention twice weekly. Again these periods need to be long enough to enable some discussion about content of the present book, selection of future reading book and diagnosis and teaching of specific weaknesses.
3 Listening to children read individually may be supplemented by:
   occasional small group reading if children are at the same stage in a book;
   children reading to one another or to another adult or taking their book home to read;
   children using their reading skills in other areas of work in the classroom, e.g. reading notices, instructions, their own stories.

INDIVIDUAL ATTENTION FROM OTHER ADULTS

1 A well-briefed voluntary helper or ancillary may offer a valuable one-to-one relationship for a child, e.g. discussing a story or picture, working with simple construction toys or puzzles.
2 Regular contact with one adult, not necessarily the teacher, may boost a child's self-confidence and thus his ability to learn.

WITHDRAWAL OF GROUPS

There needs to be regular contact between the class teacher and the withdrawal teacher, e.g. a meeting at the beginning of term to consider the child's work together and plan a joint approach to meet his needs; brief weekly meetings to exchange information about developments and concerns. Even if the withdrawal teacher only works part-time, such contact is part of her commitment to the work and her job satisfaction will be increased if she is treated as one of a team. Clearly contacts must be modified if the withdrawal teacher is to relate to a number of different classes.

1 When a group is withdrawn the class teacher will be able to concentrate on the remainder of the children; this can be a good opportunity for small group or individual work.

2 If less or more able children are withdrawn the aim should be to play down any emphasis on their differences. If room size allows, the withdrawal teacher may be able to work alongside the class teacher at particular times rather than take the children out of the room.

3 In order to minimize disruption for the less able children, the class teacher may choose to work with them and leave the withdrawal teacher to take the remainder of the class.

4 A cooperative approach may enable one teacher to take a large group of children, releasing the other to work with a small group.

5 Hymn practice and occasional assemblies may also provide occasions for the teacher to withdraw children with special needs.

Admission, accommodation and transfer of children

ADMISSION

Children need to remain with their first teacher for at least a year. Where there is more than one intake a year this may mean some form of vertical grouping (see below).

The teacher will have built up a profile of each of her new children before they start school; she will know which children have had no pre-school group experience and plan to keep a particular eye on them.

During the first few weeks the assistance of an ancillary helper or an established mother helper or secondary school pupil is particularly useful whilst the teacher is establishing daily routines, e.g. dressing and undressing for PE, moving into the hall for assembly. Children may need to be reassured by physical contact. The children should enter the reception class already familiar with the classroom and the teacher. A phased introduction to the rest of the school can follow together with the opportunity to meet some of the other teachers.

1 *Playtime* The reception teacher needs to be in the playground to remain with the new group of children for the first week. In a large school it may be a good idea to have a separate playtime for the youngest class or not to have a playtime until the children have become familiar with other school routines. Children who find playtimes particularly difficult may be placed under the supervision of an older child or a brother or sister.

2 *Self-sufficiency* The first half-term will probably place priority on teaching children self-sufficiency skills. Daily practice and plenty of time

will be needed for finding apparatus and putting it away, looking after personal possessions and using books and equipment correctly.

3 *Contact with parents* The reception teacher can reassure new parents by using every opportunity to communicate with them when they collect their children at the end of the session. She should aim to say something to each parent during the course of the week. If personal contact is difficult because parents are working, a small home/school notebook may be kept in the child's school bag, and any necessary messages written in it by parents and teachers. Parents can be encouraged to be involved in the child's learning from the start. The children can take home their 'reading book' from day one (this is likely to be a sequential picture book which can be shared with parents).

ACCOMMODATION

A mixed style of accommodation may work best. The total group of children in the school will need to be considered, bearing in mind the numbers of teachers and teaching spaces available. Perhaps mixed age-groups will be adopted with the younger children and single year-groups in the top classes.

The size of the teaching spaces needs to be considered. The primary aim in first schools should be to keep class sizes as small as possible. However, if one of the teaching spaces is very small it may be decided to have a floating teacher to withdraw groups of children from other larger classes.

Children's and teacher's personalities may influence grouping. Where there are parallel age-groups there may be opportunities to place 'difficult' children with a teacher who is temperamentally suited to meeting their needs: distractible children should be dispersed amongst different classes: where a group of children are known to be difficult the group should be kept small.

Generally the teachers of the youngest children should have the smallest groups – particularly if there is no regular ancillary help available.

1 *Temporary flexible grouping* Cooperative planning may enable different groupings for specific activities, e.g. the headteacher, two class teachers, and two parents working with a group of 90 children in the hall. Children may be paired to work on problem-solving, leaving the third teacher to join the group, or work with a few children with special needs, or assist a teacher in another class.

2 Two classes may combine to share a practical area for part of the day. Two or three classes may combine for an 'activities' afternoon when teachers are available to take interest groups for various creative work.

3 *Mixed age-groups* Criteria for determining mixed age-groups can include: sex, age, physical size, personal interests, friendship groups, ability. There needs to be sufficient space and variety of apparatus to provide for all levels of development.

4 *Horizontal grouping* works well for activities which relate closely to a certain level of development, e.g. PE, stories, poetry. Where children remain in the class for more than one year, certain topics can be repeated as

part of a spiral curriculum. For example, with a topic like 'Ourselves', the youngest children can concentrate on basic physical similarities and differences which can be reflected in art work, maths and descriptive language; the older children could do more observational work focusing on measurement, individual likes/dislikes and interests. In this way class work is given a greater cohesion and discussion can develop within the whole group.

5 *Timing* needs to be considered. In an integrated programme, the youngest children can take a break from an activity while the older children have the opportunity to sustain it. If the programme is split, longer time slots should be provided for the older children who will have a greater span of concentration.

TRANSITION AND TRANSFER

Internal transition
A few children at a time can be discussed with the next teacher, who might visit the class to familiarize herself with those children before discussing the next group. The next teacher will need the fullest information about children who are difficult, e.g. personal likes and dislikes, 'successful' approaches with them. Children who seem to be 'thrown' by change during the year may be the ones who will need particular attention when the time comes to move class.

1 If possible the next teacher should visit the children's present classroom to make a note of the environment, teacher expectation and routines, some of which could be incorporated into the children's regime during the next year.

2 The summer term is a good time for the children to become familiar with their next class and their prospective teacher by, for example, taking messages into the classroom, or the teacher taking storytime with her prospective children.

Transition to middle school
Regular inter-tier meetings between middle schools and feeder first schools will provide opportunities for discussion of similar approaches to be adopted in basic skill subjects, as well as information which first schools consider essential to pass on in the interests of the child, and which middle schools find useful in promoting continuity of learning, e.g. areas of experience covered, tests used.

1 A series of termly visits will enable the middle school teacher to focus on prospective children and for the first school teacher to see her former children settled in the next phase of education.

2 Exchange teaching could be arranged in the summer term between the top-year teacher of the first school and the first-year teacher of the middle school.

3 Where schools are designed on a pyramid basis, i.e. several first schools feeding one middle school, various consultations and in-service projects

could develop horizontal continuity, for example, discussion of expectations, curriculum guidelines, criteria for assessing children.

4 Joint in-service for first and middle school teachers could stress the curriculum principles which are relevant for children of all ages.

Transfer

1 When transferring the child may be encouraged to take samples of his work from the previous term, dated and commented on by the teacher. This may be packed into a special file and addressed 'For my new teacher'.

2 The teacher may allay some of the child's anxieties about moving by talking to him about his new school. She may know of a teacher there or comment positively about the geographical area to which he is moving.

3 A child coming from another school will need a brief tour of the parts of the school that will concern him immediately, and time to talk about his previous school and to show his previous work to the new teacher.

4 A reliable, friendly child can be responsible for showing him all new routines during the first week. (The teacher may need to check that this is succeeding and that the new child is aware of what is expected at transition times, e.g. changing for PE playtimes, lunchtimes.)

5 An informal meeting with the child's parents and new teacher can be arranged at point of transfer or soon after. If there have been problems at the previous school, parents may need reassurance that the child will have a fresh start in his new placement.

6 A small group of reliable parents may have the task of helping settle new children and their families into the area. With encouragement and guidance from the headteacher these parents could:

> keep a watchful eye on a new child during his first few days at school if they are already parent helpers;
>
> prepare a small booklet for new families coming into the area offering information about local facilities, e.g. doctors, dentists, shopping area, activities such as Cubs, Brownies, swimming;
>
> run a coffee morning or evening in one of their homes for parents new to the area to both welcome the family and offer them practical information.

ORGANIZING THE ENVIRONMENT

The building

Specific staff meetings could look at a particular space within the school to decide whether it is being fully used, and if not, whether it could be developed. If building design is preventing staff adopting a particular teaching approach, certain adaptations might overcome the problem, e.g. team teaching in a traditional building ideally requires two or three linked classrooms. A small classroom may be extended by imaginative use of furniture to provide a book area or practical space in an adjoining wide corridor.

1 Many old buildings have high ceilings which make it difficult to display

suspended work. Large box structures, attractively covered with cork or hessian, may be permanently suspended from the ceiling and children's work can be attached to them.

2 Plants and hanging containers will enhance a dull area. Provided there is no fire hazard, doors to small rooms can be removed to make them more easily overseen and accessible to a main teaching area.

3 If the building is new, the architect and adviser might like to come and explain the philosophy behind the design.

4 The school entrance should be clearly marked if it is not immediately apparent to visitors.

5 A welcome sign by the entrance can be made and illustrated by the children. Flowering shrubs or tubs and plants immediately outside the entrance will help to create a bright impression.

6 The school office needs to be clearly signposted.

Circulation

An observation of children moving around the school will identify where there are congestion problems. Staggered playtimes and lunch hours can help (although then staff will need to come together as a group at the end of the day). If the building design is poor, a system which avoids unnecessary circulation around the school needs to be agreed, even if this entails some inequalities in allocation of teaching spaces.

1 Children need space to keep their coats and personal belongings tidy. Coat-hanging space needs to be dispersed as much as possible.

2 It helps if cloakrooms have both an entrance and exit, and if their use can be staggered at certain times of the day.

Teaching spaces

Where teaching spaces vary in size and convenience there will need to be agreed criteria for their allocation to particular groups of children, e.g. the youngest children generally need more space and to be kept within sight of the teacher; older children may be able to have their class as a home base and work in other spaces – library, practical area, corridor. Where space is scarce it may be useful to consider using the staffroom and headteacher's room as teaching areas at certain times in the week. Teachers could invite colleagues into their teaching areas and ask them to appraise the layout critically.

1 Teachers can look at a range of other classrooms and see what they offer children. Is each piece of furniture being used? Could it be usefully removed to create more space? Do all the children need a chair? Are different working areas clearly identified? Are different size teaching groups catered for? Can storage facilities be improved?

2 Using graph paper, different layouts can be planned to create more space, or more privacy.

3 Records of decisions about particular furniture arrangements and how they succeeded or failed can be kept for future reference.

4 Carpets and curtains will make a classroom both less 'institutional' and quieter to work in. Large cushions for the book area and curtains can be made from tye and dye or batic projects tackled by the older children.

Practical spaces

There needs to be an area within or adjoining the classroom, with suitable floor covering, where practical work can be tackled in small groups.

The programme of work can be varied throughout the year so that different experiences are provided and skills introduced over a period of time, e.g. modelling with dough, clay, polystyrene, soap, alabaster, papier mâché.

1 Storage facilities will need to be near the practical area. If the stock room is not convenient, immediate supplies should be easily available in a storage unit.

2 The children will need time to find materials for themselves and to be responsible for keeping them in good order, e.g. paint-brushes properly washed, clay returned in small balls to bin and lid properly replaced. Inventories of materials to be kept in each area can be displayed and checked by children at the end of the day.

3 *Storage* Where space is limited, paper can be stored suspended on a light platform lowered on a pulley system. This arrangement can also be used for storing models and wet paintings.

4 A cork-covered wall and wide shelf in the practical area enables children to display their work as they complete it. The work can then be seen by the whole group before certain items are selected and mounted for permanent display.

5 *Aprons* should have loops so they can be hung on hooks which are easily accessible to the children. A parent may be responsible for checking and repairing the aprons.

Outdoor spaces

FOR RECREATION

1 A defined hardcore area might be used for ball play and activity games, and remaining space developed for quieter leisure activities.

2 Seating may be fixed logs and wooden or concrete benches. These should be sited in the most sheltered part of the playground. Benches and tables will allow table games.

3 *Playground markings* A giant draughts or chessboard may be marked out and used with foam or polystyrene figures. Hopscotch pitches and giant footstep patterns provide for other activities. Some playground games involve keeping off the playground surface – logs and stepping stones will make this possible.

4 The playground supervision ladies might like to teach new children different games. A supply of beanbags and skipping ropes could be made available during the lunchtime. A sheltered wall covered with blackboard

paint will provide a good outside chalking area for younger children – chalks and duster can be supplied by the supervision ladies.

5 Plastic shoe-cleaning container(s) with two compartments and a handle are ideal containers for crayons, scissors and adhesives – all the materials needed for one activity can easily be carried outside.

6 The difficulties of working outside, e.g. children becoming over-excited and over-tired, rising noise levels which disturb other groups, should be discussed as a staff.

FOR CURRICULUM PURPOSES

1 Even the smallest area of playground will host a variety of minibeasts if a suitable habitat is created, e.g. damp surfaces covered with large stones for snails and woodlice, buddleia bushes for butterflies. The children will enjoy being able to collect their own specimens for the classroom vivarium.

2 The outside area can be used as an extension of the classroom. Measuring rainfall, size of puddles, work on shadows, measuring wind speed and direction with homemade weather vanes and bubble blowing, bird tables and charts – are just some examples of practical work that can take place immediately outside the classroom.

3 If teaching spaces have immediate access to outside, it is well worth paving these areas and providing some form of veranda cover so that they can be used for teaching purposes during most of the year.

4 A small gardening area (inner city schools may have window boxes) will reap dividends. The youngest children will enjoy an area just for digging.

5 Outside areas can be used to develop sensory skills – what sounds can children hear? what surfaces can they feel? – and observation skills – drawing outside brickwork, trees, shrubs, traffic counts from the school gate.

Safety

1 Very dry sand and sawdust can be dangerous play materials as they can choke a small child.

2 If a child is sick, immediately place a chair over the area to prevent a further accident.

3 Teachers will need some lockable storage for any potentially dangerous materials, children's medicines etc.

Material resources

ORDERING AND PURCHASING

1 It is wise to avoid relying solely on catalogues when choosing materials – exhbitions or visits to other schools offer a chance to see equipment in use before making decisions.

2 The local librarian may give advice on ordering reading books.

3 Termly meetings with local schools can be arranged to demonstrate new pieces of apparatus in the classroom.

4 A notebook, kept throughout the year, can be a useful way to identify gaps in apparatus and avoid making hasty or last-minute purchases.

5 Apparatus in the classroom needs to be checked regularly. Careful organization and training children how to look after and use equipment will mean that resources will last longer. Incomplete pieces of apparatus and worn-out books should be thrown away.

6 A local or county scheme for exchanging resources which are either duplicated or not wanted in the school can sometimes be organized through a surplus equipment 'fair', where all unwanted equipment is displayed and marked according to its value with vouchers. Schools can then receive and exchange vouchers depending on what goods they have submitted.

7 Some counties have a central store for 'waste' and surplus stocks from industry which can be collected and used in schools, e.g. rolls of newsprint, cork and wood offcuts.

8 Where space and manpower prohibit this, a limited scheme may be organized by teachers' centres who could collect these materials and make them available to schools annually.

USING RESOURCES

1 Children need access to a class library and a central library if space permits. Ideally the central library should be able to accommodate a whole class in order to teach and demonstrate reference skills.

2 Some apparatus may be underused by children. This can be remedied sometimes if such apparatus is introduced again perhaps by another member of staff who is using it particularly imaginatively.

3 Occasionally the apparatus is just not suitable and it should then either be discarded or exchanged for something more appropriate.

CATALOGUE AND RETRIEVAL SYSTEM

1 One member of staff could develop a central resource for more expensive single items of equipment, e.g. cassettes, filmstrips, language masters. Such equipment needs to be thoroughly checked and maintained, and any faults reported to the appropriate person immediately.

2 The central school library should be a dynamic and exciting area of the school. The teacher in charge may use different approaches to encourage children to use and enjoy books, e.g. quizzes, reviews of books by children for other children to read, pictures of children's authors, displays of new books.

3 Children could use the library during lunch hours if a parent is willing to oversee this arrangement.

4 Project resource packs can be built, containing cassettes, charts, suggestions for outings, lists of reference books and a brief report from the teacher on the approach used, with samples of children's work.

STOCK

1 Again, one member of staff will probably have overall responsibility for

ordering and keeping the stock cupboard in good order, but all staff will need free access to stock.

2 If quality of stock varies – there may be deterioration in quality or colour of paper – this may mean looking to a different source for the next order.

3 Teachers can share responsibility for what is in the stock cupboard by, for example, leaving a note when supplies of a certain material are low.

4 Staff meetings should include some discussion of stock, e.g. is the width of the Sellotape suitable? do we need more exciting materials for art and craft?

5 It is often a good idea to keep some particular materials for half way through the year, e.g. new exercise books, painting sticks, to provide a stimulus both for the teacher and the children.

APPRAISAL QUESTIONS

TIME
What range of activities do the children have to select from after they have completed their main task? How many of these are occupational/educational? Can I improve on the grading of these activities?

How effective are the tasks I have offered to groups today in developing collaborative learning?

How many times was I interrupted by other children in the class whilst I was teaching today? For what purpose? How could I avoid such future interruptions?

TEACHING AND LEARNING
How can I obtain more information about experiencees gained by other children in a parallel class?

How well informed am I about what the younger children and older children are taught in the school? How can I become better informed?

What are my criteria and purpose for grouping children in my class?

How much of my time is given to class teaching, group teaching, and teaching individuals? Could I improve this balance?

If my age-range is mixed, what group of children am I most concerned about? Why? How can I provide better for this group?

CURRICULUM ORGANIZATION
What range of activity have the children experienced today? What proportion of their time was spent in sedentary activity? How closely did the programme of work today relate to my guidelines?

ENVIRONMENT
When did I last ask a colleague to look critically at my classroom layout?

When did I last use a language master/cassette/cine-projector/overhead projector?

What prevents me?

How can I plan to use one or more of these as teaching aids in my classroom?

How many children lost articles in the cloakroom today? How could this be prevented?

At our next staff meeting what suggestions could I make to enhance the appearance of our school?

FURTHER RESOURCES

BOOKS

DEAN, J. (1972/4) *Room to Learn*; *A Place to Paint*; *Room Outside*; *Working Space*; *Language Area*; *Display* Evans
Essentially practical booklets with good suggestions and illustrations for improving organization.

BENNET, N., ANDREAE, J., HEGARTY, P. and WADE, B. (1980) *Open Plan Schools* NFER/Schools Council
Offers a comprehensive picture of current practice, highlights successful ways of working, and identifies problem areas for teachers working in open plan schools.

GALTON, M., SIMON, B. and CROLL, P. (1980) (eds.) *Inside the Primary Classroom*; (1981) *Progress and Performance in the Primary Classroom* Routledge & Kegan Paul
Volumes 1 and 2 of the Observational Research and Classroom Learning Evaluation Project, a large-scale observation study of primary classrooms, focusing on the relative effectiveness of different teaching approaches.

WATERS, D. (1980) *Management and Headship in the Primary School* Ward Lock Educational
The task, role and responsibilities of the primary headteacher in the 1980s.

YARDLEY, A. (1976) *The Organization of the Infant School* Evans
A basic introductory book suitable for students and interested parents.

KITS

ROWELL, J. (1976) *Place and Space: A Design and Furnishing System* Globe Education
A kit, incorporating gridboard and furniture symbols to allow planning on paper.

4

PERSONAL AND PROFESSIONAL DEVELOPMENT OF TEACHERS

INTRODUCTION

Work can be one way of providing for what Herzberg describes as 'that unique human characteristic, the ability to achieve and through achievement to experience pyschological growth. The stimuli for the growth needs are tasks that induce growth.'[1]

The dynamic nature of teaching gives it an added potential for pyschological growth. Because the work is so personally demanding teachers need to take advantage of this potential and exploit all opportunities for their *own* growth. Children will be best served by teachers who themselves are personally and professionally fulfilled.

Recent developments have accentuated the need for teachers' professional growth. The rapidly changing nature of society and the vast amount of new information and research about education means that increased demands are placed upon the teacher. The emphasis on children learning rather than being taught requires a close look at methodology, and the increasing amount of curriculum material being published means that teachers must be sufficiently informed to select wisely what to offer to children.

An added reason is the increasing demand for school accountability. In 1976 the Ruskin speech started the move towards an extension of central government's control over what happens in schools. Teacher accountability can be seen as three-pronged: a contractual accountability to the employer; a personal accountability to oneself as a professional and to the school; a moral accountability to the children and their parents. John Elliott sees these last two elements as being of greatest significance and argues for a responsive school accountability rather than external bureaucratic controls.[2]

The movement towards accountability has increased public interest in schools and all that they do. The 1980 Education Act has sharpened this focus with its stress on the central role of governors and parental choice of schools. Many parents are now very aware of their rights and teachers and headteachers are being questioned much more closely about their work. Matters are complicated by the fact that many questions from parents may be the result of popular media exposure about educational matters rather than informed enquiry.

These increased demands can only be met by teachers who are well informed, with a clear rationale for working, which they can explain both to other professionals and to the public. This is particularly important for first school teachers whose way of working is not always as easy to understand as the secondary subject-based curriculum.

Teachers who are functioning in this way are developing professionally. A staff of such teachers results in a 'thinking school' which looks constructively at its own performance and moves progressively to meet new challenges.

Teachers will not achieve this level of professionalism and competence alone. We suggest that support is needed in the following areas.

INDUCTION

The move from initial training to employment is a time when the teacher ideally builds on her knowledge of child development, curriculum and methodology and is helped to apply it in the reality of daily school life. However sound the training, the teacher's attitude and approach to her work will be largely moulded by her early years of teaching. Because of her vulnerable position as a newcomer she is forced to fit in with the school regime. If the regime is one where the needs of children are given low priority, where administrative efficiency and senior staff comforts are paramount, the young teacher will find it difficult to bring her educational goals to the fore: 'The kind of school where the new teacher is welcomed and valued for himself is one where there is respect for all who work there, both staff and children, where non-conformity in intellectual matters, and in personal appearance is accepted, and where leadership functions not as a straitjacket, but as a constructive aid to work.'[3] Where the school provides a model of good practice the new teacher is helped with teething troubles, grasps the practicalities and moves on to the next stage of development.

IN-SERVICE EDUCATION

Lady Plowden identified three periods of growth in a teacher's career:

The first, the academic acceptance, without full responsibility for implementation, of what I think I can best describe as the best primary practice: second, the realistic interpretation of this within the school situation, which may or may not be favourable to what has been learnt in college. But it is the third stage which is vital if standards are to be kept high and there is not to be stagnation of thinking. This is when the philosophy behind the day-to-day work must again (and again) be considered and what each individual child is doing measured in the light of this philosophy. It is at this stage that the teacher needs to re-assess his own strengths and to be aware of any weaknesses.[4]

The James Report advocated three cycles of training involving initial training, induction of new teachers and suggested that the 'highest priority' should be given to the expansion of the third cycle of opportunities for the continued education and training of teachers.[5]

Thus firm approval was given to in-service support and training for teachers and by 1975 the term 'in-service' was used to cover a range of activities. Stephens offers one interpretation: 'I use the term in-service education to mean the development of the individual which arises from the whole range of events and activities by which serving teachers can extend their personal academic or practical education, their professional competence and their understanding of educational principles and methods.'[6]

Recently the thrust for professional development has been through school-focused in-service. The SITE (Schools and In-service Teacher Education) project helps schools to evaluate and identify their own professional needs and with the aid of a co-ordinator these needs are met through LEA resources. Clearly there is much to be said for placing this professional responsibility on schools, although the ideal situation which enables every school to have 'tailor made' in-service provision may prove costly and complicated for LEAs to manage.

Essentially we now recognize that teachers need a diversity of provision to meet their professional needs.

CAREER DEVELOPMENT

In-service training will focus initially on heightening the teacher's professional skills in the classroom. There must also be provision for the teacher who wants to gain promotion. Whilst not all teachers have the inclination or the talents to take on positions of leadership, some able and ambitious teachers fail to gain promotion because they have not received guidance or had the opportunity to develop. A teacher should be able to look to her headteacher and local education authority for some form of counselling about promotion prospects. The LEA should provide training for leadership and management; the school should offer scope for the teacher to practise her newly-acquired skills. Advice should also be available about applying for posts and attending interviews. The teacher who wants to develop a career will stand the best possible chance if she is given this support, if she uses every opportunity to learn from different school experiences, and if she plans her promotion route in advance.

WORK APPRAISAL

The 1960s saw a time of tremendous innovation and change in schools. Expansion was multifold; finance was available for curriculum development; teaching posts were available; and there was a high degree of mobility within the profession. The accent was on experiment and development but without much attempt to monitor the resources being poured into the service and the methodologies being adopted.

Despite this growth a number of government documents after 1977 intimated that schools were not keeping up with public demands. One of the initiatives developed by central government was the Assessment of Performance Unit which was set up to monitor standards in schools[8] (see p.104).

Many LEAs have responded to *The School Curriculum* which requires them to 'look to the content and quality of education' in our schools. One response has been evaluation documents for schools which, through questions and checklists, form a basis for external, joint and self-appraisal. All these approaches have a place, but if the crucial requirement is to heighten the quality of education offered to children then the need is to help the development of the teacher's own professional skills.

THE TEACHER AS A PERSON

The process of enabling children to learn in the best possible setting requires the teacher to give a great deal of herself. The younger the child the more physically demanding the job – the emotional demands are there regardless of age. So the teacher needs to be someone who can give a great deal because she also receives a great deal from her work.

In Chapter 1 (p.18) we quoted Dr Kellmer Pringle's[9] list of children's basic needs. Teachers have these needs too; and they will be recognized and met in schools where rigorous yet caring attitudes apply to adults and children alike.

WHAT THE THEORY SAYS

INDUCTION

> . . . The first year of teaching is and always has been a formidable and even painful experience for many teachers. Everywhere efforts are now being made by schools and local authorities to help the probationary teacher to cope with his new role. . . . In most teacher-training courses there have been reforms designed to bring theory and practice into close relationship and to give student teachers more direct experience with the children they are going to teach. Yet the fact remains, that the first year of teaching still comes as a shock for many and, indeed, the evidence of our study suggests that it is becoming more and not less difficult. . . .[3]

This statement is just as relevant today, particularly with reference to the current recruitment and induction procedures adopted as a result of the financial climate. In 1972 the White Paper supported the James Report proposal for 'a planned re-enforcement of the process of induction in the first year in school'.[10] Recommendations included a lightened teaching load for newly qualified teachers and the 'committee's wish to see the teaching profession itself playing a major role in the induction process. The government agree that professional tutors will need to be designated and trained for this purpose.'[10]

These statements were made during a time of rapid teacher expansion. Today many authorities are not employing newly-qualified teachers, and where they are intitially employed it is often on a temporary contract without even the security of completing their probationary year in one school. Thus although schools and LEAs now have only a few new teachers to cater for, because of reduced resources provision may not be in any way improved since the 1972 recommendations.

Despite the lack of finance both LEAs and schools must be aware of the continuing anxieties experienced by the majority of new teachers.

In 1973 new teachers in Northumberland's junior and first schools identified their main concerns as: 'Dealing with groups of wide ability range; awareness of children's previous learning; lack of specific techniques; individual discipline problems – later replaced by "inadequate organizing ability".'[11]

A study on the first year of teaching mentions difficulties in the teacher's relationships with pupils and staff:

> When he (the teacher) is introduced to the unofficial lore of the school he must beware of being manipulated to the extent that his

independence is threatened. On the other hand he has to accept that having taken on a teaching post he has a responsibility to become a functioning member of the whole staff group.[3]

Whilst the major recommmendations of the James Report are unlikely to be fully implemented in most authorities it is important that the few resources left are channelled into appropriate support for new teachers.

Survey findings from LEA induction programmes suggested that:

> Positive support from the school is welcomed, usually highly regarded and preferred above external provision both by the probationer and other staff. It is suggested here that schools should adopt an active approach to induction. Experienced staff can do much to help probationers at classroom level with on the spot advice and their close knowledge of the children's abilities and particular problems. Probationers indicate that they welcome advice on specific aspects of class teaching in preference to more general advice and also the chance to watch or teach with experienced staff.[13]

LEA support should therefore be focused on helping schools to develop these support strategies.

Ideally external courses for newly-qualified teachers need to be during school hours, as the new teacher usually finds the first year very tiring. In the same survey the new teachers were very critical of the external courses provided for them:

> Comments frequently criticized the presentation methods, the theoretical approach, the irrelevance of much of the work and the repetition of work done in training. Their suggestions for improvement included more workshops and practical sessions with fewer lectures, more use of practising teachers on the courses, more discussion and more opportunity to raise particular issues in order to obtain direct help upon these.[13]

The assessment procedure can present worries for new teachers particularly if they are not clear what is actually going to happen:

> There seems to be a lack of clarification to the probationers of the procedures, roles and responsibilities of those involved in assessment. Specific feedback about progress from responsible persons was asked for by probationers in several open-ended comments, e.g. requests for 'encouragement' and someone to tell me how I'm doing.[13]

Finally, whatever help is offered during the first year of teaching should build upon what has been offered in training and should be part of a continuum of professional development.

Falling rolls in schools are now levelling out and LEAs expect to employ increased numbers of infant and first school teachers in the late 1980s. It is an appropriate time to prepare carefully for a sensible and supportive introduction to work for the large majority of those who will be new teachers.

IN-SERVICE EDUCATION

The term in-service education 'arises from the whole range of activities by which teachers can extend their personal education, their professional competence and their understanding of educational principles and techniques'.[5]

This broad interpretation will vary according to the stage of development of the teacher; how long she has been teaching; her past experiences in school; her own personality and ability to seize opportunities for professional growth; her ambition; and finally it will relate to the resources available and the sensitivity and imagination with which these resources are deployed to meet teachers' needs as expressed by themselves and as perceived by others.

School-based and school-focused in-service

The school is increasingly seen as the first and possibly the most important source of in-service education. Keast and Carr identify two elements which distinguish school-based in-service from other forms:

(i) The course members are teachers from one school. It may be that almost the complete staff is involved as in a junior or middle school (or first) or, alternatively, a faculty or some such substantial number of secondary school staff: such a group has been described as a 'functional group' within a school.
(ii) The teachers themselves have agreed on the subject of the course and the subject will reflect the needs of the school as perceived by the teachers. (The course is then distinguished from a group of teachers collectively working on, say, an OU course.)[14]

These elements are very important because if all staff can share a common experience and be party to new information there is more chance of this being disseminated throughout the school and having some effect on the children. Teachers are also much more likely to be motivated to work at something that they have identified for themselves rather than something they see as being imposed from outside.

However, the strengths of a school-based approach can be matched by its weaknesses. If schools look only at their own situation they become insular and the fund of expertise they have within their own school will be limited. Keast and Carr add a third requirement to their school-based in-service courses: 'The teachers or their representatives invite somebody external to the school to give some leadership to the course'.[14] This external input may not provide the leadership element but rather inject new ideas when staff feel that they have exhausted their own.

It can be dangerous to assume that schools will always clearly identify their own professional needs.

> The assumption that a school encompasses a breadth of expertise and specialisms within the teaching staff capable of identifying problems across the whole curriculum may hold for a large comprehensive school but it is less likely to be found in the smaller primary schools. It is even less likely to occur in two- to three-teacher rural schools. The expectation that teachers in small rural schools can show the full range of understanding for curriculum change and implementation is in the main unfounded.[15]

These weaknesses of school-based in-service can be partly overcome by a somewhat broader approach in which work is school-focused. Thus INSET can take place in or out of school by a variety of means and involving a greater flexibility.

Whilst professional development is a complex matter and achieved in many and various ways, both school-based and school-focused approaches allow maximum scope for individual and corporate growth to affect the school. Starting from where she is the teacher can develop a wider understanding of her own children and provide for their learning in a familiar setting. A staff can learn more of how to work as a body, sharing skills, relating to one another and moving forward to joint decision-making. These moves must have impact on the service that the school offers the community.

HELP FROM OUTSIDE AGENCIES

Most staff find it difficult to have a wide perspective on educational developments and may require the help of an outside agency to identify the possibilities of professional development and to help provide the way forward. The DES-funded SITE project already referred to (p.158) placed the onus on teachers to state their in-service priorities but provided the services of a consultant to assist in planning a programme to meet these needs. In most cases the consultant was from a higher education establishment and one such consultant describes how her role was explained to school staffs:

> A distinction was made between consultancy tasks and processes and those of counselling and advising with the emphasis put on consultancy as a staff support or back-up operation which would aim at offering them as professionals, i.e. who would have to make their own decisions, (a) some help with their immediate specific concerns, (b) a long-term developmental and training element in relation to the underlying wider issues, which might also enable them eventually to build up or continue their own staff support groups without the regular presence of a consultant.[16]

Other examples of schools benefiting from higher education establishments may be through local initiatives or DES regional courses where a school identifies its in-service need and places a bid with the LEA and university providers for some assistance. Clearly the school that has reached this stage has already done a great deal of work in staff development. Keast and Carr consider that

> . . . a school is certainly ready for a school-based course if the school
> is already characterized by some of the following:
> (a) staff participation in curriculum and organizational planning;
> (b) cooperative approaches to teaching as opposed to teaching in
>   isolation;
> (c) regular discussions of educational and pedagogical matters;
> (d) a staffroom climate which allows uninhibited discussion;
> (e) teachers who have developed the skill of learning from each other
>   and from teachers in other schools;
> (f) a staff which has developed a theoretical basis for their methods
>   which they can communicate effectively to the local
>   community.[14]

The forms of support for a school identified to date require teachers to be sufficiently confident to expose themselves within a staff setting which may be chaired or led by what they perceive to be an expert. It may be less threatening for some teachers to work on a one-to-one basis with either a college tutor or an LEA advisory teacher.

In some cases the greatest benefit may be given by practical assistance in the classroom. Andrew Salisbury describes a three-pronged approach to developing maths with a group of rural schools in Suffolk: '(a) a working party looking at common core curriculum and the problems of transfer from school to school, (b) a short series of lectures after school, (c) my visiting schools and offering to help in any way including teaching'.[17]

Cooperative ventures with other schools
If neighbouring schools join together for common in-service purposes they can gain many of the advantages of social-based in-service together with the opportunity of a wider viewpoint. If these meetings are school-based staff have an opportunity to visit another school and at least look at the physical environment even though the meeting may be after hours and children are not present. In other areas, schools may group together for a specific in-service purpose with a time limit. Where a pyramid structure of schools exists, in-service can be valuable for a group of first and middle school teachers, together with some staff from the secondary school that they feed.

In Norwich a group of first school headteachers started a self-help in-service project which is described as follows:

A letter from the LEA about 'self-help' in in-service activity encouraged teachers to start thinking about the organization of their own meetings. The teachers' centre coordinator was available for consultation about speakers who might be invited to add sessions on particular topics, LEA advisers agreed to lead some sessions themselves: a small amount of money was made available by the LEA to each first-school group for incidental expenses. . . .[18]

Content for these meetings was as a result of issues identified by school staffs. Attendance was generally good and heads suggested that 'A strength of the meetings is that they are attended by a number of teachers from the same school . . . and there is, therefore, a natural basis for collaborative follow-up work. Moreover some teachers would not attend any in-service were these meetings not held.'[18]

However although the strength of the meetings was that they provided a local response to teachers' requests, this resulted in a 'range of session titles that may appear to be somewhat unconnected and even random'. The author suggests rightly that 'In no way can the content of the meetings be said to reflect or represent a policy for the professional development of the teachers involved. What the meetings do achieve, however, is a foundation of interest and openness on which more substantial patterns of professional development could be built. They are a necessary beginning.'[18]

Small school cooperation

All schools can benefit from working cooperatively but the small rural school will find this approach particularly useful. Small schools can offer a great deal to young children within an informal and uninstitutionalized setting. They also have problems. It is very difficult for two or three teachers to attempt to cover a full first-school curriculum with the depth of expertise that is required today. Teachers themselves are aware of the dangers of their position.

> If you're not careful, you can become introspective: your ideas are not exactly old-fashioned – not that that's particularly bad – but you're probably not particularly outward looking, and you do not accept new ideas readily. And then when you do go out and find things are being said that you don't agree with, you might become even more isolated, and tend to shy away. So it's this problem of the small Norfolk schools, with people feeling isolated, that has to be overcome.[19]

Ambrose and Baker argue the case for professional help for small rural schools:

> Rural isolation imposes on teachers limitations in the maintenance of professional contact with their colleagues. Teachers' centres and institutes of higher education are often geographically distant from

these schools and opportunities for extended teacher release are made difficult by their very smallness. For rural schools the roles of advisers and in-service tutors in helping to identify areas for INSET work are far greater than in urban areas.[15]

Whilst it is important that, despite geographical difficulties, LEAs offer external stimulus and support to isolated schools, groups of schools can themselves gather strength from working cooperatively. Curriculum, organizational and economic initiatives can be developed, at the same time maintaining the autonomy of each small school. Financial support will be required to cover travel costs and teacher cover, but these costs may be small in comparison to the development of a group of schools and the enriched and extended programme that can be offered to children.

INTER-SCHOOL VISITS

Whatever the size of school many teachers admit to suffering from isolation, although this is overcome to some extent by open-design buildings and headteachers who see their role as that of encouraging staff to share expertise. The fact still remains that teachers in traditional buildings are largely ignorant of how their colleagues operate with children and how their own methods and style of teaching compare.

Visits to other schools give the opportunity to see other classrooms and offer stimulation in terms of physical organization and environment. However, the greatest value is derived from visits to see other teachers in action. At present resources are scarce to release teachers during the school day, so where this is possible, it is important that visit pays dividends. Jean Rudduck points out the possible limitations of school visits:

> The visit is popular as an event but it seems that casualness of planning often limits its potential. Visitors are often uncertain how clearly they should state their interests (and indeed were sometimes uncertain what their interests were: 'Everyone else was going on school visits so I felt I should have one too'); hosts are uncertain whether to put on a show or allow the visitor to take pot luck. This uncertainty often leads to awkwardness and disappointment.[20]

Teachers in Partnership was a small research project to develop and try out different approaches to collaborative in-service work, school visiting being one such approach. The author stresses: 'It's not that the approaches are novel but that their potential is often underreached. The familiarity of the idea tempts organizers and practitioners not to work out afresh for each occasion the logic of learning: planning is skimped and opportunities are lost.'[20] The study emphasized the need to turn *ad hoc* visits into planned events in which 'tasks, roles and responsibilities are carefully defined'.

The main recommendations include structuring the teacher visitor's observations. The teacher has a list of questions she might like to ask herself:

1 What kind of topics or issues lend themselves to exploration through observation?
2 What kinds of evidence will best illuminate the topic or issue that was the starting-point for the observation?
3 How will the teacher observer record evidence – that is will she make mental notes (and if so will they be committed to paper later)? and will she take field notes (and if so what kind of thing will be recorded, and how can one ensure that it will make sense later)? Will it be helpful to take sketches or take photographs?
4 How will the teacher observer manage herself in the situation in which she is observing so that her influence on the learning and teaching is minimal?
5 Will the teacher observer need to check out her observations by talking to teachers and/or pupils?
6 Will the teacher observer's purposes allow her to learn through observation or should she be a participant observer, taking part in the teaching or sharing some other professional duty?[20]

The benefits of teachers visiting in pairs and in having the support of the staff when reporting their observations are emphasized. Finally the onus of responsibility is placed firmly on the headteacher: 'If the visit is to be seen as more than an outing – however well deserved an outing may be – then the headmaster may have to accept responsibility for finding ways of helping teachers to make the most of their experience.'[20]

SHARING OBSERVATIONS
Teachers' isolation can extend to a lack of feedback about their own per-formance in the classroom. Again the headteacher performs an important role by encouraging staff to accept and welcome her presence and involve-ment in sharing teaching throughout the school: occasionally, however, status may act as a barrier to full and frank discussion with the teacher.
A further study from *Teachers in Partnership* looked at the feasibility of teachers observing one another in the classrooms. Their starting point was 'What are the ways in which teachers can learn from each other within the school setting to improve the practice of teaching?' The project monitored pairs of teachers who alternated roles of 'observer' and 'teacher':

The teacher who is to act as 'observer' is invited into the classroom of the colleague to comment on issues designated by the teacher as a source of concern in his or her teaching: the partners meet after the observation to discuss the observer's comments: the observer shapes observation and commentary to the agreed focus (i.e. the problem or topic nominated by the teacher) the teachers agree not to discuss their observations outside the partnership.[20]

The study findings indicated that a trusting relationship between these pairs is crucial to any successful developments and that the teachers who are most likely to benefit from this approach are those who are interested in deepening their own professional understanding of work rather than seeking easy 'tips' from teachers.

The teachers who took part in this study were mainly from secondary schools: the same potential benefits will apply equally to first school teachers although release from a full teaching programme for the 'observer' will be a major problem. The study suggests: 'Ideally if a headteacher perceived the potential of the scheme it could operate as part of the school's policy for the in-service development of staff and appropriate organizational plans could be made to support the partnership.'[20]

It would be valuable if an LEA could resource a group of schools to mount a pilot scheme enabling teachers to experiment with a form of in-service in which they rely very heavily on each other's professional expertise.

TEACHERS AS RESEARCHERS

In a climate of accountability there is a strengthening argument for the teacher to increase her own reflective skills, to be increasingly aware of not only what she is doing but why. Such skills are necessary to reinforce the teacher's professional principles which she must maintain against all external pressures. Educational research should aid classroom practice and support teachers. All too often in the past this has not happened and teachers themselves have been faced with reports placing additional requirements on them without offering any assistance as to how they might cope.

Jon Nixon sums up the disenchantment of many teachers:

> Much educational research, both in principle and practice, remains an activity indulged in by those outside the classroom for the benefit of those outside the classroom. Teachers, if they are considered at all, are seen merely as consumers, never as the producers of original research.[21]

John Elliott, always a strong advocate of teachers' reliance on their professional skills, described the alternative approach:

> The truth is that teachers have consistently failed to see how the abstract generalizations of traditional empirical research apply to the concrete and complex situations in which they have to operate. The teacher-as-researcher movement, with its focus on the practical educational problems arising from the particular situations and with its aim of illuminating such situations for those involved, offers an alternative solution to the familiar 'applicability of findings' issue.[21]

Jon Nixon describes the approach:

By investigating and reflecting upon their own classroom practice, teachers may increase their understanding of the classroom. Understanding why a particular child is upset or withdrawn may not imply a different course of action on the teacher's part, but it does help that teacher make sense of the child's behaviour.[21]

Published reports of action research projects reveal few from first school practitioners, and yet teachers of young children have traditionally been committed to their work and remain so today. What is needed, therefore, is not additional commitment but more effective ways of gathering data in the classroom, looking critically at implications, and greater confidence to share professional findings with colleagues. Action research is surely the way forward for many teachers who wish to develop themselves and also to assist colleagues.

TEACHERS AS LEADERS AND CONTRIBUTORS TO IN-SERVICE

One of the problems the LEAs have to face in planning in-service is providing the manpower to meet the demand. Whilst advisers and other outside agencies can provide some support, sustained work with small groups of teachers is not always possible unless manned by advisory teachers. An acceptable alternative in some LEAs is to train a body of teachers as group leaders or in-service consultants. Apart from the obvious benefits of having a trained body of people available to disseminate in-service there can be advantages for the teachers themselves. One such scheme monitored in Essex recognized that

> Such schemes depend heavily on the energy and commitment of a number of teachers for whom there is virtually no financial reward. However, there are other payoffs: for instance the experience might count in the highly competitive market that we now have and at a time of low teacher-mobility the opportunity to meet and work with other teachers in professional settings outside the confines of one's own school is an incentive not to be underestimated.[18]

This particular scheme highlights some of the organizational issues that have to be faced in selecting, training and deploying such teachers. For instance will the teachers 'be selected by advisers, will heads be invited to recommend suitable teachers or will they advertise for volunteers?' When planning the teacher tutors' training it will be necessary to define the tasks that they will perform and the related skills required:

> It may not be realistic in the short time available for training, given that teacher tutors have full-time teaching jobs, to do more than help them find ways of presenting classroom experience so that it offers other teachers possibilities for development and help them discover and use in in-service activities the potential of their own personalities and styles. Such an aspiration would require that attention be given,

on the training courses, to techniques of communication, including skills in lecturing, answering questions, handling discussion and making effective use of examples of pupils' work.[18]

Finally, close liaison between in-service providers needs to ensure that once these teachers are trained they not overused.

To sum up: the success of having teachers actively contribute to and lead in-service sessions is dependent on them having a clearly defined role and working to a particular brief. They should be well supported in their work and not exploited, bearing in mind that whatever the commitment it will be in addition to their full-time job of teaching.

Local in-service

SHORT NON-RESIDENTIAL COURSES

The past four years have seen an emphasis on school-based in-service and the school does seem the logical starting-point of the teacher's professional development. However a sensitive LEA will recognize that various routes to in-service provision will be needed to meet diverse needs. Ideally dissemination of a project should affect an entire school staff and result in beneficial change in the school; this cannot always be possible. Sometimes a teacher's professional needs and interests may not be shared by her colleagues; occasionally she may need to look at the educational scene in a different setting and with another group of people. If staff relationships are somewhat strained the opportunity to put forward a viewpoint in a more anonymous situation can be helpful. We have already explored opportunities for a teacher's viewpoint to be widened by working co-operatively with neighbouring schools. There should also be a place for teachers, as a group or as individuals, to attend school-focused in-service education which is provided through a short outside course.

> On the short outside course teachers have access to ideas that they can explore in the company of professional colleagues and whose experiences are likely to be less familiar. . . . The present study reveals the deep sense of professional isolation that many teachers still feel: this makes attendance at outside in-service meetings a crucial aspect of professional life and an important condition of professional development.[18]

Financial stringencies have meant that opportunities to release teachers to attend in-service sessions during the school day are increasingly restricted. It remains a dilemma for in-service providers to decide how this valuable resource is to be used. Should staff be released who are reluctant to attend courses in their own time but who badly need refreshment? This would support Rudduck's suggestion that course attendance becomes a matter of professional obligation: 'There would seem a need to move forward from benevolent opportunism – where some teachers attend some courses of interest to them – towards a more systematic attendance pattern of courses designed to fit a policy for rational curriculum development which has the support of the school.'[18] Alternatively resources may support the enthusiastic teacher who gives unstintingly of her time and whose development and increasing skills may affect other colleagues in school.

Certainly teachers prefer courses during school hours and much more satisfactory work results when course members are fresh and able to work over a period of time. Teachers are sometimes quite willing to meet for a full day during a weekend. However, more and more short courses are forced into the slot after school hours and this trend seems likely to continue.

This type of course is studied in Jean Rudduck's work. Although the end of course comments are from secondary teachers there is no reason to believe that the criteria for judging effectiveness would be any different for first school participants.

1 Course members respond well to a course which demonstrates that the course leader has put a lot of effort into its preparation. The evidence for sound preparation includes appropriate handout, overhead projector transparencies, lecture notes and resources for discussion.
2 Course members respond well to a course where the content is thoroughly researched and professionally presented.
3 Course members respond well to sessions which are varied in rhythm and have a range of activity – this seems to be particularly important when teachers come, rather tired, straight from a full working day at school.
4 Course members respond well to lectures – if lectures are the appropriate medium – which are lively and provocative and which generate confidence in the speaker.
5 Course members respond well to advisers' attempts to build in opportunities for discussion – even though they acknowledge that as participants they do not always make the most of these opportunities.
6 Course members respond well to attempts to test theory by reference to practice, preferably if the practice can be illustrated from their own classroom.[18]

THE TEACHERS' CENTRE
In 1967 the Schools Council recommended the establishment of facilities to assist local groups of teachers to consider curriculum development:

The Council's hope is that teachers will, more and more, meet in groups to discuss curriculum problems and that local education authorities will do all that is practicable to encourage such groups, and in particular help them with the use of accommodation, apparatus and secretarial assistance as may be necessary.[22]

This then was the starting-point for the establishment of local teachers' centres. Subsequently they have taken on other functions, primarily the provision of short in-service courses for members, but they also act as a meeting place for teachers and house curriculum resources.

During the period of contraction some LEAs decided that teachers' centres were an extra that could be dispensed with. There are now areas of the country where they no longer exist, and where they do remain it is in a varied form.

The geography of Britain, political as well as physical, has ensured that the roles selected for emphasis by individual wardens and LEAs have varied widely. Some have stressed subject-centres, while the majority have decided on multi-purpose centres. Some have put their money and people into providing resources while others have stressed their in-service role and local curriculum development. The needs of beginning teachers are recognized, and since the James Report some teachers' centres are now seen as 'professional centres'. Social needs of teachers are provided for in some centres, while in others the only provision is the tea-urn. Some teachers' centres have a full-time warden, an assistant warden, a full range of ancillary staff, while others may have only a part-time warden or secretary.[23]

A broader and deeper view

It is important to emphasize the variety of organizational patterns of in-service education that exist. We will identify certain approaches in the knowledge that some LEAs may have a different approach to planning and presenting courses, which will come under our headings.

We have looked at developments starting in and focusing on the school, and also at short local initiatives which teachers may attend as individuals or in staff groups; we will now turn to opportunities for teachers to gain a broader and deeper experience outside their school. Two approaches will be discussed: the residential short course which recruits teachers from the county, region or on a national basis; and the extended part-time course which may be accredited. The former, whilst brief, offers teachers the chance to mix with a broad range of colleagues in a setting where they are removed from the normal demands of work and home. The latter should enable a more gradual and deeper understanding of education, with the stimulus of academic study.

THE SHORT RESIDENTIAL COURSE

This may be organized by the LEA, a regional planning group, by educational trusts or the DES. It generally offers the teacher three or four days of intensive input and group work. The setting may be a higher education establishment or a comfortable residential centre, but the aim of the course leader will be to provide a pleasant environment, a range of new people and stimulating professional experiences to aid professional growth. A well-planned residential course can have immediate impact on a teacher but this impact may quickly dissipate:

> The very detachment and euphoria which make time-limited systems (e.g. the temporary course) so fascinating and productive help to blind the participants to what they will be up against when they return to 'ordinary' life with its role conflicts, work pressures and vested interest. . . . At best, the decisions reached on the cultural island [the short course] may be unworkable, inappropriate, or very difficult to communicate to those on the mainland [the school and classroom].[24]

It may be enough if the short course recharges individual teaching batteries. However, if it is to have a more lasting effect on the individual teacher, or cause wider ripples of change within the school, then particular strategies should be added in terms of follow-up sessions, group rather than individual attendance, and good support from the headteacher in any subsequent staff dissemination.

THE LONG COURSE

By long course we mean any course which extends over a year on a part-time basis. These courses are usually provided through higher education establishments although LEAs may have some influence in the planning and organization. Long courses were traditionally offered to teachers who were released from school for full-time study. Financial constraints have stopped a number of these and the courses have had to be reshaped for part-time attendance.

> For the teachers, a substantial course no longer means extra time to think and adjust, but rather a full week's work in school and, in addition, evenings attending the course and others for private study, possibly with occasional vacation blocks as well. Those who obtain partial leave for a day or half a day a week are often freed merely by blocking free periods rather than by diminution of teaching time, or may feel pressurized because attendance is only possible through the willingness of colleagues to take on extra work to allow their release. This confines the applicants to the very determined, the very healthy and to people who are very committed to the type of study on offer. It is a challenge to the course designers which is far more demanding than in the past.[25]

What are teachers' initial motives for enrolling on a B.Ed. course?

> They are mixed. Many of them are clearly instrumental. The rapid move towards a graduate profession means that many people are frightened of being left on the shelf with a certificate. Promotion prospects are getting scarcer and, therefore, another qualification

can be a help. There is a salary increment. Status matters. Against these, many teachers will say openly that they were getting stale, that they need tuning up, that they felt the need for a better understanding of what it was they were trying to do, and that they felt the need for an intellectual challenge and a stimulus of academic study.[26]

Through sustained study a teacher will have the opportunity to link theory with practice over a period of time, to reflect with colleagues on aspects of the education system and in addition some courses may offer extrinsic rewards in the form of accreditation. These are all incentives for enrolment but many of the benefits that exist in day release or residential courses will be less apparent in a part-time course. The camaraderie of being students, of gelling as a group and being removed from school and its stresses in order to stand back and look at oneself and the broader educational scene – this is helpful to teacher development. On a part-time course the group spirit will develop but only gradually: the tired teacher at the end of the day is more likely to have an eye on the clock during evening meetings – there is always tomorrow's class to consider. Moreover there is less likelihood of reflective and leisured reading with immediate opportunities to discuss and clarify thoughts with tutors and colleagues. The demands and stresses on the teacher of part-time study are considerable and any commitment needs to be considered carefully. From the provider's point of view the part-time course can only recruit locally and this can be restrictive.

The great benefit of the move away from the full-time college course is that course work can be firmly anchored in the classroom. This does require a new attitude from course makers and tutors alike as one provider comments:

> Tutors learn to be supportive, but not dominant: teachers at first find that they as the experts with knowledge of their classes, must play a leading part in the devising of the learning experience, and then, stimulated to further efforts, find considerable satisfaction in the process. Heads learn not to expect an array of new ideas for the curriculum, but rather to observe a process of analysis and judgment of the value of regular classroom pursuits.

DISTANCE LEARNING

The Open University has in recent years offered teachers a new perspective for in-service development. The concept of distance learning, which presents theoretical constructs for an individual teacher who has to rely mainly on this printed material for guidance and clarification, is clearly a very limited one. It may offer some personal illumination but unless the theory happens to link up with that teacher's practice, and without the opportunity to share the course experiences with others, it is unlikely that professional development will be very great.

However, the great strength of such distance learning materials is that they can be used flexibly and recent courses have made it possible for teachers to start with their own classroom problems using the material as a support in helping to foster further awareness and improve performance.

In the case of the curriculum course, six basic questions have been identified which open up pupils' daily classroom experience to inspection by the teacher. To answer these questions, teachers must learn to carry out accurate observations without interrupting their normal work, recognize the assumptions they make, devise means of gathering further evidence, employ ingenuity and care in making assessments of pupils' progress and clarify the criteria they use in judging the value of the curriculum they provide.[27]

In this case distance learning is providing school-focused action research projects in which large numbers of teachers may take part.

The success of this approach is dependent on the same type of support required for other areas of in-service. A committed staff and supportive headteacher using distance learning materials are likely to ensure that the school benefits as well as individual teachers. Advisers and other LEA INSET leaders may wish to adapt the materials to suit the needs of a particular group of teachers.

SECONDMENT

Whilst the process of professional development should be constant and built into the school there is a place for the teacher stepping away from the classroom and undertaking a substantial full-time course. The James Report rcommended that one term in every seven years should be used for the teacher's own development. Financial constraints have prevented this but many authorities offer some full-time secondments for teachers applying for courses of study. Martin and Surrell (both of whom have taken a year off from school for further study) are firm advocates of this provision:

We would like to stress the intrinsic value of externally-based education-focused full-time courses in contrast to school-based activities and the stimulating temporary distancing from the hectic 'chalk face' which helps to foster increased objectivity, to broaden educational horizons and to promote significant personal and professional development.[28]

However, the authors also pinpoint the pitfalls of the teacher being away from colleagues for over a year in some cases and then re-entering the school. They identified the difficulties of adjusting from an environment of intellectual rigour to the hectic pace of school life, the problems of missing a year's contact with children in the school, the hostility and suspicion shown by some colleagues. On returning to school after a stimulating and successful period of secondment teachers will be keen to influence others and bring about change in their school.

Martin and Surrell stress that the main problem on returning was frustration at not being immediately effective and having to tolerate the school viewpoint which may be based more on practice than on intellectual debate:

'Having survived the traumas of this energy, enthusiasm and confidence sapping vicious circle of frustration, one emerges with a renewed vigour to take things step by step and to attempt to disseminate some of the valuable experience of the previous year in the realization that 'slowly but surely' is perhaps a more efficient, effective and realistic maxim in the longer term than the impatience born of youthful exuberance rekindled by contact with education students and university life.'[28]

Secondment of teachers on full salary with other expenses paid is a costly procedure. It can be most valuable for the teacher and school if planned and handled sensitively and in these cases the benefits accrued justify expense.

CAREER DEVELOPMENT

Any programme for professional development should not only help teachers to do their present jobs well, but also provide a training for those who wish to work towards gaining additional responsibility and thus have a greater influence on what happens in school: 'Helping teachers to work more efficiently means raising their general level of professional competence and so turning jobs into careers. Too often in education the teacher is left to look after her own future.'[29]

Career development is dependent not only on the teacher's motivation but on the opportunities for increased responsibility within the school. The teacher needs to be more aware of how she is performing and helped towards acquiring the skills necessary for promotion.

It is crucial that there should be a determined move on the part of teacher trainers and employers to encourage a coherent, planned career pattern for first school teachers. Olive Banks, writing in 1968, described the low status of primary teachers as being partly due to the low expectations of women:

The fact that many women in the profession see it as a temporary job rather than a permanent career also has a profound effect on their expectations. The initial salary, the length of training, the possibility of rejoining the profession after a break of several years: all of these considerations are of more importance than ultimate salary or promotion possibilities.[30]

Since that time there have been certain developments. The recent period of contraction meant that only the more committed teachers were prepared to train and then gain a foothold in the profession by means of temporary contracts: more women are choosing to combine careers and producing families and a shared approach to parenthood makes this more possible. The NUT Research Study on *Promotion and the Married Woman* identifies that out of a sample group of 960 primary and secondary teachers aged between 20 and 30 years '3 per cent of this age-group are working part-time and several have already had a break in service to rear a family and return to work. These are the "new" category of working women teachers – mothers with the possibility of up to 30 years of service ahead of them.'[31]

Moreover this research study repudiated the myth that most women teachers are married women with children: 'This description applies to only 8 per cent of the under 30s and just over half of the 31–50 age-group, . . . thus at any point in time the "average" woman teacher is as likely as not to be childless. Such figures make a mockery of the generalization about married women.'[31]

In 1964 Brookover and Gottlieb stated:

> Teaching is associated with motherhood, with the training and socialization of the young, and with the protection of the needy. So firmly entrenched is this popular image in our society that it becomes difficult for a man who wants to enter the field to withstand the social pressures against doing so.[32]

Today's society has a less stereotyped view and is slowly being acquainted with the skill and academic rigour involved in teaching young children. Hopefully the future will see more men look to a role in early childhood education. Strong, articulate leaders of both sexes are needed to press for the respect and resources which are the due of this phase of education.

Every teacher who has a professional commitment to the job should be offered support for career development by the school and the local authority. Whilst the school should provide opportunities for responsibility and shared decision-making at all levels, the local authority should provide training in management to enable teachers to develop their leadership roles.

The role of the school

> It is the task of the head to enable his staff to produce the work of superior people and this will require more sophisticated forms of leadership. Ways need to be found to develop the teachers into a good team who are committed to the aims of the school and use their collective energies towards reaching them. At the same time the head has to look at each individual member of staff (teaching and non-teaching) and examine ways of enabling them to do those things even they didn't know they could do.[29]

If the headteacher is to enable her staff to develop fully she must ensure that there is wide delegation, so that teachers can take on areas of responsibility at all levels. The demands on headteachers today are many and complex and most recognize that the school can only function effectively if decisions are shared.

Arthur Razzell, himself an experienced headteacher, states:

> I feel we are moving steadily towards the position where primary schools will see it to be highly desirable if not essential to function as a team of professionals sharing fully in the decision-making. The day of the autocratic head setting his personal thumbprint clearly on his school is almost over.[33]

Although first schools pride themselves on being informal institutions, a staff structure where areas of responsibility are clearly defined will enable every teacher to see to whom and for whom she is responsible. If these lines of communication are made clear it is less likely that confusion and indecision will arise. Development of good relationships will then enable the structure to be interpreted flexibly without stifling individual initiatives. It is also important for the teacher to be clear about the varying aspects and perimeters of her job. A written job description can never be a definitive document but it does offer guidance to a new person settling into the job and can act as a point of reference for discussion as the professional role develops. Headteachers should aim to be aware of the career aspirations of every member of staff and to provide all the teachers with the opportunity for broad and varied experience which will enable them to be strong applicants for promotion.

The role of the local authority

> In our experience there is certainly a dearth of career guidance for teachers. This is an area which could well be developed by INSET. At present most people who train as teachers and work in schools hope to move on from Scale 1 but rarely have a clear pathway in mind. There must be a potentially vast field of varied career opportunities about which the majority of teachers know nothing. Good industrial practice attempts to place suitable people in suitable posts, and this simply is not done as a rule in education, which must lead to reduced efficiency.[28]

This description of the *ad hoc* approach to career development by two secondary school teachers applies just as much to teachers in early childhood education. Very rarely does a teacher take up a post with a view to it fitting in with a particular career pattern. It is accepted that some schools will offer rich experience for professional development whilst others will provide very limited opportunities. The teacher in the former school will be well prepared for promotion while her colleague in the latter may be unsuccessful not because she is less worthwhile but because she has been less fortunate in her place of employment.

MANAGEMENT COURSES

A career teacher will be looking to in-service support both to develop her curriculum and leadership role. In the past teachers in senior roles in schools learned solely through their mistakes and successes. It is now recognized that there are certain skills attached to good leadership that can be identified, practised and refined.

Management involves getting things done through other people. An effective leader needs also to be a good manager and one criterion by which his work might be judged is his effectiveness in delegating tasks and enabling others to take them to a successful conclusion.

There is a sense in which every classroom teacher needs to be a good manager of children. Every headteacher needs to be a good manager of adults and this is also true for others holding senior posts in schools.

The ability to lead is sometimes thought to be no more than a matter of innate qualities of personality which you either have or have not. There is a modicum of truth in this view, and some brilliant leaders certainly succeed because of their personalities. Leadership is not exercised in the abstract, however, but in the performance of specific tasks. You may find it easier to perform these tasks if you have certain qualities of personality and you may be able to cultivate appropriate qualities to some extent. There is a limit to a person's ability to do this, however. It may be more profitable to consider the skills and knowledge needed to perform specific leadership tasks effectively and to concentrate on those. It is not unusual for someone to develop personality traits as a result of practising appropriate skills and using knowledge.[34]

Most local authorities are developing some courses to help develop these skills for teachers in posts of responsibility, for deputy head-teachers and headteachers. There needs to be appropriate training at each level of responsibility but the Surrey Inspectorate identified three common aspects:

1 Work on evaluation of his own school situation by each member leading to appropriate work on identifying targets, problem-solving and forward planning and some follow-up.
2 Work on developing the interpersonal skills of presentation, group leadership and interviewing.
3 Work on staff development as related to those teachers for whom he is responsible.

First schools are generally small units and many industrial management techniques will not be appropriate to them. However, certain lessons can be learned.

There is a discipline related to good management which would not come amiss in some schools. But we must resist any temptation to complicate it – so much of it is simply good commonsense anyway. No one ever became less effective by learning about a job, and most people improve. By synthesizing their own set of principles of management, headteachers can avoid at least some of the pitfalls and traps awaiting them. More positively, they will learn what to do, how to make effective decisions relating to the purpose of the school, and how to work with and through others to reach the agreed goals.[29]

WORK APPRAISAL

Judgments or evaluations must be made if decisions are to be taken about future action. We have already looked at the teacher's role in monitoring and assessing children's development in order to plan for the next stage (see p.133). Here we focus on the wider significance of evaluation and the part it plays in deepening the teacher's awareness of other aspects of her work, thus increasing her professionalism. The ways in which information is gathered for evaluation will vary. Wynne Harlen suggests that it is hard evidence that is required.

In looking hard at what we already do the questions to ask are of the kind: are judgments based on relevant evidence, or on the general impressions influenced to some degree by prejudice or by non-relevant aspects? We know this happens in relation to judgments about schools. The same questions should be asked about the basis for decisions about schools. The same questions should be asked about the basis for decisions about changes in teaching materials and organization at both class and school levels.[36]

Whereas an external evaluator will offer this evidence and an objective view, it may be a limited one which springs from the inability to appreciate the fine nuances of a situation which are apparent to those working within. However teachers will recognize that to some extent their own professional careers are dependent on local authority advisers seeing them in the classroom and making judgments about their performance. So long as this information is fed back to the teacher and preferably time allowed for discussion, it can form a valuable basis for an individual to look at her own practice with additional insight.

The profession, and in particular the headteacher, also has a responsibility to look at each teacher's progress:

The teaching profession differs from many other bodies today in having little or no system for the appraisal of individuals. Where there is appraisal it tends to be unsystematic and sometimes unsupportive. Teachers are to some extent held back by the view that it is unprofessional to see a colleague teach or to make an appraisal of his ability to feed back to him in a supportive way. Now that teacher movement is more limited, it is important to examine ways of improving performance. Regular individual appraisal is a way of working which should be considered.[37]

THE TEACHER AS A PERSON

Although there are obvious dangers in applying management studies, some helpful parallels may be drawn when looking at the ways in which people respond to work and (as far as this book is concerned) offer the best quality education to young children.

The teacher is both a manager of her class and also a product of management. In this role of manager the teacher needs to be able to motivate her children and colleagues and also to be motivated herself. Rensis Likert looked at the style of managers in industry who were deemed most successful in motivating employees and offering them job satisfaction:

> The research findings show, for example, that those supervisors and managers whose pattern of leadership yields consistently favourable attitudes more often think of employees as 'human beings rather than just as persons to get the work done'. Consistently, in study after study, the data shows that treating people as 'human beings' rather than as 'cogs in a machine' is a variable highly related to the attitudes and motivation of the subordinate at every level in the organization.[38]

The study goes on to look at the employee's perception of this manager.

> He is supportive, friendly, and helpful rather than hostile. He is kind but firm, never threatening, genuinely interested in the well-being of subordinates and endeavours to treat people in a sensitive, considerate way. He is just, if not generous. He endeavours to serve the best interests of his employees as well as of the company. He shows confidence in the integrity, ability and motivations of subordinates rather than suspicion and distrust. His confidence in subordinates leads him to have high expectations as to their level of performance. With confidence that he will not be disappointed, he expects much, not little. (This, again, is fundamentally a supportive rather than a critical or hostile relationship.) He sees that each subordinate be promoted by training them for jobs at the next level. This involves giving them relevant experience and coaching whenever the opportunity offers.[38]

This description could well fit a successful teacher, headteacher or adviser and it is important that some attempt is made to identify how that style of management is developed.

The qualities described are those of a manager who has a good self-image. Only with a degree of inner confidence can a person afford to be generous and supportive to others. We can assume then that in order to be successful a teacher (manager) must be gaining a great deal personally from her job. However, the successful and fulfilled teacher may not necessarily be one who looks for promotion or increased status:

> It is important to distinguish between two kinds of rewards. The first type are those that are extrinsic to the individual. These rewards are part of the job situation and are given by others. Hence, they are externally mediated and are rewards that can best be thought of as satisfying lower-order needs. The second type of rewards are intrinsic to the individual and stem directly from the performance itself. These rewards are internally mediated since the individual rewards himself. These rewards can be thought of as satisfying higher-order needs such as self-esteem and self-actualization. They involve such outcomes as feelings of accomplishment, feelings of achievement and feelings of using and developing one's skills and abilities.[39]

In our first schools there are a group of teachers who are masters of their profession, and who derive great satisfaction from their work without wanting or achieving senior positions in schools. The sensitive head-teacher and adviser will use every opportunity to make these teachers feel valued members of staff.

REFERENCES

1 HERZBERG, F. (1972) 'One more time – how do you motivate employees?' in L. Davis and J. Taylor (eds.) *Design of Jobs* Penguin
2 ELLIOTT, J. (1979) Accountability, progressive education and school-based education *Education 3 – 13* 7, 1
3 HANNAM, C., SMYTH, P. and STEPHENSON, M. (1976) *The First Year of Teaching* Penguin
4 PLOWDEN, B. (1973) Aims in primary education *Education 3 – 13* 1, 2
5 DES (1972) *Teacher Education and Training* (The James Report) HMSO
6 STEPHENS, J. (1975) 'Some current issues for teacher in-service education' in E. Adams (ed.) *In-service Education and Teachers' Centres* Pergamon
7 BOLAM, R. and BAKER, K. (1978) *The Schools and In-service Teacher Education* (SITE) Evaluation Project OECD/CERI International Seminar Paper
8 KAY, B. (1976) The Assessment of Performance Unit: its task and rationale *Education 3 – 13* 4, 2
9 KELLMER PRINGLE, M. (1974) *The Needs of Children* Hutchinson
10 DES (1972) *Education: A Framework for Expansion* HMSO
11 McCABE, C. (1978) A new look at the problems of the probationary year *British Journal of In-service Education* 4, 3, pp.144–50
13 BAKER, K. (1978) Survey findings from LEA induction programmes *British Journal of In-service Education* summer
14 KEAST, D. J. and CARR, V. (1979) School-based INSET: interim evaluation *British Journal of In-service Education* summer
15 AMBROSE, B. and BAKER, R. (1980) School-based INSET in rural primary schools *British Journal of In-service Education* autumn
16 HANKO, G. (1981) SITE Project: consultancy, support and training courses for teachers of children with special needs in ordinary schools *British Journal of In-service Education* spring
17 SALISBURY, A. (1979) Tractors, Fanny Craddock and mathematics *Cambridge Journal of Education* 9, 2/3
18 RUDDUCK, J. (1982) *Making the Most of the Short In-service Course* (Schools Council Working Paper 71) Methuen
19 Head of a small rural first school quoted in 17 above.
20 RUDDUCK, J. (1982) Teachers in partnership *Journal of NAIEA* spring
21 NIXON, J. (1981) (ed.) *A Teacher's Guide to Action Research* Grant McIntyre
22 SCHOOLS COUNCIL (1967) Curriculum Development: Teachers' Groups and Centres (Schools Council Working Paper 10)
23 WILLIAMS, J. (1981) Teachers' centres in the UK: an antipodean view *British Journal of In-service Education* 7, 2

24 MILES, M. B. (1964) 'On temporary systems' in *Innovation in Education* New York: Teachers College Press
25 GRADY, A. (1980) In 1980 the long course is school-focused *British Journal of In-service Education* 6, 3
26 EVANS, N. (1979) Fact, fiction, or both *Cambridge Journal of Education* 9, 2 and 3
27 ASHTON, P. and MERRITT, J. (1979) INSET at a distance *Cambridge Journal of Education* 9, 2 and 3
28 MARTIN, S. and SURRELL, G. (1979) A year off: retrospect and prospect *Cambridge Journal of Education* 9, 2 and 3
29 WATERS, D. (1979) *Management and Headship in the Primary School* Ward Lock Educational
30 BANKS, O. (1968) *The Sociology of Education* Batsford
31 NUT (1980) *Promotion and the Woman Teacher* NUT/Equal Opportunities Commission
32 BROOKOVER, W. B. and GOTTLIEB, D. (1964) *A Sociology of Education* New York: American Book Company
33 RAZZELL, A. (1979) Teacher participation in school decision making *Education 3–13* 7, 1
34 SURREY INSPECTORATE (1980) *Leadership* Media Resources Centre, Glyn House, Church St., Ewell, Surrey
35 SURREY INSPECTORATE (1980) *Management in Education* (see 34)
36 HARLEN, W. (1978) *Evaluation and the Teacher's Role* (Schools Council Research Studies) Macmillan
37 SURREY INSPECTORATE (1980) *Evaluation* (see 34)
38 LIKERT, R. (1970) 'New patterns of management' in V. Vroom and E. Deci (eds.) *Management and Motivation* Penguin
39 LAWLER, E. (1969) Job design and employee motivation *Personnel Psychology* 22, pp.426–35

IN THE CLASSROOM

INDUCTION

The introduction to the school

Starting a job for the first time is always daunting. The new teacher is aware of her lack of experience, the need to acquaint herself with a mass of information about the school, the staff, the children and parents; and overall is the knowledge that she has to be judged on her performance in the classroom. The following suggestions, which apply to any new member of staff, may help 'settle' a new teacher in.

THE FIRST VISIT

After the interview, the first visit should be a relaxed and semi-social occasion. The new teacher could be invited for an initial chat with the headteacher, a walk round the school and then join the staff after school for tea or a glass of wine as a welcome into the school.

The aim of this visit will be to meet the staff as people and to gain some idea of the geography and the ethos of the school. During this visit the head should introduce the new teacher to her 'mentor' (the teacher with a specific responsibility for newly qualified teachers). The mentor's task is to provide the first line of support during the teacher's first year in school. Initially this will mean ensuring that the new teacher has the information and resources for the job in hand. It could also include offering information about the area, e.g. details of flats to rent, transport, doctors and dentists. Whilst teachers will expect to make their own arrangements for many it will be their first experience of setting up home – any domestic problems are best resolved before teaching begins.

THE SECOND VISIT

If a second visit can be arranged it should focus on gathering information. The mentor could take the new teacher into her class for a session. The new teacher may have prepared a list of questions which can be tackled after school over a cup of tea. Many of these quesitons may arise as a result of the school documents.

DOCUMENTS

Documents are most useful if they are talked through with the new teacher. They may be given to her at the end of her interview or on her first visit to school allowing her to read them at leisure and mark any points that she wishes to raise. School documents will vary. We suggest that the following will all be useful to a new teacher:

1 A job description.
2 A staff handbook providing details of daily administrative routines and school policies. (It is most important that this is kept up to date.)
3 Curriculum guidelines (see p.138).
4 A plan of the school and of the classroom, with a list of equipment.
5 A list of children who will be in the teacher's class with recent records and samples of their work.
6 A personal welcoming note containing some practical details, e.g. coffee money arrangements, locker in staffroom, provision for educational journals in staffroom, and an open invitation for the new teacher to ask for any additional information.

These documents are only *additional* to discussion held with members of staff – they are of limited use as the sole means of information.

PREPARING FOR THE CLASS
The new teacher should, if possible, be given an age-group with which she has had some previous experience. Ideally the class should be of a reasonable size (under 30), a chronological age-group, and in a well-resourced classroom. Any new teacher should be given the maximum opportunity to succeed.

The teacher may need to spend at least one day in school preparing her classroom before term begins. She may need to be advised not to be over ambitious for the first term, but to concentrate on meticulous planning and preparation, which will stand her in good stead for any other problems that might occur.

Continuing school-based support
As the new teacher settles into school particular problems may emerge. She may find it difficult to strike the right relationship with the children. She may have ideals about teaching children individually and allowing learning through concrete experiences but find that her organization does not make this possible. She may have concerns about individual children whom she feels she is failing as they are not progressing. In addition she may feel that her philosophy and practice are alien to some other members of staff. These difficulties all involve a crisis of confidence and it is essential for the new teacher to have the support and sympathetic ear of the teacher mentor. The latter needs to be sensitively supportive whilst not undermining the new teacher's autonomy. However, if classroom doors are open and the head and other teachers freely visit each other, there should be no opportunity or need for any teacher to keep her weaknesses to herself.

Continual help may be given by

1 encouraging the new teacher to look at other classrooms and if possible to see other teachers working;
2 the teacher mentor going through lessons and reviews with the new teacher;

3 advice about a child's progress, about management of a difficult child,
   about classroom organization;
4 the head or teacher mentor regularly withdrawing a small group of less
   able or more able children from the new teacher's classroom;
5 a team teaching approach;
6 time given to listen to problems and regular morale boosting, e.g.
   respect for the new teacher's views and expressed appreciation for the
   contribution that she is giving to the school.

External support

The LEA has a responsibility for assessing the newly qualified teacher
during the first year of teaching and all LEAs provide some form of
induction for new teachers. It is important that this is seen to be realistic
and appropriate rather than merely an additional commitment for the
teacher. The following approaches may be helpful:

A SOCIAL OCCASION

This can be a way of welcoming teachers to the authority. It is a chance
to meet other new teachers and to learn about some of the resources
available within the county. This information should also be displayed in
a handbook for teachers. As with new parents, teachers can only cope
with a little information at one time. Anything that they need to know
should be told them but also given in written form for future reference.

REGULAR MEETINGS OF NEW TEACHERS WITH AN ADVISER OR INSPECTOR

If possible these should take place during school hours and be carefully
planned to provide practical assistance for the teachers. They can include
workshops, talks and demonstrations by experienced practitioners as
well as discussions on common problems of organization and methodology. The first of these meetings should ensure that assessment
procedures are clearly explained.

VISITS TO OTHER SCHOOLS

These should be carefully planned with particular needs in mind. Host
schools should be briefed as to what the new teacher is focusing on and a
follow-up session will provide an opportunity for the teachers to discuss
how the visit helped them rethink their own situation. Schedules or
observation sheets may be helpful to teachers.

ADVISERS' VISITS TO SCHOOL

These will mean that the teacher is visited in the classroom and has the
opportunity to discuss the visit with the adviser at leisure afterwards.
When teachers have no 'non-contact' hours this can be difficult and it
may be necessary for the adviser to arrange a subsequent visit or to call
after school hours in order to talk. Some advisers hold regular 'surgeries'
which offer an opportunity for any teachers to be seen individually and to
talk about professional concerns away from the classroom.

SUPPORT BY ADVISORY TEACHERS
Where provided, this is helpful for teachers who are experiencing difficulties. The advisory teacher will offer practical support in the classroom
and is in no way concerned with assessment of the new teacher. Support
may include demonstration teaching, a team approach, discussion of
particular weaknesses with regard to organization and planning of
rooms, practical hints. Any support offered should be carefully co-
ordinated with the support offered within the school. The advisory
teacher will liaise with the teacher mentor.

IN-SERVICE EDUCATION
The expectation and policies of the headteacher regarding her role in
developing teachers' professionalism is crucial in a growing school.
However motivated and able the staff, their energies will only be
frustrated if they are not supported in their efforts to keep up to date and
to try out new approaches and new materials with children.

School-based and school-focused in-service

THE STAFFROOM
1 The staffroom setting can do much to help teachers' development. It
should be an attractive and pleasant place in which to relax (soft furnish-
ings and flowers can help). It should also house information. In addition
to current notices the staff board could have a section for short topical
educational articles. There could also be a staffroom folder for such
articles which need to be regularly changed and contributions offered by
all teachers.
2 Educational publications are expensive and the staff should decide on
their priorities for ordering. It may be possible to exchange publications
with a neighbouring school.
3 Books are costly but essential – a 'book' fund could be set aside, a new
book bought once a month, and staff might take turns to select, read and
review it.

IN-SERVICE STAFF MEETING
Although the attendance at in-service staff meetings cannot be imposed
contractually it should be made clear to new teachers at interview if they
are expected to attend. Regular weekly meetings after school can offer a
constant, gentle opportunity for the development of all staff. The
following points may be helpful in planning such occasions:

1 All staff need to be consulted about the most convenient evening for
them – not everyone will be satisfied but at least they will have been
consulted.
2 A regular meeting pattern. If meetings are cancelled, teachers may not
feel inclined to support others.
3 A comfortable meeting room and refreshments. An occasional cake or

glass of sherry to 'celebrate' the completion of guidelines or the beginning of term adds to goodwill and a positive attitude after a tiring day in the classroom.

4 Time for discussion but a deadline to finish. The agenda needs to be clear and realistically timed. It is preferable to meet less frequently and have meaty issues to discuss; on the other hand an overfull programme will not allow time for all staff to contribute their views at leisure.

In-service meetings will need to be sensitively planned to meet staff needs. Most staffs are a mixed group of people ranging from the teacher who is constantly aware and eager to refine her skills to the cynic whose opposition to change often springs from a deep feeling of inadequacy: in between these extremes are teachers with a range of attitudes. The skilful headteacher and curriculum consultant will plan in-service for a mixed-ability group and will ensure that everyone's viewpoint is treated with respect and that everybody's expertise is used.

Meetings may involve the following approaches:

1 A workshop with encouragement for teachers to try out initiatives in their classrooms and report back at the next staff meeting. (For example, teachers may make workcards for problem-solving, have three weeks to try these with children and monitor the effects.)

2 A brief curriculum paper may be given by a member of staff. This needs to have been read by all of the teachers beforehand so that the meeting can be used for discussion.

3 Children's work may be brought to the meeting and discussed.

4 A member of staff may have attended an external course and her report may trigger off a series of school-based initiatives. For example, a course on developing learning skills through art and craft may lead to teachers reporting on their approach to art and craft with their children; the curriculum consultant will identify strengths and weaknesses within the school; children's art work may be looked at with regard to progression and followed by discussion as to how the school can develop art and craft. The teacher who attended the course may recommend that some of the contributions that she found useful, e.g. a particular speaker or a workshop approach, be used in the school.

5 Teachers find it difficult to keep in touch with current research and publications. Headteachers may take a lead here by reading much of the material themselves and providing summaries for their staff. Alternatively teachers may be requested to read a book or article relating to their own area of expertise and summarize it for colleagues.

OPENING UP

The headteacher sets the tone of the school and will encourage easy relationships and trust amongst staff. She will also help teachers to be aware of the complexity of teaching and to appreciate that they will be better armed for the job if they join forces rather than operate individually. This 'open' approach to teaching and learning can operate in the following ways, bearing in mind that some of the greatest benefits will be in the discussion that takes place during the planning and evaluation of events.

1 *Sharing of resources* A central resource area will give teachers access to all materials in the school. Various members of staff may demonstrate pieces of apparatus that they have found particularly useful and, having gained confidence to use these items for herself, a teacher may develop other uses, e.g. language masters are commonly used for word recognition with younger children – teachers of older children may also find them useful as a resource for a word bank or for tables practice.

2 *Helper or assignment cards* may be produced by one teacher who uses them for a pilot scheme and then shares them with other colleagues after particular strengths and weaknesses have been explored.

3 *Sharing content and method* Teachers of parallel age-groups might offer their children similar experiences through a topic approach or through planning for a joint assembly. A time set aside for the whole school to be involved in a topic (e.g. water) encourages a spiral curriculum.

4 *Different methods of working with groups* e.g. listening to more able readers in groups, training children to work in pairs, may be planned by two teachers and the results compared.

5 *Sharing the children* (see p.140) Teachers may grow to appreciate the benefits of sharing children with colleagues. Opportunities may be made for flexibility of groups enabling one teacher to work with a small group of children. Personality conflicts may be overcome if they exist between a particular adult and child. Occasionally in a chronologically age-grouped school, teachers with different age-groups may combine: the older children can work with younger ones in the same curriculum area – the older children will grow in confidence and younger ones may be motivated by the older child.

Help from outside agencies
Having established a professional confidence amongst staff the move to bring an outsider into school should be taken gently. It may be helpful to invite someone with whom staff are familiar and for whom they have a professional respect. A bad experience with a visitor who is detached from the classroom or a muddled thinker will lead to disillusionment and a setback in professional development.

The school may find it useful to list all the support agencies in the locality – HMI, local inspectors/advisers, university, institutes of higher education, drama centres, educational psychologist, parents (in a professional capacity). Bearing in mind that it is necessary to communicate through correct channels and that most of these people have heavy commitments, all are potential contributors to in-service.

LINKS WITH ADVISERS/INSPECTORS

1 An adviser/inspector may act as a catalyst in initiating discussion, e.g. an adviser may outline his ideas as to main objectives for free/creative writing. Such a broad perspective can then be followed by sessions of detailed planning for each stage of development. If the objectives are provocative staff may retaliate with their own suggestions and lively debate develop.

2 Outside involvement may prove helpful where there are mixed staff attitudes and constant friction prevents development. For example, where some teachers see children's learning as passive and others support an active approach, an adviser may enter the arena to support the best practices of both (thus preventing loss of face on either side) and at the same time make it clear that teachers should be sufficiently open-minded to try a different method.

3 A staff may sometimes not appreciate the need for appraisal. They may be unaware of how their practice has slipped in a certain area. An adviser, by talking about initiatives in other schools and illustrating this with practical examples, may provide a necessary jolt. (Visits to other schools will also help.)

4 Specialist advisers may also be called in to contribute to development of curriculum guidelines or to offer advice on curriculum material.

ADVISORY TEACHERS

Whilst an adviser may have only limited time, an advisory teacher may be attached to a school for a longer period and offer the following types of support:

1 Attendance at a number of in-service sessions to make a contribution and to bring in resources from outside as and when required, e.g. a range of published curriculum material to consider together with reports as to how it is used in neighbouring schools; suggestions for school visits that may be particularly relevant for that staff.

2 After discussion with the headteacher, scale post-holders could be released from their classes to develop curriculum work in other classes. The advisory teacher will teach the scale post-holder's class whilst this is happening and also work closely with the post-holder to develop her leadership role.

3 *Development of pre-school initiatives*. The advisory teacher may have the flexible role of, for example: providing supply cover for the reception teacher to release her for pre-school work, accompanying the teacher on playgroup visits, collaborating with the teacher in developing pre-school guidelines and contributing to parents' sessions.

4 *Classroom support*. A teacher developing a new initiative, or a weak or inexperienced practitioner may all benefit from extra teaching support. The approach will vary according to the need and personality of the teacher but whatever the strategy it should both support and also develop the teacher's own skills thus enabling her to cope single-handed in the

future. For example, the advisory teacher may help the teacher to develop an approach with a disruptive group of children in the class which can then be tried out with the advisory teacher monitoring the work of the rest of the class.

LINKS WITH HIGHER EDUCATION ESTABLISHMENTS
The type of link must depend on the willngness and resources of the institute. An example of a successful scheme offering all-round benefits is working at the West Sussex Institute, where tutors are taking part in school-based work by teaching classes, using team teaching and developing discussion with staff. A teaching fellow is also appointed from the staff of one of these schools to work with B.Ed. students at the institute for one day a week and develop this work with the students in her school for a further day a week.

The following initiatives from schools may help to develop contacts:

1 A request through the LEA for establishment representatives to join headteachers' meetings to discuss developing links.
2 Extension of existing links with tutors – some may be longstanding where tutors have used the school as a training base for students and supervised school practices.
3 An occasion at the end of term when establishment staff are invited into school to look at children's work and stay for a buffet supper.
4 An invitation, for certain tutors, to a school-based seminar on a curriculum topic.
5 A tutor and group of students could be invited into school to work jointly with staff on a particular project, e.g. a weekly workshop for a mixed age-group of more able children.

Institute initiatives could include:

1 A regular occasion when teachers are invited into college to talk with staff, e.g. after school hours for a cup of tea.
2 Publication of a broadsheet providing schools with information about institute events/research projects.
3 Opportunity for teachers to use reprographic and other institute resources.
4 Open meetings for teachers and institute staff with a national speaker invited.

Cooperative ventures with other schools

MAKING A START
Staff can discuss and decide on a number of priority concerns for in-service. Having identified these, a working lunch or after school meeting with the headteachers and deputy heads of two neighbouring schools could follow at which each school's proposals could be discussed and compared and an in-service programme compiled.

CONTENT AND APPROACH
These will affect the number of sessions required, e.g. a request to see progression in PE sessions may be organized by three demonstration lessons with different age-groups followed by a discussion looking at the capabilities of the children and the skills expected of them. A request to look at art and craft in the curriculum may require a number of sessions, including a talk on the principles underpinning art and craft, and demonstration lessons followed by practical workshops.

TIME
It is important that teachers are given time to accommodate any new ideas and make them applicable to their own situation. At the end of a session tasks may be suggested for them to try out with their own children, e.g. painting and sketching as a result of close observation; painting after listening to a piece of music. A joint display of work achieved can be mounted for a small exhibition and children from the schools involved brought to view it. Teachers and children will be stimulated by the scope and variety of work.

VENUE
Meeting at each school in turn will provide a change of venue. A cup of tea to start gives teachers a chance to relax and allows time for others to arrive from their school. A small display of material or new books will provide a focus of interest, and in addition most teachers do appreciate the chance to meet colleagues socially. The opportunity to look around each school is usually welcomed; this is best offered after the main session so that teachers can look at the layout of classrooms and displays of children's work at leisure.

BACK-UP
Although regular meetings should ensure that teachers become familiar and relaxed with one another, some individuals will never be sufficiently confident to express their views out of their own school setting. It is necessary then to follow up the cooperative in-service discussion within each school staffroom.

FEEDBACK
Useful feedback as to the success of the session can be gained from teachers in the staffroom the day after the session. Headteachers might like to note this and if the criticism is constructive it can be used to improve following sessions.

Small school cooperation
As with most initiatives a cooperative venture will develop best if the need is identified by the staff and supported by LEA rather than imposed. The scheme is more likely to succeed if each initiative is tried and monitored before being extended to other schools.

STARTING-POINTS

The physical limitations of small schools may be the starting-point for cooperation, e.g. one school might offer the other the use of their playing field or school hall for PE; two schools could share a minibus for swimming lessons.

Schools may visit one another annually for an 'outing': this gives the children the opportunity of acting as visitors and hosts, the benefits of being in another school and the opportunity to join together for games, treasure hunts or a visit from a music or drama expert.

RESOURCES

The purchase of large items of equipment is sometimes beyond the finances of a small school. Joint purchase of a photocopier, heat copier and jumbo typewriter conveniently placed in the largest school, or allocated to schools on a termly basis, will immediately broaden opportunities for children. A shared resource centre for filmstrips, charts and cassettes can be planned and used jointly by two or three schools.

JOINT CURRICULUM INITIATIVES

These may arise following the need for each school to have curriculum guidelines. Teachers with particular curriculum strengths can exchange schools weekly as a pilot project, e.g. art and craft with music or science. This can eventually operate as a straight exchange with teachers meeting to discuss the work undertaken. However, initially the scheme needs to be carefully planned with supply cover to enable the teachers involved to visit one another's classes and observe teaching.

Joint topics may be mounted between schools and a joint exhibition open to the public. Joint music festivals and carol concerts will enable more ambitious schemes to be arranged. Joint parent meetings occasionally will enable a speaker to offer a subject/film/demonstration to a wider audience.

JOINT STAFF MEETINGS

If held once a term six or more teachers from three schools can enjoy the stimulus that their own school's meetings cannot provide. These occasions may be hosted by each school in turn. Teachers attending courses may report back to these larger staff meetings, professional books may be reviewed and new apparatus and materials discussed. Teachers of parallel age-groups in different schools will benefit from discussion and comparison when planning and reviewing work.

Inter-school visits

Visits need to be an integral part of school-focused in-service and planned to meet specific needs.

The headteacher will have a total view of priorities for the school year and how school visits can help to gather information in working towards these priorities. For example, enhancing the school environment:

teachers who are reluctant to 'waste time' in self-help decorating projects may be enthused by visiting an old school which has been transformed by carpeted areas, cork tiles, paint and hanging plants.

Heads will have their own view of how visits can benefit them, e.g. a new scale post-holder may gain confidence by seeing how a teacher in another school occasionally works alongside colleagues to provide support. This outside visit may be more effective than advice from other scale post-holders within her own school.

A consultant teacher may look at new material being organized and used by the children in another school, and then talk with the teacher afterwards about its strengths and weaknesses.

Ideally teachers will need a full day's cover to enable them to visit and observe at leisure and gain something of the ethos of the school whilst feeling that their own class is in good hands. Cover may be provided in the following ways:

1 The LEA could be approached with an outline plan and a request for supply support.
2 Students on final school practice may provide opportunities for teachers to leave their classes.
3 A school assembly or film for a larger group of children might allow two teachers to be released to visit a neighbouring school for a limited time.
4 The headteacher may cover one teacher's class.

MAXIMIZING THE VISIT
The teacher(s) concerned can note down what they want to see and what they hope to gain from the visit. Advisers will have a broad view of schools and can suggest where particular strengths are to be found.

1 The host school will need notification of the visitor's requirements so that they can plan accordingly. It may help if specific questions are sent in advance so that teachers can give them some thought. A particular teacher may be most at ease and articulate with visitors – other staff may be inhibited and need more time for preparation.
2 The time of day chosen should enable the visiting teacher to gather as much relevant information as possible.
3 Visiting teachers should realize that they may be offering something to the host school. Their questions and appreciation of the visit, their very presence, can all be a stimulus to the host teachers and encourage a reciprocal invitation.

AFTER THE VISIT
1 A 'thank you' picture postcard sent to the children of the host school is always appreciated.
2 Teachers will want to report back on their visit to the rest of the staff. They may recommend that other colleagues visit the host school; they

may suggest a change in their own school following the visit; they may merely spell out how the visit has helped their own professional development.

3 At the end of the year the programme of visits can be reviewed and the benefits assessed by the staff.

THE HOST SCHOOL
Receiving teachers for a visit may provide an occasion for a buffet lunch or glass of sherry and a general boost for the staff. Host teachers may also benefit by being required to clarify their practice in order to answer questions from visitors. The headteacher could suggest that staff be prepared to stay for a short while at the end of the day to discuss any issues that visitors wish to raise as a result of the visit.

It can be valuable and relevant for visitors to sit in on staff meetings, either as observers or contributors where this is useful.

Sharing observations

The ability to admit to professional problems and to look to a colleague for assistance and possible criticism requires confidence and this approach is only likely to succeed amongst staff where there is already a tradition of collaborative work. It will be helpful if teachers

1 are used to the headteacher regularly joining the class and working with a group of children,
2 have open access to one another's classrooms in order to share ideas about display and physical organization,
3 through regular meetings and other informal contacts have established an easy and frank relationship where strengths and weaknesses are discussed, regardless of hierarchy.

The headteacher will know her teachers as personalities, and so should be able to identify at least two compatible teachers who are likely to be interested in sharing observations before she offers the suggestion to the whole staff, emphasizing that the scheme is voluntary.

The choice of problem to be observed needs to be appropriate to the observer's expertise, e.g.

1 The teacher's problem is that she cannot deal with a group of disruptive children within the total class. The observer has particular strengths with disruptive children and will focus on this group.
2 All children are relying too heavily on the teacher for support with their learning. The observer is required to focus on how else this support can be offered.
3 Timing of children's assignments. Those who complete their main task quickly are not working positively afterwards. The observer is asked to focus on secondary activities, their value and structure.

The number of occasions that the observer is able to be in the classroom will be strictly limited by organizational constraints. However, if possible the occasions should be flexibly timed to allow the observer to gather maximum information.

Both partners will need to have a professional respect for one another, an ability to temper honesty with tact and a sense of humour, apart from a real desire to improve their own professional performance.

Teachers as researchers
The idea of starting classroom enquiry may come from:

1 A course where teachers are required to develop a piece of classroom research and report on it.
2 A staffroom discussion where the headteacher suggests that teachers follow a particular line of enquiry, e.g. how each member of staff receives their children at the start of the day – how does this reception add/distract from the pattern of the rest of the day?
3 One teacher having read about such initiatives and deciding to develop an enquiry independently in school.

Teachers need to look closely at the nature of the enquiry and then decide how best to gather information, e.g checklist when looking at types of language used by children; questionnaire and discussion with parents when focusing on their role as helper in the classroom; diary when making observations and commenting retrospectively.

It may not be easy to identify the best method of enquiry initially. It may be helpful if:

1 The staff are consulted – the teacher states what it is she wants to look at and asks for suggestions about how she approaches the project.
2 Two or three teachers focus on the same area of enquiry but adopt different methodologies.

It is usually better to examine a limited area in depth rather than attempt to be over ambitious, e.g. What encourages children to ask probing questions after a story – preparation before the story? delivery of the story? follow-up tasks set by the teacher relating to the story? What effect do first-hand experiences have on children's art work? Request paintings from children without any preparation, make the same request after children have handled objects, listened to music and discussed their experiences. Evaluative skills may be extended to whole-school research projects, e.g. continuity of curriculum throughout the school – how is the continuity maintained and what is needed to strengthen it?

Schools and LEAs should encourage teachers not only to undertake their own research projects but to share their findings. Staff meetings should encourage teacher reports followed by staff discussion. Teachers' centres can support by duplicating teachers' reports and producing termly publications of local action research. Advisers may organize conferences for the dissemination of action research.

Teachers as leaders and contributors to in-service

STARTING IN THE CLASSROOM

Teachers are always asking for practical courses – what they want is material and advice to help them to teach children tomorrow. They are keen to see other schools and they appreciate listening to someone who has sound classroom experience. These requirements point to the value of experienced teachers sharing their own classroom experiences with a group of teachers. The example outlined below may serve as a model for this approach:

Classroom management sessions
Broad aims
1 To provide a simple and inexpensive school-focused form of in-service for a group of schools.
2 To offer teachers in-service which is practical, appealing and non-threatening.
3 To work with teacher contributors offering them the opportunity to develop teaching and communication skills with a group of colleagues.
Strategy
The adviser identifies a cohesive group of schools and approaches head-teachers. Adviser, with headteacher, identifies noteworthy practices in each school. Experienced teachers in the schools are invited to talk about their work in the classroom. Meetings are arranged with these teachers to offer guidance on the content and presentation of their contribution. Each teacher is requested to give her rationale for working and then to focus on an aspect of good practice previously identified – these areas may include developing children's self-sufficiency in the classroom; providing children with a balanced programme; developing collaborative work in groups; planning work for a vertical age-group; point and purpose of display; self-evaluation. The teachers will usually require initial encouragement and good notice in order to have time to prepare their contribution thoroughly.

Each session should be based in the teacher's classroom after school hours. The teacher's contribution may be approximately 20 minutes, leading on to discussion and questions. The adviser or headteacher should act as chairperson, thus providing continuity. The final session may take place in the neutral setting of a teachers' centre when course members are required to reflect on the various practices they have heard and to identify any aspect which caused them to alter their own practice. They may also be invited to suggest other strategies of sharing teaching experiences, e.g. this may lead to requests to see the teacher contributors working with children in their classrooms.

A further meeting with the teacher contributors will enable them to be thanked formally and also to explore with them how the experience has helped to develop their professional growth, e.g. clarification of their own teaching practices; growth of confidence when facing an adult audience.

TEACHERS AS COURSE LEADERS
The opportunity to see teachers offer a one-off contribution and to share their reaction to the experience may help advisers to assess these teachers' potential for more sustained work. This may include:

1 Disseminating national projects with small working groups of teachers.
2 Running curriculum workshops in areas where they have particular expertise.
3 Leading groups of teachers in follow-up work following a county or DES/regional course.

Qualities required of teacher leaders are:

1 An enthusiasm and commitment to do the job thoroughly.
2 Professional credibility with colleagues, e.g. seniority of status, own sound practice and length of service.
3 Curriculum expertise.
4 Leadership skills with adults.

Support in the form of regular group meetings is required to train teachers in communication and chairmanship skills; to brief teachers closely about the job required of them; to continue to support the teacher leaders whilst they are taking sessions. The atmosphere at these meetings needs to be relaxed to encourage problem-sharing. Resources need to be easily available, e.g. all duplicating arranged, audio-visual equipment set up in advance, workshop materials supplied.

Initially the adviser should visit the group to make it clear to the teacher leader that she is there in a supportive capacity to iron out any difficulties with the group. New teacher leaders may work more confidently in pairs; they may also benefit from one or two 'trial' sessions with an experienced teacher leader.

LOCAL IN-SERVICE

Short non-residential courses

TIMING AND FREQUENCY OF SESSIONS
If teachers cannot be released from school for in-service, their views on the timing of courses should be sought, e.g. immediately after school; mid-evening sessions; or part or full-day courses during the weekend. It is impossible to please everyone but variation in timing does mean that teachers with different commitments have the chance to attend.

1 If headteachers are convinced of the worth of the course for their staff

they may be prepared to release teachers for the last hour of the day to allow sessions to run from 3.00–5.30 pm.

2 If course members are required to tackle school-based tasks there might be a two-week gap between sessions to allow time for this. Otherwise weekly sessions are best to maintain the continuity.

3 The maximum length of an after-school session should be about two hours. Teachers arrive direct from a working day and will need refreshment and a short time to adjust to the course setting.

4 Any session held over a weekend needs to be particularly well planned to enable the best use of time, e.g. a day course may include a brief 45-minute lunch break with sandwiches and wine provided on the premises to enable relaxed discussion with course contributors during the break.

5 All sessions need to start and finish promptly, with provision for course members who wish to stay afterwards for individual questions and discussion to do so.

COURSE INFORMATION

1 This should be sent out in good time for teachers to organize other commitments if they wish to attend.

2 It should define the intended course membership and the main areas of study to be covered.

3 It should define the style of the course, e.g. group participating. Speakers will need to indicate the level of commitment required of course members, e.g. if teachers are expected to undertake tasks in between sessions.

SIZE AND SELECTION OF GROUP

The optimum group size will depend on the aim and style of the course, e.g. if the intention is to disseminate information mainly through a series of speakers, a large audience may be accommodated; discussion is best managed if the audience subdivides and the speaker spends some time with each sub-group; if the course is to be a workshop or dependent on teacher contributions, a group of more than fifteen may prevent less confident teachers from contributing. If the course is oversubscribed a decision must be made whether to 'squeeze in a few extra', refuse some teachers a place or, if numbers merit it, re-run the course. This last alternative may demand more of the course leader's time but is preferable to overcrowded sessions.

Selection of teachers for a course will again depend on course aims but may involve the following criteria:

1 Representatives from different schools, if a variety of experiences are to be shared.

2 Representatives from schools who share a similar situation, e.g. open plan buildings.

3 A mix of strong and less confident teacher contributors.

4 Teachers who share a curriculum responsibility or status (occasionally a mix of hierarchy levels may be successful if the course is a curriculum workshop or a reading study group).
5 Teachers with a mix of experience.

CONTENT AND STYLE
1 It is important on a short course for teachers to get to know one another as quickly as possible. The initial meeting might start with course members being paired off and after a few minutes conversation being asked to introduce one another to the group.
2 Course members should be briefed about the content and style of the sessions – a programme of such information can be given at the first session.
3 A preliminary meeting or questionnaire sent to interested teachers could be a means of gathering main concerns on which to focus course content.
4 Generally course content should take some perceived teacher needs as a starting-point and use these for development. Theory and practice should be emphasized together; it is reassuring if the course leader makes it apparent that he is familiar with practical teaching situations. He might like to illustrate a point by requesting a teacher to describe her own experience (e.g. Mrs Smith might like to give a brief description of the way in which she organizes her groups for maths work).
5 Opportunities should be made for sharing experiences, e.g. teachers might be asked to identify (anonymously) their greatest problem in the particular area of study, and these issues selected in turn for discussion by the group.
6 A variety of activities including outside speakers, films, discussion groups and group tasks, will provide a balanced programme. Teachers are more likely to forget their fatigue at the end of the working day if they are involved in activity.
7 School-based tasks to be tackled between sessions should be realistic and a firm requirement made for all teachers to be involved if the activity is central to the course. Sufficient time needs to be allowed at the next session for all teachers to report back; this may be achieved more efficiently if sub-groups are formed.
8 With limited time discussion should be clearly structured and preferably centred around the task. The groups may select their own chairman but if group dynamics are likely to be difficult it is preferable to have identified and notified strong chairmen in advance.
9 Plenary sessions on short courses may waste time but all work done by groups needs to be recognized, shared and used. Ten minutes at the end of each session will allow each group to identify three main points. Flow-charts of main points may be displayed for the whole group to consider briefly and then collated and handed out to course members at the next session.

PHYSICAL RESOURCES

1 *The setting* The venue will depend on the type of course. Management courses may be held in the neutral setting of a teachers' centre whilst curriculum sessions are best based in a resource centre or in school where materials are to hand. Whilst school venues are always popular a teachers' centre may provide welcome physical comforts in the way of easy chairs and a bar or refreshments.

2 *Documents* Handouts are always welcome. Their purpose needs to be made clear to course members. These could be:

A list of the main points of a talk, thus enabling teachers to concentrate on a speaker rather than take notes.

A collation of group findings and points from the previous session, thus assisting the continuity of the course.

A list of further references following a particular session, e.g. a collection of quotations.

A booklist, which may be provided at the first session or as a source of reference at the end of the course. If teachers are recommended to read books from the list at the beginning of the course, this material should be referred to at subsequent sessions.

The teachers' centre

CREATING A PLEASANT ATMOSPHERE

1 Some centres are housed in unattractive buildings but attention to detail inside can help greatly. Displays of children's work, fresh flowers and friendly staff, warmth, cleanliness and easy chairs can all work wonders.

2 Clear notices about facilities and how to use them, and a programme of events for week displayed are helpful to the busy teacher.

3 Occasional social functions may be an added attraction to accompany a large exhibition or display of materials.

ADVISORY LINKS WITH CENTRES

It is in the teachers' interest if all in-service provisions liaise closely to present a coordinated programme of courses and advisers and teachers' centre leaders can work closely together towards this end. Whilst advisers will use the centre for many of their own courses, teachers' centre steering-groups will ensure that teachers' practical needs are met through short courses. Advisers should be kept informed of these courses and may attend some to identify a number of starting-points for development. Advisory initiatives may include a regular 'surgery' held at a centre. This enables any teacher to talk with the adviser with or without an appointment about any matters relating to personal or professional development.

TEACHERS' CENTRE PUBLICATIONS

These will vary from a simple course programme, published termly, to a range of professional documents disseminating curriculum information. These publications will help to set the 'tone' of a centre and will reflect the personality of the centre leader. Some suggestions for inclusion are: provision for schools to advertise surplus materials and to request others; reviews by teachers of new professional books, educational reports and apparatus newly acquired in school; suggestions for, and review of, educational visits for different age-ranges; reviews of visits to residential centres with children; brief reports from teachers on courses attended the previous term (these can be useful for would-be course members if the course is to be repeated).

TEACHERS DEVELOPING AND SUPPORTING THEIR CENTRE

The teachers' centre leader will develop his centre in his own particular style assisted by his steering committee. However, the way in which teachers see their centre as a resource and use it for their own needs will affect its life and style. Most teachers' centre leaders are very willing to supply courses if teachers identify what they want. The headteacher will need to take a lead in the staffroom to encourage teachers to make suggestions – the centre will only be as good as the support it receives.

1 Having put forward suggestions teachers can ensure that a course is tailor-made if they form a planning group to identify issues for inclusion.
2 If a school staff request a particular course they may decide to attend as a full group and to make the occasion an evening out by sharing a meal or a drink each session.
3 Some of the larger centres receive a range of professional journals that most schools cannot afford. Teachers might arrange to visit the centre monthly purely to have a cup of tea and look at the journals: a designated teacher may have the job of feeding back any interesting articles to the rest of the staff.
4 The centre may be used by a group of schools for a joint display of work. LEA officers and members of the public could be invited to come and see the work and gain insights into how young children learn from teachers.
5 Teachers can ask for exhibitions of materials and books at the centre and make a point of visiting any such exhibition before purchasing goods. Rural schools may ask for a minibus to bring the exhibition to their school for the day.
6 Teachers' centres may have a suggestion box in the entrance hall, together with pencils and paper, so teachers can jot down any suggestions for development.

The short residential course

SOCIAL ASPECTS

These are unique to a residential setting and should enable a group to 'gel' easily and encourage individuals to mix socially.

1 There should be comfortable group rooms, with attractive displays of books and children's work, a bar and lounge facilities in the evenng – perhaps with music and/or light entertainment.

2 Course leaders will need to circulate amongst course members, introducing those with similar experiences. Some teachers will find a residential setting initially very difficult and will appreciate sensitive and friendly support on the first evening/day.

3 Some teachers find adjustment difficult, yet they may be the very people who eventually benefit most from a residential course. Clear concise instructions of times and venues for meals and course sessions, with a sketch map of the building, may be reassuring as will the opportunity to approach the course leaders easily if there are any domestic problems.

THE PACE OF THE COURSE

Course members cannot work non-stop and be productive. However, any free sessions need to be carefully planned so that teachers do not feel that they are wasting time. It may help to have a film/slide show on offer, or open the college library. Alternatively school visits may be an option which provides a break from course work.

LINKING COURSES TO CLASSROOM REALITY

Course leaders should have visited as many teachers as possible in the classroom prior to the course in order to be aware of their problems and weave them into course content.

1 An inspirational or provocative speaker can be used to heighten awareness, followed by structured small-group work when teachers share experiences and place what they have heard in the context of the classroom, e.g. after hearing a talk on language and the value of the child expressing his own aims, teachers might discuss how this can be managed in the classroom.

2 A three- or four-day course may permit some extended workshop sessions in which teachers produce materials to take back to their classrooms, e.g. an individual programme of work for the child with a particular learning problem.

3 Throughout the emphasis should be on identifying steps towards good practice rather than stressing an impossible 'ideal' which may make teachers feel inadequate.

FOLLOW-UP SUPPORT

If a group of teachers from one school have attended the course, they are likely to support one another once back in the classroom. An individual teacher is more likely to feel isolated and soon lose the impact of the course.

1 It will help if the course leaders can suggest specific tasks for course members to tackle when they are back at school and then visit teachers in

the classroom to see how these initiatives are developing. Resources may be given or loaned to help such initiatives (e.g. cassettes, headphones and junction boxes) if they are not available in the teacher's school.

2 A follow-up meeting a term later will enable course members to present work they have been doing in school as a result of the course.

The long course

THE COURSE MEMBER

Enrolment on a long part-time course should preferably be undertaken when the teacher has no other unduly pressing personal or professional commitments. The following checklist may help cover other points.

1 Does the headteacher support the application? This can be helpful if her expertise is required or if time is needed in school for curriculum tasks.
2 Has the teacher considered all courses open to her – has she sought advice from her headteacher and adviser?
3 Has the teacher clarified why she is applying for a particular course? If it is for a further qualification it is important that she considers an award which is nationally recognized, e.g. a part-time B.Ed., rather than a local Certificate of Further Professional Study. If the reason is academic study or to look in depth at a curriculum aspect, she requires a range of information about the course content and method. If it is to embark on school-based or focused work she must check that the course design is sufficiently flexible to accommodate this.
4 Has information been offered from a colleague who has recently completed the course? On what grounds was the course recommended?
5 What distance will the teacher be required to travel each week?
6 What proportion of work must be tackled during the term and what can be completed during the holidays?
7 Is there a colleague from school or living locally who will also be applying? Moral support on a long part-time course is important.

THE PROVIDERS

Higher education establishments have to contend with the constraints of their own particular problems of staffing and expertise when planning long part-time courses. With this in mind the following points are worth mentioning:

1 Travel problems may be considerable for course members. A questionnaire may locate groups of teachers eager and willing to tackle a part-time B.Ed. or equivalent if the study centre is local, in which case a local, rural outpost could be established.
2 Recruitment should be considered carefully. A broad view can be offered if the group represents a range of schools. Minority groups should be avoided, for example, two first school teachers might feel overwhelmed when putting a viewpoint to a large secondary group.

3 If the course is to be school-focused it helps if the tutors familiarize themselves with the teachers' schools.

4 Teachers should be encouraged to discuss school-focused areas of study with their headteachers. The tutor may be able to meet with heads to brief them about the sort of support that would be appreciated and explain how the school-focused work could benefit the school. It is important that on return to school the teacher's newly acquired skills and expertise should be used and valued.

5 Some short orientation sessions before the main course begins could offer insights into the requirements of the course, e.g. the approach to reading, the need to think and talk at the level of principle rather than anecdote. This could save valuable time on the course and offer teachers some time and guidance to adjust.

6 A gentle reintroduction to academic study may be offered through an initial requirement for course members to tackle a fairly straightforward written assignment, e.g. a book review, a synopsis of their own professional development to date.

7 Teachers having committed themselves regularly to part-time study may appreciate opportunities for continuing after the course has officially finished. These may be provided through a self-help support group who could look to the institute for occasional help and administrative assistance.

Distance learning

INFORMATION ABOUT THE COURSE

Teachers need to gather all possible information about the course before committing themselves. Two teachers who have previously tackled the course could be invited to talk to an interested group of would-be members. Their accounts could usefully include any problems of isolation, and link in study with school practice as well as actual quality of content. Some of these problems could be discussed with a view to finding practical ways of overcoming them.

SHARING STUDY

Wherever possible distance learning should be a shared experience. Teachers need the opportunity to view video programmes together and discuss points of interest immediately. Reading will be of more value if books are reviewed with colleagues.

Two or more teachers from one school studying together will find that daily contact makes discussion easier. School-based research studies may be jointly planned and monitored. Groups of teachers from an area may meet together with an adviser to review their response to the course. Such meetings, by encouraging constructive criticism and evaluation of course content as well as individual progress reports, will help to overcome problems of isolation.

USE OF MATERIALS

It may be that distance learning materials can be adapted to meet specific needs in in-service education. Recent materials such as the curriculum evaluation project provide excellent starting-points for teachers to ask questions about their own performance in the classroom. It is not always necessary to follow the course outline closely. Occasiohally one video programme or an observation schedule may be useful when schools are planning their own in-service programme. The intention is to bend the materials to the teacher's own purpose.

Teachers who have studied through distance learning may identify particularly useful content or tasks which could help colleagues from school in other areas, e.g. self-assessment techniques. Headteachers should positively encourage Open University students to report their progress, frustrations and successes at staff meetings.

Secondment

PREPARATION AND APPLICATION

Initially the teacher will need to find out if the local authority has funds to support long-term salaried release from school. If this is not possible the teacher may wish to apply for unpaid release, knowing that there is the security of a job to return to at the end of the course. A simultaneous application must be made to the county for secondment and to the college or university for a place on the course.

The teacher will need to seek advice from as many sources as possible as to the calibre and relevance of the course. She will have to make decisions about location of courses and the possibility of living away from home.

The providing institution should be considered from the point of view of what support it offers students, e.g how well staffed is the course, do the tutors have relevant expertise, is there opportunity to visit other educational establishmenis, are library facilities good, is the course well respected by the local education authority? In some cases higher education establishments have liaised closely with local authority advisers to ensure that long courses meet particular criteria.

RETURNING TO SCHOOL

The return to school is going to be a sensitive time. If the course has been successful the teacher will have changed and is likely to have some different attitudes towards the job. Some teachers will expect promotion as a result of secondment. This is not always possible and it is important that if the teacher does return to her previous post she has room for development. A gentle re-introduction to school may include a meeting with the headteacher at the start of term, during which the teacher can be briefed as to what changes have taken place in school during the year she has been absent.

Shortly after, a further talk with the headteacher can enable the teacher to discuss and evaluate the secondment. As a result of this, decisions may be made about disseminating some of the material to the rest of the staff. The teacher may talk generally about her experience of secondment to colleagues, or certain changes which the teacher wishes to initiate and which are supported by the headteacher could be gradually introduced, e.g. the suggestion that staff read professional books, including research, and share this reading with others at staff meetings.

The local authority may ask the teacher to share her experience of secondment with a group. This is a formal recognition that the teacher has acquired something of value to offer other colleagues and that the authority expect some feedback as a result of their support.

CAREER DEVELOPMENT

The role of the school

OPPORTUNITIES FOR DEVELOPMENT

Development of present role
The most satisfactory way of gaining promotion and increased responsibility is for a teacher to be able to demonstrate that she has already done the job successfully. Teachers without a designated post of responsibility should be consulted about their particular interests and skills and offered the opportunity to take responsibility for organizing resources and influencing colleagues. This can only happen if the headteacher is seen to support the teacher and the initiative through offering time for discussion and providing material resources.

On appointment to a post of responsibility the teacher can discuss her job description with the headteacher and offer her views as to how she would like to develop her role in the school. An open style of management will allow members of staff to develop a range of leadership skills. Opportunities should be made for individual teachers to present outlines of curriculum guidelines to which other colleagues contribute: staff meetings can be chaired in turn: individual teachers can speak to parents' groups about aspects of school life: teachers may present a curriculum report to school governors.

Career prospects
Teachers should be able to discuss their careers regularly with their headteacher: according to the size and style of school this will be a formal interview or an informal chat. The important point is that both headteacher and teacher are clear about the gaps in the teachers' expertise and experience and that steps can be taken to fill these gaps, e.g. teachers take responsibility for teaching different age-groups or changing areas of responsibility: the deputy headteacher has opportunity to become familiar with administrative routines and to run the school on a regular basis – possibly one day a fortnight while the headteacher takes his class.

Applications for promotion
The headteacher should encourage interested staff to discuss possible applications with her with a view to identifying what is required of candidates and whether the application is realistic. The teacher should be encouraged to find out as much as possible about the post and the school and to consider whether such a move would provide job satisfaction and the right type of experience, e.g. a young scale-two teacher in a large school may apply for a deputy headship of a three-teacher school. Whilst this can be seen as promotion in terms of experience she could gain more from taking on year leadership in her present school and taking part in a school-based in-service development in a school with a large staff.

Teachers should feel able to show their letter of application to their headteacher and to ask for guidance on the interview procedure.

The role of the local authority

KNOWING THE TEACHERS
Many teachers feel that they are an unknown quantity to their local authority. This may not be the case, however, as advisers will gather information from various sources about a teacher's performance: a well-respected headteacher will be asked for an opinion; the teacher's attendance and response on courses will be noted as well as any initiative that she has developed in their school. It is possible to develop a reasonably accurate profile of a teacher's abilities without seeing her in action in the classroom. However, this is not ideal and local authority representatives should aim to see teachers in the classroom as much as possible. It is obviously helpful if an individual's professional competence is known to a person on the interview panel when it comes to applications for jobs.

COUNSELLING

Availability of advisers
It should be possible for a teacher to have access to her local adviser for professional help. In practice most advisory services are short-staffed and many individuals become heavily involved with county procedures which prevent them having leisurely contact with schools and developing close relationships with the staff. An economic way of seeing teachers is for the adviser to hold a regular 'surgery'. Teachers can then book an appointment for a specified time to see the adviser but the last hour of the surgery can be open to anyone who wants to call in casually. Frequency, venue and timing of surgeries will vary, but weekly sessions at the local education office or teachers' centre from 4.00–6.00pm is usually convenient. An adviser may wish to change the venue from time to time if she has a large geographical area to cover.

Headteachers should be notified of such arrangements and may find it useful to offer their teachers the chance of a 'second opinion' on a professional matter. Although it remains the teacher's right to talk to an adviser in complete confidence, it is courteous to notify the headteacher of an intended visit.

Areas of communication

The adviser's view on career development complements that of the school. After the school has offered the teacher all possible experience, the adviser may be able to arrange:

1 Exchange teaching – two local schools might exchange teachers for one day a week over the period of a year.
2 Temporary exchange of teachers between schools for a year.

In both cases the exchange may offer two teachers experience of new children and parents, buildings, styles of management, colleagues, curriculum expertise, or a different age-group.

3 In-service courses relevant to the teacher's next stage of development may be discussed.
4 Applications for posts may be considered in the light of the adviser's knowledge of the school's needs and the teacher's experience.
5 After an interview at which the adviser has been present the teacher may find it helpful to have some appraisal of her performance if she has been unsuccessful.

MANAGEMENT COURSES

The local authority should provide a rolling programme of management courses at all levels to support teachers as they accept more senior posts in school. These courses should help teachers to reflect on their present role and see how it could be developed, as well as looking to the next stage of promotion. Although a measure of preparation for the next level of responsibility is helpful, in some cases the candidate will need to be in the post before she can fully appreciate the skills necessary for the job and have the opportunity of putting them into practice.

1 *Courses for consultants with posts of responsibility* should focus on the skills necessary to

　　1 draw up, develop, implement and evaluate curriculum guidelines;
　　2 work with and influence colleagues in the appropriate curriculum area;
　　3 provide in-service training for colleagues.

2 *Courses for deputy headteachers* should focus on the skills necessary to

　　1 liaise between the headteacher and staff;
　　2 assist in making, implementing and evaluating school policy;
　　3 provide in-service training for colleagues;

4 assist in selection procedures for new members of staff;
5 prepare and implement an induction course for any new members of staff.

Both types of courses need to be planned bearing in mind that definition and development of roles will vary according to the individual school. The format and content of such courses can be explained to headteachers either by letter or preferably by personal contact with the adviser. Head-teachers should be encouraged to make it possible for the course members' newly-acquired skills to be developed back in the school.

3 *Courses for headteachers* should focus on the skills necessary to

1 act as curriculum leader for the school, including oversight of organization, support and evaluation of the teaching and learning;
2 develop public relations with school and community;
3 select, deploy and professionally develop members of staff;
4 plan ahead for all aspects of school development.

In addition to courses for new headteachers there should be provision for in-service management courses for experienced headteachers who have witnessed a change in their role-expectation in recent years.

WORK APPRAISAL

EXTERNAL APPRAISALS
A formal inspection or evaluation by HMI or the LEA is something that not many teachers welcome. However, there is the positive aspect of having one's practice looked at by other professionals with a view to receiving some advice.

Preparation for the visit is helpful and the teacher should look carefully at her work to identify her own strengths and weaknesses and to clarify her curriculum, organization and fulfilment of any leadership role. In the 'thinking' school teachers will already be doing this as part of their job and the evaluation will mean no more than 'tidying up' of ideas.

Evaluators are usually working under pressure of time and it is helpful for them to have as much evidence of the school's way of working as possible. All policy documents should be presented, together with any other written information, e.g. notes of staff meetings, procedures for linking with the community, details of extra-curricular activity, staff development schemes.

It is also important for teachers to have the opportunity of talking with the evaluators in order to answer any questions which may have arisen as a result of the day's observations, or to present additional information which might not be apparent to an outsider. Teachers may also note down their particular professional problems as resource and in-service support might be offered to the school as a result of the evaluation. Joint evaluations will enable teachers to make their own statement of practice which is then matched to the adviser's or inspector's report. The final statement should be the result of considerable discussion between school staffs and the evaluators. It is this discussion and decisions made about the way forward which are the most valuable elements of the exercise.

STAFF APPRAISAL

Teachers, like other employees, need guidance in their work. The headteacher will be respected for adopting a frank and honest approach to staff performance. Any criticism should be direct but coupled with offers of support to overcome weaknesses: achievements should not be taken for granted – teachers need and respond to praise and recognition.

The headteacher may talk with staff individually at the beginning of September to gain insight into their priorities for the year. Alternatively staff may submit a written note which can be discussed, e.g. consultant teachers state their aims for innovation in the school; an assistant teacher outlines a new form of organization for her daily programme. At the end of the year the headteacher will review these aims to see what has been achieved. If the headteacher has been actively involved with staff she will have a clear idea of each teacher's progress: it is important, however, that individual teachers have the chance to clarify their own thoughts on the year's development through discussion.

Appraisals may successfully take place with the deputy headteacher or between pairs of teachers if the relationship is right and both wish to benefit from the experience (see p.196).

SCHOOL APPRAISAL

If the intention is to appraise an aspect of the school the headteacher can call on the staff to offer a professional viewpoint, e.g. what evidence is there of our school having successful links with parents?

An adviser may be requested to observe differing expectations of children's behaviour within the school to provide evidence for the staff and on which to take appropriate action.

SELF-APPRAISAL

Teachers need help to ask themselves pertinent and formative questions about their own performance, e.g. Which child took most of my time today and why? An answer to this question may lead to another, e.g. How could I make provision for this child not to be so demanding tomorrow? These questions may be discussed and tried as a start and the most useful ones retained in a folder.

Teachers should be encouraged to share their self-appraisals with colleagues. Too much introspection is unhealthy but occasionally a staff could individually state their own main strengths and weaknesses. The strengths could then be shared with others and in return advice could be offered for the weakness.

THE TEACHER AS A PERSON

Establishing relationships

On taking up a new appointment a teacher or headteacher has the immediate job of developing a relationship with colleagues. The aim should be to develop trust and confidence in individual staff stemming from their belief that the person appointed has the personal and professional qualities needed for the job.

A teacher newly-appointed to a school with a consultancy role will need to pay attention to the following points:

1 She should be seen as a friendly and flexible person in the staffroom. Colleagues will appreciate it if she seems pleased to be included on the staff and given the opportunity to work with them. A new teacher can create this impression by commenting positively about the good things that are happening in the school, e.g. the easy relationships with parents. She should avoid the temptation of talking at length about her past school experience, particularly if it compares favourably with her new situation.
2 She must strike a balance between being too dominant in a staffroom and being overshadowed by older, more experienced members of staff, e.g. at a first staff meeting it is better to listen rather than contribute. However, the headteacher may want the teacher to introduce herself more formally to the staff at this meeting by briefly explaining her background and expertise. She needs to make it clear that she has been appointed to help her colleagues. An immediate offer of practical help will help to convince teachers of her intentions, e.g. a suggestion to develop a resource area in the school.

A new headteacher will have similar priorities.

1 She will need to get to know her staff as people as soon as possible. If the relationship with the outgoing head is sound, a few comments about each teacher's background and personality may be helpful, although the new headteacher will need to form her own opinions.
2 She should have an individual, informal interview with staff at an early opportunity. These interviews can be staggered over a period of time and held at the end of the day accompanied by a sherry or coffee. The head needs to be able to show genuine interest in the person. Some teachers will be very guarded and reluctant to share any details of family or personal and professional background at this stage. Probing questions are not usually successful – sometimes the headteacher may elicit further information by sharing one or two of her own experiences. Although the meeting should allow the teacher to talk at length about her strengths and weaknesses and career ambitions these issues are best dealt with later. The main purpose of this occasion is for the headteacher to become better informed about the teacher and for the teacher to feel that she matters and that she has a supportive leader.

Maintaining relationships

The quality of relationships within any establishment is crucial to successful working. Whereas any teacher will consider this in her own class and when liaising with colleagues, for a headteacher the maintenance of sound relationships is fundamental to the development of the school. A first school staff are likely to be a varied group of people. The opportunity for early retirements in local authorities has meant that younger teachers are now able to be recruited and to balance the older, more experienced staff. Personalities may differ as well as professional ability. The head's task is to encourage each teacher to have self-respect through doing a good job of work and to be enthusiastic to continue learning both for his or her own benefit and for the benefit of the children. This enthusiasm to learn will include acknowledgment that colleagues have skills to offer, which in turn leads to a staff with professional respect for one another.

TEACHERS NEED CARE AND CONSIDERATION

The staffroom is an important room in the school: it needs to be a pleasant, comfortable room where staff can relax and talk to each other. Teachers should always be consulted before visitors are invited into it. Staff morale will ebb and flow as in the classroom. Long periods of wet weather, pressures from the local authority, the serious illness of a colleague, or exhaustion at the end of term are likely to be 'difficult' times. A delicious cake at coffee time, or the suggestion that everyone contributes towards a special staff lunch can act as a boost.

Most teachers are more likely to work hard after school hours if the occasion can be combined with a social event, e.g. an in-service session at school followed by staff going out to supper; in-service planning in the headteacher's home over a bottle of wine; an occasional day when all staff visit schools outside the authority and meet afterwards for a theatre visit.

ACHIEVEMENT LEADS TO FURTHER SUCCESS

Teachers know that for a child the route to learning is to discover his strengths and build on them. The adult learning route is identical. The headteacher needs to exploit individual strengths and enable these to be shared in school. The mathematics consultant who feels that she has gained the respect of colleagues and helped them to develop the subject with different age-groups will have sufficient confidence to admit to her weakness in music and respond to any advice offered.

Some teachers will have less obvious strengths or may be unduly modest about their expertise. Some teachers may appear confident with a group of children but very reticent when asked to exchange views with adults. The headteacher will be aware that these teachers will need time and particular encouragement to realize what they have to offer. Occasionally they need to be approached individually and requested to take on some specific responsibility. If they succeed and gain praise and recognition, their development is likely to accelerate.

RANK CAN BE A BARRIER TO COMMUNICATION

As people move up the career ladder they achieve higher status and they also take on greater responsibility. The headteacher's and adviser's responsibility is to help the teachers to develop professionally and become high quality practitioners. Teachers' growth is helped by the feeling that they have professional challenges to meet but that they will have support in meeting these challenges.

In the education service roles are not strictly defined. Headteachers and advisers have status and expertise – it is largely up to the individual to determine which is going to dominate in a leadership role. Whilst teachers will defer to rank, they will respect expertise and recognize that they are more likely to learn from a senior colleague who has something other than rank to offer them.

Some teachers will neither be able nor desire to achieve senior positions. Nevertheless expertise is within everyone's reach if appropriate support is given by senior colleagues.

If the headteacher is human and approachable, if she admits to weaknesses and can identify colleagues on her staff who can do some things better than she can, this will encourage teachers in their efforts. This approach does not ignore rank: the headteacher is paid and expected to take the responsibility for final decisions. However, high quality practice is dependent on the headteacher using her leadership skills to enable others to grow.

SEPARATION OF PERSONAL AND PROFESSIONAL ROLE

The person in a senior post will need to relate closely and openly to colleagues in order to get to know them. The use of Christian names in a staffroom and the opportunity to meet one another's families will help teachers to get to know each other as people. There will be occasions, however, when senior staff, and in particular the headteacher, have decisions to make which are strictly professional, e.g. teachers are not returning to their classrooms promptly after coffee break; a teacher has to be redeployed. In these cases the children's needs must come first. The headteacher will find it easier to make such decisions if she is clear in her mind about the two roles which she plays. In a personal capacity she is Mrs X: in a professional capacity she is Mrs X the headteacher, paid to take responsibility and to run the school. If these roles are clearly explained to staff, they will be more likely to respond appropriately in both a personal and professional capacity.

TEACHERS' PERSONAL NEEDS

The professional first school teacher gives a tremendous amount of herself. Batteries need recharging not only at a professional level but at a personal level. Every teacher will have her own way of using leisure. The important point is that outside interests and enthusiasms *are* developed. The interested and interesting teacher is a person in her own right: she is aware that any enrichment of her own life can be fed back into the classroom. Her own interests may be transmitted to children: qualities of sensitivity and understanding which she develops will help her to relate to children, colleagues and parents. In this way the teacher's personal and professional development are inextricably linked.

APPRAISAL QUESTIONS

INDUCTION
What were my main problems when I started teaching? How could I use my own experience to help other new teachers?
What written documents are available for any new teacher or ancillary helper entering the school?

IN-SERVICE EDUCATION
How could we make staff meetings more professionally satisfying? e.g. Is there sufficient time allocated for the meeting? Are staff sufficiently prepared when coming together to discuss a curriculum issue?
When did we last meet with/visit local schools/the staff of the middle school?
How are the courses I am attending this term meeting my own needs/the needs of my children/the needs of my school?
Have I informed anyone if I have found the course unsatisfactory?
How can I best disseminate recent course information to colleagues?
What would an extended course offer me at this stage in my professional life?

CAREER DEVELOPMENT
What will I be doing in ten years' time?
What experiences do I need now in order to strengthen my application for promotion?
From whom have I sought advice about my career development?
If I am not interested in/not likely to gain promotion, how can I ensure that I do not become stale in my job?

WORK APPRAISAL
What are my priorities for the current year? How far have I achieved them?
What are my strengths/weaknesses as a teacher?
What have I done to rectify my weaknesses? What should I do now?

THE TEACHER AS A PERSON
What activity/interest am I pursuing this term for my own pleasure?
Have I become more or less satisfied with teaching and why?
How many good days have I had this week?
How many bad days?
If there are a majority of bad days what can I do to help redress tl balance?
How do my colleagues regard me? How do I regard my colleagues?

FURTHER RESOURCES

BOOKS
NIXON, J. (ed.) (1981) *A Teacher's Guide to Action Research* Grant McIntyre
Unfortunately no first school contributions but insights into, and examples of, teacher research projects.
SHIPMAN, M. (1978) *In-school Evaluation* Heinemann Educational
Some helpful suggestions on how schools can organize their own evaluation.
RUDDUCK, J. (1983) *Teachers in Partnership: Four Studies of In-service Collaboration* Longman Resources Unit, 33–35 Tanner Row, York YO1 1JP.

PUBLICATIONS
British Journal of In-Service Education published three times a year by Studies in Education Ltd, Wansford Road, Driffield, North Humberside.
Forum Discussion of the new trends in education. Published three times a year and available from 11 Pendene Road, Leicester LE2 3DQ.
Inspection and Advice Journal of the National Association of Inspectors and Educational Advisers, published twice a year by Studies in Education Ltd.

FILMS
Video Arts A selection of films designed to develop leadership and communication skills. Video Arts Ltd, Dumbarton House, 68 Oxford Street, London W1N 9LA.

5

PARENTS, SCHOOL
AND THE COMMUNITY

INTRODUCTION

'Not only do the teachers need to work together, but teachers, ancillary workers, parents and the community need to understand and support the work of the whole school.'[1]

First school teachers know that the Christmas sale or the summer fête are exhausting fund-raising occasions. They also know that the goodwill generated is as valuable as the extra money for commodities for running the school.

But if the vision of parents, teachers and the community working together with mutual understanding is to be translated into reality then thought must be given to two sets of ideas. First, teachers need to make clear in their own minds why such cooperation is desirable; second, they need to work out ways to bring it about.

How does an individual teacher see her professional role in relation to laymen in general and parents in particular? She may see herself as an explainer, a manager, an expert. In this case she is sharing information and she may well feel this is the limit of her participation.

On the other hand, she may go a little further, trimming her professional work in the light of what she sees and hears and actively participating with parents and the community. People and events will have a value for her as part of school life and she will share experiences. Sometimes she may even ask parents and other non-professionals for advice which will have a direct bearing on her classroom procedures. 'If a community school develops a life of its own, the professional role of the teacher has begun to change in far-reaching and fruitful ways.'[2]

Real understanding and genuine support require teachers to think carefully and set up a framework within which they are happy to operate. Every school needs to formulate a policy (not necessarily committed to paper, or deeply theoretical) agreed upon by all the teachers and the receiving school. This will ensure that unpredictable situations which need to be settled quickly will be dealt with consistently; as will parents.

Not all schools will wish to have highly developed, time consuming and emotionally demanding community involvement. Some schools have made outstanding contributions in this field (and it is heartening to see such success). A modest commitment is all that is appropriate in some schools but even then other teachers' experience is worth its weight in gold. Therefore we have set out some ideas under headings which we hope might form the base-line for individual thinking or discussion with colleagues.

SHARING INFORMATION

Although home and school are the two most important factors in the well-being of young children, they are not interchangeable, only complementary. School cannot attempt to replace family life and families cannot truly duplicate the role of the school.

The bond between a child and his parents is unique. In the home the child is loved simply because he is the offspring of his parents. The quality of that affection and the way it is expressed varies, but the family unit has bonds to be found nowhere else in the child's experience. No school, however caring, can offer children such a relationship. In short, 'Family living gives meaning and purpose to life that the child cannot obtain from any other source.'[3]

How is the role of the school different from that of the home? School offers the young child an introduction to group life. He learns new ways of living. He meets children of his own age and acquires fresh social skills. If he is successful he achieves a special security, a new confidence arising from being accepted among his peers. His teacher, while affectionate and concerned, because she is also trained and experienced, is able to assess him in the light of her knowledge of other children of the same age. Her relationship with him must be temporary.

If the roles of school and home are different, why should they work actively together? The answer is that both school and home share mutual aspirations for the children. They have a common goal to which both contribute, albeit in different ways.

Parents are eager for happy, well-adjusted, vital children who are going to enjoy life and find satisfaction and fulfilment. Furthermore they recognize and encourage these traits which reassure them that they are successful parents. If cognitive advance is important, so is a healthy personality.

What do schools wish for children? If they view learning as a life-long process they will want children to grow up able to 'solve their personal problems and play a significant part in the solution of problems of the world'.[3] In this case the acquisition of knowledge will be seen not only as an end in itself but as a vehicle for healthy living.

If both parents' and school's aspirations for the child are to be realized then sharing information is crucial.

SHARING EXPERIENCES

A great deal has been written about home and school and in particular the role of parents in school. As yet no theoretical framework has emerged. Stuart Maclure doubts 'whether or not it is worthwhile erecting an elaborate theoretical structure on the fairly simple perception that parental and peer-group support and encouragement are essential ingredients in successful teaching and learning . . .'.[2] Nevertheless, some teachers are uneasy because the role of the school seems to be expanding and professional life is becoming blurred at the edges. They feel inadequate in an area for which they have not been trained and the fluid, undefined boundaries of their new role with parents can make them anxious.

This is why we have tried to explain that while school and home have different roles, they are both working towards the same outcome and neither can achieve it properly without the other. Both are dynamic forces working to produce knowledgeable, well-adjusted children who will no doubt become parents themselves (and may even become teachers).

A vision of a wide role will create more common ground. A perception of a narrow one reduces overlap. If the teacher sees herself merely as a trainer or instructor the need for her to work with parents is far less pressing then if she sees herself as a facilitator, enabler and inspiration to the children.

Homes have frequently to adjust to the requirements of the school (e.g. mealtimes, holidays, clothes). Schools also need to adjust to the changing circumstances of the home. The secret is to maintain the speciality of the school role but dovetail with the changing needs of the parents. An example of this might be the question of punctuality in a particular school.

Teachers complained that children were arriving later and later in the morning. This not only interrupted the routine but raised the level of tension in the classroom. The headteacher was asked to write to the parents of persistent offenders and generally to 'tighten up on time-keeping'. The head knew that growing unemployment in the area meant that parents had no reason to get up early and that most of the children who were late came from families where father was out of work. Changing conditions in the home had repercussions in school. She therefore declined to write a letter of complaint about punctuality but suggested other measures. She positioned herself in the cloakroom at the start of school and spoke to individual children and parents. She arranged an early morning assembly once a week. She offered incentives to individual children to arrive at the correct time. She suggested to a group of parents that they stayed in the morning to see the school in session. She made selected home visits. An authoritarian, inflexible view of her role as trainer of children in punctual habits was not appropriate but at the same time she needed to explain to parents the damaging effect a late arrival would have on their child. She tried to share the home experience and react accordingly without compromising the needs of the school.

SHARING DECISIONS

As in every sphere of first school work, a theoretical framework needs to be translated into practice. This is best done if teachers think through a brief but clear set of ideas which serve as a mental checklist. A piecemeal approach to home/school involvement which has not really been thought through runs the risk of staying at the 'mixing the paints, cutting the card' level. As Ronald Meighan remarks in 'A New Teaching Force': 'Effort is not so much in question as the vision and design. You are not likely to reach the moon in a T model Ford however hard you try . . .'[4] – nor are you likely to arrive at mutually satisfying joint decisions unless there is a framework within which to operate.

Sharing information is a good place to start and then perhaps 'cooperation may be extended beyond the sharing of information to the sharing of experience'.[5] Active and joint decision-making will need to be approached cautiously but need not be on a large-scale at first. It might involve only one child or a small group of children to begin with.

If a school accepts the principle that children, parents and teachers will benefit from collaborating then the machinery for advance is there. The First School survey reports:

> At least a quarter of the schools had established links with individuals or groups in the locality. Most often, these were old-age pensioners for whom entertainment and gifts were provided, but links were also made with handicapped children resident in community homes, as well as with members of village associations. Funds were collected for charitable organizations.[1]

Finally why do we include 'the community'? Reasons range from advertising the school to helping the less fortunate, from extending the child's horizons to accepting help from outside groups.

Home learning and school learning, although they overlap, have different characteristics. One is the context: 'At home the contexts and people for learning from are manifold; the house, garden, street, car park, shops, waste ground, fields, the neighbours . . .'.[7] Another is the time scale: 'At home, learning is whole, it is spread out and can take place over days or weeks. At school it is short-burst, fragmented and compacted into segments of time.'[6] Thirdly, 'at home (it) is idiosyncratic and personal. . . . At school the curriculum is standard for all, the topic is usually a class project and all are expected to be interested in it.'[6]

A child in his home is also in his community – the two cannot be separated. The home and community offer patterns of learning not to be found in school. So one reason for beginning work in harmony with the community is to offer the children the continuity of learning as a whole experience.

Furthermore, if the home and the community not only share information but also experiences and decisions then the professional role of the teacher is changed. Work in Haringey, Eric Midwinter's work in Liverpool, the work at the Red House in Doncaster,[7] Bassey's survey[9] all point to the fact that there is, as yet unplumbed, a pool of energy and talent amongst parents and the community at large which could transform the work of the teacher and unleash exciting new possibilities for the children.

WHAT THE THEORY SAYS

SHARING INFORMATION

Sharing information about the school with parents

WRITTEN INFORMATION

Any headteacher who has an interest in developing home/school relationships recognizes that the better informed parents are about their child's education the more likely they are actively to support the school's policies and programme. This way of thinking has been highlighted in the Taylor Report which emphasizes parents' right to such information: 'Every parent has a right to expect a school's teachers to recognize his status in the education of his child by the practical arrangements they make to communicate with him and the spirit in which they accept his interest.'[9]

All schools should provide written information for parents.

The task of extending and improving the quality of a school's written communications is one where, with some effort and imagination, considerable and even dramatic improvements can be made. Unlike many suggestions for innovation and change, our proposals do not call for complicated organizational changes or additional staffing and resources. More than anything else they call for the harnessing of the goodwill and honest intentions which we believe the vast majority of teachers have towards their parents and the wider community. . . . Written communications represent one form of tangible evidence about what a school believes and does. At worst, they may be a little more than glossy, rather empty window dressing. Our hope, on the other hand, is that they will provide an important opportunity to reappraise what a school has to offer and to relate this, in appropriate ways, to the lives and experience of parents and the wider community.[10]

Depending on the catchment area it will be more or less successful as a form of communication. However successful though, it should only be regarded as one means of contact.

THE LOCAL 'GRAPEVINE'

Parents will talk together in every school catchment area: however, it is important that the informal exchange of information is not a substitute for the contact with school. The easier the access that parents have to teachers the less chance there is of unrealistic and damaging rumours being spread around.

HMI noted: 'In almost all schools there was an easy informality in the relationship between parents and staff: parents were seen to come readily into school and were made to feel welcome.'[1] This in itself fuels the knowledge about a school. The parents as well as their children become agents between the school and the community. Families moving into an area are most likely initially to seek information about the local school from their neighbours. Parents who have had a welcome reception will be good ambassadors.

QUESTIONS PARENTS NEED TO ASK

'If parents are to be fully involved in the life of the school, their views and their support called on, they are entitled to have full information about the running of the school, who is responsible for the school, who administers it, what are the sources of finance and so forth.'[11] However carefully the school offers information, and however comprehensive it tries to be, there will still be gaps in parents' knowledge.

The Education Act 1980, followed up by television and radio programmes on 'How to Choose a School', are concrete events which demonstrate the right of parents to ask for information. The school can no longer expect to dispense only that information it chooses. The information parents need in the first school seems to fall into two categories.

First of all there are the major questions – 'Who will be my child's teacher after the holiday?' These are usually dealt with systematically by the headteacher. But all first school practitioners know there are other questions which crop up through the day-to-day work and handling of the children which may appear less important but which are vital: questions about wearing coats at playtime, waiting for older brothers and sisters at the end of the day, the seating arrangements in the classroom; in other words questions which set a parent's mind at rest, clarify a misconception or articulate a request.

It is wise to remember that:

> The obvious language difficulties facing the parents from ethnic minorities who have no English, only a very basic English, or a form of English such as Creole which is not acceptable in schools, are faced also by a working class parent. . . . Where schools fail to give a clear account of themselves, this gap widens, and the fear which keeps such parents away from schools and away from being seen to participate in their children's education earns them the description of uninterested, couldn't care less, not one of the 'good' or 'helpful' parents.[10]

Working relationships can be improved. An excellent framework for teachers is to be found in *Parent – Teacher Relationships*, by Stout and Langdon:

> Even though the importance of good parent-teacher relationships

has been recognized comparatively recently, no teacher needs to build them entirely on a trial-and-error basis. Research in this specific field is limited, but the findings in many other fields point this way.[12]

We have taken some headings supplied by Stout and Langdon and expanded them.

1 *Assume parental cooperation* Teachers should assume that parents want to cooperate with them. The vast majority of parents have a positive, constructive attitude towards the school and individual teachers. They will respond eagerly to suggestions, invitations and requests, showing generosity and thoughtfulness. They will recognize difficulties teachers have, and will try to be friendly, interested and helpful. Working from this positive assumption teachers are likely to be successful in their dealings with parents.

2 *Think of learning as cooperative* Home and school are a continuous experience for children, the one always supporting and complementing the other.

3 *Think of parents as people* Sometimes it is helpful for the teacher to try and imagine what it is like for parents whose remembrance of their own school days may be less than happy to be obliged to leave their young children in the care of someone they do not as yet know very well. Parents who are slightly aggressive, shy, or appear uncooperative are often waiting for the teacher to break the ice. Tension, lack of imagination, a retiring personality, heavy family commitments, may all contribute to a seemingly uncooperative attitude.

Cleave, Jowett and Bate remind teachers that although 'most staffs expressed an openness towards parents "They can come and see us anytime they want" many parents did not feel they could . . . for most parents access was complicated by feelings about the staffs' professionalism, their own self-image and memories of their own school days.'[5]

4 *Use the resources available* Stout and Langdon suggest that 'The classroom teacher does well to find out the interests and skills of parents and to let them know how glad he would be for their help. Good relationships thrive on just such working together.'[12]

INFORMATION PARENTS CAN GIVE
One way of evaluating routines and involvement is to keep a box where parents can post their written suggestions.[11]

Organized sharing: PTAs
Many schools prefer to indicate their willingness to link with parents through an association. The First School Survey reported that

23 schools had formally constituted parent/teacher associations the membership of some of which included friends of the school whose

aims usually expressed the intention of bringing about a closer cooperation between home, school and community for the benefit of the children and whose main activity was usually fund-raising. A number of these associations were very supportive in the school . . .'.[1]

Schools need to be aware that although a formal association with a committee may prove a convenient way of communicating with a group of parents it may not be the most flexible, effective way of encouraging a full parent/teacher partnership. The success of an association may depend on the catchment area of a school. Some parents respond eagerly to a formalized committee framework: others would reject such an approach or feel ill at ease.

Regular parent/teacher contact
Most first school teachers are sensitive to the value of a developed relationship with parents based on regular contact:

> Most of the teachers had a considerable knowledge of the home circumstances, needs and problems of the children in their classes. Much of this was the result of frequent, often daily contact with the mother or another member of the family, particularly in the case of the youngest children. . . .[1]

USING THE COMMON DENOMINATOR
Stout and Langdon[12] have isolated some common denominators, 'useful hints of things to do and not to do'. Although these refer not only to sharing information but also to sharing experience and decisions, it seems an appropriate place to include some of them in our discussion.

1 *Respect* 'Parents want their child's teacher to be a person who likes children and commands respect both of children and of adults.'[12]
2 *Relieving anxiety* 'Parents want to feel assured that the classroom teacher will let them know if anything is not going well with their child.'[12]
3 *Honesty* '. . . honesty begets trust, and trust is a bulwark to good relationships. We must expect that sometimes the teacher will be mistaken in judgment and faulty in conclusions, but even so, his honesty and sincerity give parents assurance. Parents also can make mistakes with complete sincerity of purpose. But when both sides are honest, the way is open for discussing differences and coming to an understanding.'[12]
4 *Encourage questions* The study by Cleave, Jowett and Bate[5] indicates that whereas teachers see themselves as approachable, parents do not always share this view. So teachers should not assume they are approachable but should take note of how parents approach them, when, and for what reasons.

Sharing information about the children with parents

INDIVIDUAL CHILDREN

Discussing the two worlds of pre-school and home, Blatchford, Battle and Mays suggest that 'persistent and explicit attempts to let parents know how their child is getting on are required'.[13] Cleave, Jowett and Bate, dealing with slightly older children ask, 'But do parents want a stake in their children's schooling? One thing was clear from our study – they at least wanted more information.'[5]

Having accepted that parents need information, how can this best be given and what demands does it make on teachers? Obviously, the needs of the catchment area have to be borne in mind. In a middle class area, where every family has a telephone and most run two cars, arrangements will be very different from an area where mothers work an evening shift or work regularly during the day.

We have already said that the key period for establishing a good relationship with parents is *before* the child starts school. However, once this crucial stage is passed, information from parents to school and vice versa needs to be continued. We will discuss some ways to do this to which teachers will undoubtedly add their own successful techniques. Quite as important as the method of communication is the detailed thought and planning that goes into each occasion.

The First School Survey found that

> in 26 schools parents were able to discuss their children's progress at almost any time without prior appointments. A few schools expected parents to use only the time at the beginning or end of the school day for discussion. In nearly half of the schools parents were requested to use occasions arranged by the school or to make appointments if they wished to discuss their children's progress.[1]

CHILDREN AS A WHOLE CLASS/YEAR GROUP/TEACHING GROUP/SCHOOL

Catchment areas vary enormously. A formal talk which might be successful and indeed satisfying in one area would be a near disaster in another. In the section 'In the Classroom' we suggest a range of activities, some quite modest, but with the explicit aim of sharing information with parents. Which are most suited to the catchment area will depend on the history of parent/teacher relations in the school, the expectations of the parents, and the managerial skills of the teaching staff in arranging and hosting different functions. For example, is the headteacher uncomfortable in large groups or does she respond well to a hall full of people? The important thing to be remembered is that every activity will need to be thought through carefully in detail, preferably with a colleague. Nothing should be left to chance.

Tizard, Mortimore and Burchell recommend films and videos:

A film about the class is a guaranteed way of attracting parents to school. In our project we found that between 75 and 100 per cent of families would come to film meetings, provided that they were offered at least two different opportunities to attend.[11]

USE PARENTS' KNOWLEDGE OF THEIR CHILDREN
Tizard, Mortimore and Burchell state:

> It is as essential for parents to have opportunties to contribute their knowledge of their children as it is for schools to provide parents with full information about the children at school. . . . A parent may also be able to suggest explanations for troublesome aspects of her child's behaviour at school, because, for example, she may know that he is terrified of a certain child, upset by being called a 'wog', or bored by work which is not demanding enough for him.[11]

Ought the school to make deliberate attempts to encourage parents to give information to the class teacher and head? Cleave, Jowett and Bate found

> Some mothers had reason to speak to the teacher or head about specific matters such as the child's reluctance to come to school, his worries about dinner, his ailments or his progresses. Occasionally notes were sent but more often contact of this nature was personal. Headteachers tended to be approached less often than class teachers, several mothers expressing awe of them.[5]

Sharing information with the community
Why include 'the community' with 'parents and school'? In *All Things Bright and Beautiful*, Ronald King describes

> An annual exhibition (which) was staged in the entrance of the main library in Newbridge. The preparation for this was spread over a long period of time and had a theme, including 'pirates' and 'the sea'. Mrs Brown, the headteacher, admitted this was not representative of the year's work and that it showed more creativity on the part of the teachers than the children, but like the teachers she claimed that the children took pride in the product, and had badgered their parents into going to the exhibition, the first time either had been into the library.
> Another purpose of the exhibition was to correct the 'image' of the school. She reported with some satisfaction comments she overheard at the exhibition, expressing astonishment at the origin of the work (What there!). . . .[14]

A headteacher of a SPA school in a large northern town asked the children what they would most like to do out of school. The reply was surprising: 'Go to Whites (a large plush department store) and have a drink in the restaurant.' Accordingly the teacher telephoned the store to make arrangements for a group of twenty children, together with adults, to go at an off-peak time. The manager made it quite plain that the children would be unwelcome and he did not wish them to come although he could not absolutely refuse. How often do the general public see the children with their teachers? What impressions do they get?

SHARING EXPERIENCES

Parents and the school

We are concerned here with fabric, funds, and general organization of the school. Roland Meighan notes that parents have traditionally been seen as part of the problem of teaching, not part of the solution. The one area where their help has always been sought is in the realm of fund raising. In the last few years the unofficial school fund (monies raised by parents and friends of the school) has increased in significance and has come to be relied upon by headteachers to alleviate the lack of official resources. Bazaars, sales, auctions, nearly new sales, coffee mornings, bring and buy, fetes, besides raising well-needed money have been happy social occasions for the whole family.

Another area of shared experience is service in terms of time and expertise – painting, mending books, making curtains, putting up display boards, cork surfaces, sorting and mending equipment.

A third category – more personal, less frequent, but very real – is the unexpected response to school needs and the sharing of experiences which almost always springs from the child as a link between his teacher and his home.

The ethos of the school is contained in all these activities – the way they are initiated, the personalities involved and the care with which they are stage-managed.

Tizard, Mortimore and Burchell comment:

> One traditional preserve of the teacher is the staffroom from which both parents and children are usually excluded. We had found in our project that parents helping in school usually resented being excluded from the staffroom at coffee time so we asked both parents and staff whether they thought this practice was correct. Two of the heads thought it was necessary to protect the staff's privacy, but all the other teachers and all but four parents thought it was impolite. Some parents also saw visiting the staffroom as a chance to get to know the staff better.[11]

Parents and the children

Why do 'middle class' children on the whole achieve rather better at school than their 'working class' counterparts? May one of the reasons be that the aspirations of the parents differ? Or is it because the techniques of helping children learn are more likely to be present in middle class areas? Jones (as reported by Meighan) says:

> In both the middle classes as a whole and the working classes as a whole the range of motives is rather similar. The majority desire that their children succeed at school, while another group is indifferent and a small number is rather opposed to school. The middle class parents, some of whom are teachers anyway, are able to turn their desire into reality . . . by surreptitious teaching of reading, writing and arithmetic . . . as well as exploiting holidays, weekends and television viewing as sources of general knowledge and discussion. One of the achievements of the playgroup movement has been to pass on techniques to parents who previously lacked them.[4]

Not only this, but some parents misunderstand the purpose of school activities altogether. Their perception of the learning outcome is quite different from the teacher's. As Tizard, Mortimore and Burchell point out:

> A number of mothers offered explanations for the provision of play materials which were far removed from those of the teachers. They illuminate the gap between the teachers and the mothers. . . . Thus the provision of water was explained as 'to get them interested in washing-up', sand 'to remind them of the seaside' . . . and so on.[11]

If sheer information, offered through experience, enhances parents' perceptions of how and what children learn in school, is it the job of the school to provide such experience? How does this affect the role of the teacher? Ought these shared experiences with the parents to extend into organized learning – reading, mathematics, science? Ought it in fact to embrace the whole curriculum? Are there ways of offering these experiences which are superior to others? These are key questions which need to be asked before teachers embark on a programme of shared experience with parents.

In Chapter 1 we commented on Teresa Smith's coinage of the 'professional' approach and the 'partnership' approach when working with parents. It is pertinent to consider this again. Either teachers offer parents a chance to help in school, but engage in fringe activities, leaving the teaching to the professionally-trained personnel, or they adopt a wider, more time-consuming mode in which they explain, take advice from, and work cooperatively with the parents. It is impossible not to rely on parents to make decisions, however small, if they work in the latter way. Of course there are difficulties, which need to be recognized, but there have also been magnificent successes.

The programme of teacher/parent involvement must vary from school to school and rely on such variables as teacher time, size of school, catchment area, tradition. No school would wish to rush into a programme but there are two further points which need to be considered. The first is that in an area where both parents and teachers share similar attitudes, values, even experiences, then explicit explanation about what is going on in school is not so urgent as in an area where this is not so. It seems vital that the school, in the latter case, should attempt to explain, not only by talk, but talk and shared experience, what it is trying to achieve. Jackson and Marsden pointed out that in these circumstances a ten-minute annual interview with the teacher was a stupendously inadequate communication channel. Eric Midwinter argued that there was an urgent need to sell education to the parents – 'in essence a monumental public relations task faces all teachers.'[11]

Secondly, there are two levels of operation: the practical and the generalized. If parents are confident that the teachers genuinely desire to do the very best they can for the children, then this will generate trust, the foundation of shared experience.

Summing up the dilemma Tizard, Mortimore and Burchell remark:

> Teachers are not usually taught how to organize untrained volunteers in their classrooms, run workshops and discussion groups for parents or suggest ways in which parents can help their children at home. These activities call for different skills from managing a classroom, or working with an individual child. The teacher must also become something of a community worker and an adult education tutor.[11]

Clearly this has ramifications for in-service work and initial training. It may also generate role conflict. Having parents in the classroom and using the opportunities which occur is not only time consuming but emotionally draining. A fine professional judgment plus discussion with colleagues will help the teacher to reach a compromise.

> Many teachers may feel that parental involvement of this kind is likely not only to be threatening, but to involve them in a great deal of work . . . [but] the advantages for the child of a closer relationship between home and school have always been obvious – at present, the tremendous educational potential of working class parents has hardly been tapped. The experience of our project suggests that there are considerable advantages to the teacher also. If teachers take the trouble repeatedly to explain and discuss their work with parents, they are likely to be rewarded by the support of an interested and appreciative parent body.[11]

Sharing experiences with the community

'The schools must mobilize the support of the parents so that, together, school and home and community at large can combine to forward the process of the children's education,' writes Stuart Maclure.[2] A few simple ideas are given on pp.246–51, but individual circumstances will provide for many more.

In the report *West Indian Children in our Schools*:

> The committee highlights one of the main themes running throughout its report – the gulf of distrust and understanding between schools and West Indian parents. The failure of schools to understand the particular social and economic pressures which West Indian parents may face, together with the failure of some West Indian parents to appreciate the contribution they can make to their child's education, are both seen as factors in the underachievement of West Indian children.[16]

The task of making some parents aware of the significance of their own role is slow and initially unrewarding. Some teachers understandably choose to channel their energies into teaching the children in school. However the schools that have worked consistently to raise the level of parental consciousness and thus trigger off their active involvement in school life are quite clear about the benefits for all three parties concerned.

SHARING DECISIONS

Sharing decisions with the parents about the school and children

It is impossible to engage parents in the kinds of activities we have described without those parents making decisions, however simple. Smith argues that

> even when teachers make determined efforts to give more information to parents this is not necessarily effective in helping them to understand more about the methods and objectives of the group or their children's learning. . . . It is active involvement in these educational activities that is most likely to affect parents' attitudes, understanding and behaviour.[17]

She cites Lazar and Darlington (1979) who made a longitudinal study of the effect of such programmes as Head Start. The research suggests that pre-school programmes in low income areas had lasting effects on children's school performance. It also increased the children's own confidence and self-image 'and their parents' aspirations for future education and employment'. The ingredients which made home/school liaison most successful seemed to be parental involvement, home visits and specific shared goals.

Armstrong and Brown's study of an intervention programme in the West Riding points up the underlying principle: 'The differences lie essentially in the parents' view of education and of their own role in relation to their children's development.'[17] In the introduction to this chapter we stresed the need for the school and parents to join forces in nurturing children. We have now come full circle in recommending that lasting results in school achievement can be initiated and maintained by active parental participation.

CURRICULUM DECISIONS
Curricular decisions fall into a controversial category and are discussed at some length by Tizard *et al.*

> A new definition of professionalism is required to overcome these difficulties. The teacher would expect to use her special skills and knowledge to enlist the help of laymen, she would expect to exchange information with them, and take their opinions into consideration. Such a role would surely enhance, rather than reduce her status.[11]

Looking to the future, Atkin and Goode envisage a time when

> . . . in the same way that micro-technology will transform classrooms in the next decade or so, we believe it possible for teachers and parents working together to redefine the professional role of schools so as to transform the learning that takes place at home and school. . . . The first step, perhaps the hardest, is for teachers to listen to parents more and talk at them less and for them to begin to accept that valuable learning does actually take place in the most unlikely places.[6]

Sharing decisions with the community about the school and the children

The Pre-school Playgroup Association has amply demonstrated that 'the community', without professional help, can organize an excellent low-cost, nationally recognized service. Consumer groups, such as the Confederation for the Advancement of State Education (CASE) and the Advisory Centre for Education (ACE) intend parents to have the right to information but also the right to actively influence the professional management of schools, including the curriculum. Journals, such as the new *What Next* 'marks a departure from established periodicals. No other publication, to our knowledge, lays down a policy which aims to bring parents and educators into the tide of educational developments and debate. We believe that such an interchange is urgently needed . . .'.[19]

The 1980 Education Act further strengthens parental rights. Stuart Maclure suspects:

> We have scarcely begun to see the consequences of the modest beginnings so far made at places like Countesthorpe and Minsthorpe and Coventry and in the various Liverpool developments. So far, participation has largely been on the school's terms . . .'. If teachers choose the way of openness and dialogue, a new kind of profession-alism becomes possible.[2]

REFERENCES

1   DES (1982) *Education 5 – 9* (The First School Survey) HMSO
2   MACLURE, S. (1974) *Professionals, Experts and Laymen* (Bulmershe Lecture) Smith
3   BUHLER, C. (1953) *Childhood Problems and the Teacher* Routledge & Kegan Paul
4   MEIGHAN, R. (1981) A new teaching force? Some issues raised by seeing parents as educators and the implications for teacher education *Educational Review* 33, 2, p.141 Faculty of Education, University of Birmingham
5   CLEAVE, S., JOWETT, S. and BATE, M. (1982) *And So to School* NFER
6   ATKIN, J. and GOODE, J. (1982) Learning at home and at school *Education 3 – 13* 10, 1
7   See HALSEY, A. (1972) (ed.) *Educational Priority* (The Halsey Report) HMSO
8   BASSEY, M. (1978) *900 Primary School Teachers* NFER
9   DES (1977) *A Partnership for Our Schools* (The Taylor Report) HMSO
10 BASTIANI, J. (1978) (ed.) *Written Communication between Home and School* University of Nottingham School of Education
11 TIZARD, B., MORTIMORE, J. and BURCHELL, B. (1981) *Involving Parents in Nursery and Infant Schools* Grant McIntyre
12 STOUT, I. and LANGDON, G. (1958) *Parent-Teacher Relationships* American Educational Research Association of the National Education Association
13 BLATCHFORD, P., BATTLE, S. and MAYS, J. (1982) *The First Transition* NFER/Nelson
14 KING, R. (1972) *All Things Bright and Beautiful* Wiley
15 Cited in 12 above.
16 COMMITTEE OF ENQUIRY INTO THE EDUCATION OF CHILDREN FROM ETHNIC MINORITY GROUPS (1981) *West Indian Children in Our Schools* HMSO
17 SMITH, T. (1980) *Parents and Pre-school* Grant McIntyre
18 *What Next?* (1982) Editorial 1, 2

IN THE CLASSROOM

SHARING INFORMATION

Sharing information about the school with parents

THE SCHOOL HANDBOOK

Every school produces *a handbook* with certain information (for example numbers on roll, times of sessions) which is obligatory and other information which is included at the discretion of the headteacher. School brochures are given to all new parents and expense permitting, they may also be distributed to the local library, the social services office, feeder play groups, visitors and other interested people. Some schools have better reproduction facilities than others but certain rules of thumb are helpful.

1 The cover needs to be appealing with the name of the school dominant so that readers can see exactly what the brochure is about at a first glance.

2 Children's drawings make a lively addition to the cover but care should be taken that they add to, and do not detract from, information inside.

3 The content should be clear, brief, and easy to find, under suitable headings.

4 The size is important – will it only fit into large, expensive envelopes or is it a suitable size both for handling and storing in a drawer in a home? A4 size is clumsy and tends to get creased up.

5 A loose-leaf brochure (fastened with a treasury tag or spine binder) means that when information needs to be changed, only one or two new pages need to be inserted. (This is why it is useful to present information in sections on separate pages.)

6 A reasonable margin needs to be left round blocks of text. This makes the brochure easier to read and more attractive.

7 The handbook should be slim rather than overwhelming.

Obviously the headteacher and staff will write with the needs of the catchment area in mind, but as a general guide the tone should be informative but friendly and reflect a flavour of the school. A small collection of school brochures from other schools and LEAs can be used to compare for content, format, tone.

COMMUNICATION BY LETTER

The only way a school can communicate quickly and efficiently with the whole parent body is by letter. Sometimes an emergency letter is ready prepared, e.g. some authorities have provided schools with a letter to be sent out if a road crossing is to be unmanned. Other letters may tell of events which occur regularly in the school calendar (e.g. the visit of the photographer), request help (e.g. with jumble sales, harvest goods), or

nvitations to a school concert or parents' evening, or give information
e.g. details of a forthcoming trip).

From their first days in school children need to be trained to give the
etters to their parents and bring a reply if needed. The teacher should
make sure that she (or the children) have written the name on top of the
etter, have folded it neatly, and put it in coat pockets or school bags. If the
eacher sees letters as an important channel of communication the children
will too. If she gives them out in a rush at the school door and lets children
arry them home in their hand in wet weather she is creating the impression that letters to parents are unimportant. Absentees' letters should
be named and kept in the class register so that no family is left out or
orgotten. An enquiry in the morning, 'Did you give your letter to
mummy/daddy/grandma?' is useful. Twins should have one letter each.

If an answer is required, a tear-off slip can be provided. A closing date
or return is useful here. If the school office has duplicated class rolls to
hand it is easy to keep a check. Quite apart from this, it is good for the
hildren to see that the teacher is not only systematic but cares about each
hild. Older children, perhaps working in pairs, can be given the job of
hecking the return of slips.

It is wise to settle the school calendar in principle at the beginning of the
chool year and in more detail at the beginning of each term. The actual
ates when letters are to be sent out can be pencilled in on the calendar so
hat parents do not receive a cluster of letters all at once. Some schools
ave a half termly news sheet. This means that parents come to expect,
nd look for, a letter at certain times of the year. However there are
ituations which apply only to groups of children (e.g. trips, recorder
essons, swimming), and not all the information can be put in one news
etter.

It is a good idea to keep a copy of every letter sent to parents in a file,
umbered and dated. Besides providing a record of what has been sent, it
lso saves time and effort because sometimes last year's letter needs little
mendment. Letters which may have left the parents confused, because
n reflection they were poorly worded, can also be included with a warning
gn across them!

Consecutive letters may be duplicated on different coloured papers.
This helps in the office if replies are expected and also alerts the parents
hat it is a 'new' letter.

Although school/home letters are an essential means of communication,
is wise to exclude anything controversial or slightly sensational. It is
seful to ask several members of staff to read a newly-composed letter and
o amend it in the light of their comments. Headteachers must make up
heir own minds whether it is good policy to send a letter home from school
rom an outside body (e.g. the NSPCC, the LEA) without a short covering
ote. They must also decide whether all letters go out under their own
gnature or whether individual members of staff may write to individual
arents.

Bearing in mind that it is essential that *all* parents hear *all* the news, on occasions a door notice (i.e. Please come at 11.45 tomorrow instead of 12 o'clock. We have learned a song we would like to sing to you before we go home.') might suffice for the rising-five class.

A challenge for older children is for them to make their own letters to include all the information, carefully written and well arranged on the page. Children, however young, should never be given a letter 'cold', but instead told, 'Please, give these letters to your mummy. It's about . . .'.

Stages of information

Parents do not need to know the details of a school's organization in one fell swoop. For one thing, they will not be able to assimilate it, and for another, information is only useful when it is relevant. Timing is important here. We have suggested in Chapter 1 (p.22) ways in which children coming to school for the first time can be offered information about the school. These include home visits by teachers, school visits by parents with/without the children during the day or in the evening, and written information.

As the child settles into school the established rhythm and the tradition of the school will feature in the parents' expectations. For example, in some schools they will expect a harvest thanksgiving. If for some reason the teachers think there should be a change in the usual pattern, the parents should be told and an explanation given. Too many changes in the established pattern of the school year may be difficult for the parents to reconcile and will also contradict the 'word of mouth' information which 'stabilizes the community'.

If the parents can be received in small groups (say eight at a time) and hosted by the headteacher (or her deputy) to see the whole school at work, this is an excellent way of giving them a bird's eye view. It is always difficult to find a mutually convenient time for parents who work during the day, but if the visit is short (say half an hour) the invitation may be able to be taken up.

Keeping the parents informed about the school routines and organization is a task that needs to be worked at throughout the school year.

When the time comes for the boy or girl to move on to the receiving school both headteachers need to work together so that parents receive information well in advance. A copy of the junior or middle school brochure and a welcome letter can be sent home in May or June. The head of the receiving school can be introduced individually to the first school children and their parents. Visits can be arranged in school time so that first school children go, with their parents, in small groups to visit the receiving school. Whatever arrangements are made, it is wise to augment them gradually and in good time. Parents are always pleased to see the two headteachers working together.

Questions parents need to ask

The title of this section is 'sharing information about the school'. So far we have only talked about teachers as dispensers of information which the think the parents wish to know. It is much harder to create a situation where parents feel they can ask about the organization of the school as it relates to their own circumstances, e.g. 'Why can't Joanne bring a glass thermos flask?' There should be established channels of communication so that parents can ask for information about school organization and rules.

For safety reasons it was agreed on one large campus site (i.e. nursery, first, junior and secondary) that all children must take things home in a bag. If a child did not bring a bag (an ordinary carrier bag would do) he could not take home his model, picture, books etc. One child wished to take home his puppet but had forgotten his bag. His mother was in the playground and she stuffed the entire contents of her handbag into her pockets, gave the child her handbag and sent him back inside to fetch his puppet. The teacher refused to let the child take it, so the parent came into school rather angry and upset. However, when the teacher explained the reasons behind the rule the mother visibly relaxed, agreed with the teacher and the two parted with a laugh.

Not all parents deliver and collect their children, nor do they have the opportunity to ask about the organization of the school, even if they have pressing enquiries. The headteacher, teachers and school secretary should take every opportunity of talking to individual parents, the dinner ladies and parent governors. Teachers can let the children know how pleased they are to get letters or telephone calls as well as visits from parents. All questions need to be treated with respect, and if they are asked at an inopportune time a quick yes/no answer could be given with a definite time arranged for a further discussion. It is a good idea to commit such arrangements to paper straightaway, and if the parent does not keep the appointment to write a short letter, or arrange another time.

What about parents who do not come, do not ask, are reluctant to get involved in any way? Or difficult parents who come all too often for information, always want preferential treatment and cannot conform to the normal running of the school?

All schools will experience some of these problems and each will merit particular considerations. The important point, however, is not to allow a small 'difficult' group of parents to discourage teachers from pursuing a general policy of welcome and communication. Occasionally difficult parents may have to be made aware that teachers also have 'rights'.

ASSUME PARENTAL COOPERATION

If a young child's parents do not respond to written invitations, if an older sibling or neighbour delivers and collects the child, if there is no point of contact, then the school needs to do something constructive. A further but personal letter suggesting the first one was lost might be a beginning. If the parent is on the telephone a call might help. Failing this, a home visit is useful. If there is another reliable parent who lives nearby he/she might deliver a message. The important thing is to keep on trying!

THINK OF LEARNING AS COOPERATIVE

A note inviting the parent in to see their youngster's painting or model, written so that it requires an answer, might help to bridge the gap between home and school. Failing this, a child might take home a favourite school toy or puzzle together with a short explanatory note about bringing it back in the morning.

THINK OF PARENTS AS PEOPLE

Children talk about home, their older and younger siblings, parents, grandparents and neighbours. A vigilant teacher can sometimes use this information in a perfectly natural way to contact the parent. If the cat has had kittens she could perhaps find homes for some of them; if a new baby has arrived she could send a congratulatory card.

Just as parents have to adjust to a new teacher for their child, so the teacher needs to adjust to individual parents. It is not a sign of weakness to make exceptions to agreed policy if that exception has been given some thought. Every experienced teacher can recall a time when she needed to deal differently with one parent, for example allowing cough sweets for a day or two when the usual rule is 'no sweets in school'.

USE THE RESOURCES AVAILABLE

The teacher can sometimes find an opportunity to ask the parent into school to demonstrate skills or hobbies which she has heard the children talking about, e.g. a mother who makes lace for a hobby, a father who goes fishing. We discuss this later in the chapter.

INFORMATION PARENTS CAN GIVE

Parents often provide instant information about the fabric of the school which has escaped the attention of the staff, for example, the crossing lights may have failed, or some tiles been blown off in a high wind. If there is a genuine air of welcome and mutual concern, parents will often give valuable feedback to staff about routines and physical arrangements. For example, a parent may remind a teacher that Peter has been 'on the same reading book for ages, and he's getting fed up with it' or 'Lisa loved making the sugar mice and she told us the poem about it after tea. She likes reciting poems . . .'.

ORGANIZED SHARING: PTAs

Small, intimate groupings of parents where they feel confident to contribute are time consuming for teachers. On the other hand, an organized arrangement with secretary and treasurer, such as a PTA, may discourage other parents; it may, however, be able to organize events which the teaching staff, particularly in a small school, could not do by themselves. A written constitution can be a safeguard or a straitjacket. Alternatives to a formal PTA are *ad hoc* committees called specifically to deal with one-off events (e.g. Christmas parties) and then disbanded; single parents meetings to deal with an age group or subject; a cycle of regular parents' meetings which happen at the same time every year, or an organized sharing with the receiving school.

Before initiating a formal Parent Teacher Association it is wise to remember that it may be easier to start one than to wind one up! On the other hand, there need to be established channels through which parents can receive information about a school. Open access to the teacher in the classroom has drawbacks, especially if the parent is voluble and comes at an inappropriate time.

RESPECT

A slowness to become provoked, an unfailing courtesy, a good memory for messages, efficiency in dealing with emergencies, together with discretion, a disinclination for gossip and a refusal to get flustered, are all traits that can be consciously nurtured by teachers and which command respect. So will gentle, consistent handling of children. An attractive appearance is important – children and parents notice details like a necklace or brooch.

RELIEVING ANXIETY

This can be stated specifically: 'If you don't hear from us you can assume everything is fine. We'll do the same for you.'

HONESTY

Being honest does not mean becoming insensitive or callous. It does mean admitting occasionally to mistakes. If the view is that both parent and teacher are working for a common goal – the well-being of the child – it is much easier to be honest. A parent can be told that taking off the child's coat and hanging it up for him is something he can perfectly well do for himself, but can be told quietly and at the same time asked for her support at home so that he does it there too. Or an over-ambitious mother might be told 'To be honest, Mrs Brown, Nigel is becoming worried because I think you are expecting too much. He is a lovely little boy and getting on beautifully. Don't spoil it by rushing him along. I will let you know if he isn't making progress but right now he is fine. You can help him best by . . .'. These kinds of conversations, initiated by the teacher, may benefit from preparation, together with advice from experienced colleagues.

ENCOURAGE QUESTIONS

Asking genuine questions of the parents, anticipating hesitancy on their part to ask questions in return, and taking the initiative for them, are ways of encouraging parents to gather confidence and to ask the teacher their own questions.

Sharing information about the children with the parents

INDIVIDUAL CHILDREN

Formal occasions
Incidental, fringe, or chance meetings between parents and teaching staff, fruitful as they are, need to be implemented by formal exchanges. By this we mean organized events where teachers talk with parents about the welfare and progress of individual children. It is important to include formal occasions because some parents can only see parent/teacher contact within this framework. These parents will be sufficiently confident to attend such functions while they may not feel inclined to come to less formal meetings. As far as possible the type of occasion must suit the parents.

The main rules of thumb seem to be:

1 *Timing* What time of the day is best for parents – during school? immediately after school? evening? The same opportunity may need to be offered on several dates so that parents can be sure to come.
2 *Confidentiality* is needed in a stress-free atmosphere. Parents and staff should not be facing the clock. The teacher needs a steady, but not overlapping, stream of parents. Is an appointment system appropriate? Should the group be small, say six to eight parents so that the teacher is not over-tired? What is provided for the parents while they are waiting – perhaps light refreshments, an exhibition or just a chance to chat with friends?
3 A check should be made with the receiving school (where there may be older siblings) that events do not clash. What arrangements need to be made for the children? How often ought these opportunities to be arranged? What part of the school-year? Some peak times are a few days or weeks after a child has joined a new class or has changed his teacher, or towards the end of the school year. It is important to make arrangements for parents to see each new teacher *before* the child joins her, as well as shortly afterwards.

Open evenings
In recent years the 'Open Evening' has undergone radical change. It has become more civilized, partly because planning and thought has reduced stress, partly because teachers recognize the exchange of information means they are working in partnership with parents, and partly because it is not the sole occasion for face to face contact it once was.

1 *Teacher-preparation: an aide-mémoire* A parent/teacher chat is more likely to yield positive results if it has been well prepared. Some parents prepare for it by writing down their questions. A teacher might prepare a class roll with pencilled notes written against each child's name. Besides showing the parents that the teacher has taken the occasion seriously it will provide a nervous or busy teacher with a mental note for the things she wishes to discuss. Apart from this it is useful to make a note of points the parents make

rather than run the risk of forgetting them. The folder can then be kept with other confidential material in the school office as a record of the conversations. Some teachers feel this system inhibits parents but others find it generates confidence.

2 *In-service work* with experienced colleagues can help beginning teachers enormously. New teachers should try and react in a low key way to any unusual information they are offered or any criticism of themselves or the school. A further appointment should be arranged then and there for a few weeks' time if any stubborn difficulty needs to be resolved.

Difficult parents

Parents who do not respond to invitations need to be helped for they are the ones that teachers most often wish to see. In certain cases (e.g. where a child is disruptive) the school must make urgent and decisive moves to contact the parents. The Educational Welfare Officer, the health visitor or social worker might be co-opted to help or the headteacher might think a home visit made by herself is best. A written request is often a bad way of initiating contact in these cases as it may worry or alienate parents. Throughout all dealings with parents about their children total discretion is essential.

CHILDREN AS A WHOLE CLASS/YEAR GROUP/TEACHING GROUP/SCHOOL

Displays

Young children's work is compelling and attractive. It can be presented as a curriculum theme running through the school (for example, children's art work), or a tiny display by two or three children only. It can set out to explain the quality of children's learning or it can be purely pleasurable. An adult, adults and/or children may be on hand to talk about the display; parents may be left to wander at will; or a handout or guide may be provided, as well as labels and explanatory notes. Care should be taken to make sure the display is not too crowded, or that parents do not come and go without meeting any of the staff. Refreshments might be provided, with background music, and children accompanying their parents. From the parents' point of view this is a family occasion with no financial output, no time limit and no tension (as there might be if their own child was to be discussed) but there is, at the same time, a chance to gather information. Reluctant parents can come with a neighbour or friend. Saturday or Sunday openings might be considered.

Films, videos, pictures

A film of the class trip to the beach or zoo, a video of children exploring the school environment, slides or even colour photographs are thoroughly enjoyed by parents. Following this the head or teacher may run the film again, this time pointing up happenings and explaining the significance to the audience. Parents often ask to see 'old' films and slides to remind them what their children were like two years ago. A display can often be enchanced by a 'continuous' slide show.

Talks

Carefully structured, short, well-delivered talks work well in some areas. They might be given by heads, teachers, advisers, LEA officers or a group of heads and teachers from a pyramid of schools. Once again detail is important. For example, the room should suit the size of the group expected (two rows of people in a large hall ruins the atmosphere). Seating arrangements (rows? circle? clusters?), ventilation, an entry door at the back so that latecomers can slip in unobtrusively – all these considerations contribute to success. Generally, questions should be taken at the end, not in the middle of the talk.

1 A group of children, with the help from their teacher, can give a talk to parents, especially if they have things to show and describe.
2 A parent may give a talk to teachers. For example, in one school a good number of the children came from families who were Jehovah's Witnesses. One of the mothers came in during the lunch hour and talked to the teachers briefly about her religion and mutual arrangements were made for the children concerning Christmas celebrations.

USE PARENTS' KNOWLEDGE OF THEIR CHILDREN

Parents frequently share home information with the school. This may be because they are under emotional pressure and need support, advice or a listening ear. Teachers and headteachers will need not only to react in a mature way but also sometimes offer help through outside agencies.

Personal information is offered because parents feel it is necessary for the well-being of the children. The kinds of things which they share are major concerns – changes in their own circumstances, financial, marital, housing, health, or employment. Perhaps it is more usual for them to ask to see the headteacher in these cases, but a quiet, unhurried, totally confidential atmosphere is essential for the exchange of such information. It may be helpful to have a special notice ready to put on the head's door. Certainly the head or teacher should give their sole attention to the matter in hand and, as far as possible, avoid all interruptions. It should be made clear to all new parents, and reiterated frequently, that the headteacher is always available to discuss important and confidential matters with parents.

Individual schools need to be clear how and when a parent should be referred to the headteacher, how confidential information is to be exchanged among staff, if/when it is to be recorded.

Sometimes parents ask to see the head or class teacher on a seemingly trivial matter. Before very long the teacher realizes this was an excuse and the real purpose of the visit is something quite different. Shy parents sometimes ask an ancillary worker to 'mention it to John's teacher please': they choose the least senior member of staff to talk with because they lack the courage or social skills to seek out the head or class teacher. Whole school staffs need to be alert to parents who hesitate to leave, linger and seem to need a gentle nudge to put their worries into words.

Sometimes parents do come straight to the headteacher. The head will then need to decide how much information, if any, is to be passed on to the child's own teacher. Sometimes, because the parents are shy of 'authority' or because they have a particularly strong relationship with the class teacher, they prefer to talk to her. However, where the class teacher feels the matter is of sufficient importance she should make it quite clear to the parents themselves that she intends to speak to the headteacher. In a small school most class teachers can gain access to the head quickly and easily. In a large school this might be more difficult.

1 A 'messages' box in the head's room is a useful way of warning her of parents' visits, and she will at least know they have been in if they contact her before she has seen the teacher about details.
2 A simple, easily operated system of passing messages (verbal, telephone, written) between secretary, teachers and headteacher is vital if parent/home relationships are to be nurtured and maintained.
3 A day book (or similar) kept by the head in which she reminds herself of the things to be done, things that have happened, and in which she can sort out priorities for the next day saves time and makes sure that things are not overlooked.
4 It may be wise to have an agreement that *all* information given by parents to nursery nurses, ancillary helpers, the school secretary, dinner ladies and cleaning staff is automatically passed on to the class teacher concerned.
5 Although it may be felt that parents ought not to give or seek information from anyone else than the teachers and head, this can sometimes prove impractical. It is useful occasionally to speak with a parent and then make another appointment for a further chat.

Sharing information with the community

THE MEDIA
1 *Local newspapers* Pictures and text about school events (concerts, sales, sponsored walks/swims for charities) are often newsworthy items. Individual successes such as music and dancing exams, poster competitions may be included. Accounts of projects, trips, or cooperation between schools are not so often offered for publication. It is wise for the headteacher to see copy before it is published.
3 *Local radio* More often than not children's contributions are pre-recorded. Conversations, music, reported events can give a flavour of the school.
3 *Brochures* As already mentioned distribution of the school handbook can be generous if funds allow.

4 Films, displays Some schools feel they cannot allow a silent film to go out 'cold' but need a teacher or headteacher to introduce it. Displays in the library, church hall, foyer or window of the local shop offer information about the school to the local community.

TALKS
Teacher, parent/teacher, child/teacher talks to local groups about the work and life of the school are a mutually valuable experience.

COMMUNITY INFORMATION TO SHARE WITH THE SCHOOL
1 Details of groups like Brownie and Cub packs, Boys' and Girls' Brigade, Drum Majorettes, all organized clubs should be available in school.
2 Medical groups (such as Children with Asthma) and playschemes for the holidays (such as Holicare), together with names, addresses and telephone numbers of charities, self-help organizations, evening classes, societies and clubs, feeder playgroups should be held in school to pass on as and when an opportunity arises. Some authorities have an official booklet, but the local library usually holds all this information so it is a question of up-dating it at regular intervals.
3 *Magazines, periodicals and library books* A selection of suitable publications with a 'signing-out book' is a service some parents enjoy. This should include local publications, for example the church magazine or the community newsletter.
4 It is always useful for school staff to know what is going on in the district. Shops sometimes mount special displays, or the circus may come to town. Often these are shared experiences which can be woven into the activities at school.

SHARING EXPERIENCES

Parents and the school

HELP WITH THE FABRIC
A school is not only a place for children to learn, it is a work place for adults. Comfort, in terms of warmth, colour schemes, well-appointed furniture and equipment, quiet flooring and a pleasant, relaxing atmosphere is not only an aid to learning but a source of corporate pride.

Parents may provide not only money but the expertise and labour to transform and then maintain an old school, or add resources to newer ones. Some of this work can be done in school time, but some will need to take place in the evening, or at the weekend, or perhaps in the holidays.

FUND-RAISING ACTIVITIES

Parental participation
It is important to ask all parents to contribute in some way, and to take

up all offers of help. Sometimes it is useful to have bags of 'homework' for parents who cannot come to school to a 'work in' or get babysitters. These bags can contain one finished article and all the materials and instructions needed to make, for example, puppets, bean bags, desk tidies, teddy bears, woolly dolls etc.

Timing

The timing of fund-raising activities is important; the beginning and ending time should be clearly stated. Sometimes, if a hall or classroom is available, it is a good idea to have an all-day jumble sale (from 8.45 until 4.00 pm) so that parents can come at leisure and browse. The financial result and the way the money is to be spent should be passed on to parents and if possible a display provided of the new equipment when it has been purchased.

Children's participation

Fund-raising activities are exciting for the children and if the children play an active part are truly part of the curriculum. A Christmas Bazaar, held in the evening between 6 and 8 pm gives the children a chance to see the school in the dark, with all the lights on, and their classroom transformed into a dazzling place filled with cakes, pots of jam and sweets. The first whole sentence a little girl with impaired hearing ever spoke in school was 'My mummy is going to make a cake for the sale.'

HELP WITH CHORES

First school teachers will need to give clear instructions, provide all the necessary materials and house parents in a comfortable area. Whether the staffroom is to be extended to parents is a matter for the head and staff to decide. Working within the school environment and sharing experience about the school may be a prerequisite to sharing experience about the children and therefore moving closer to the role of 'parent as teacher'. Whether parents 'pop in on the off chance' so that a store of ready-and-waiting jobs is kept, or come on a rota basis, is a matter for the school to decide. The paid ancillary in the school will need to be reassured that the unpaid helpers in no way threaten her job. It is sometimes useful to have a place where unfinished work can be left overnight so that everything is not packed away. Teachers will soon get to know the strengths of individual helpers. They will also know that time spent in school sometimes helps parents through bouts of loneliness, home problems or simply a feeling of being inadequate or unfulfilled. Parents who help should be seen not as the low layer in the school hierarchy but as partners in the complex network of relationships. They merit courtesy (e.g. somewhere to park the car) and consideration (e.g. 'Would you like to borrow an umbrella?'). A 'parents' room' which is their own preserve, where they can make drinks, chat to one another and generally relax, can be looked after on a rota basis.

'Mummy sent this vase because I told her we didn't have one tall enough for the bluebells' is the kind of unexpected response that is heart-warming but by no means unusual in many schools. An opportunity to give on the part of parents is seen in organized PTAs, organized teacher/parent situations, but also in many small ways. A teacher who remarked, 'Oh what lovely pinks! I wish they grew in my garden' was given one or two roots the next day ready for planting. In the same way addresses, recipes, information can pass between home and school through the children.

'We mustn't keep asking the parents for money' is a familiar cry in the staffroom. Nevertheless, it is important that parents have many and varied opportunities to give to the school, if only items like clean newspapers, old boxes, wallpaper. A judicious mixture of a general approach or a personal appeal is usually best.

The kind of help requested should be varied from, for example, unwanted articles to new books for the school library. In this case the headteacher could buy some books, put the price inside and then parents could be asked to choose one and donate it to the school.

Time, services and goods from individual parents, groups of parents, teachers and governors, while the school is in session or after school, together with explanations of why they are needed and how they are to be used are the basis of shared experience about the school.

Parents and the children

THE 'HIDDEN' CURRICULUM OR 'HOUSE RULES'
There is a vast difference between reading the school brochure and actually experiencing the school in session. The best way to give parents experience of how children are handled, of the organized classroom, of the relations between child and teacher, of the atmosphere in the dining-room, of the ethos at assembly or the excitement of a concert is to invite them to share it.

1 Visits while the school is in session are best arranged in small hosted groups rather than a 'wander by yourself'. The visit could be brief but often a quick tour will focus the parents' attention on the school as a whole rather than individual children. The visit could culminate in joining assembly or having lunch with the children.
2 We would suggest that experiencing the general 'feel' of the school should come before any discussion of curriculum content, so that parents can relate specific experience to the general 'sense of purpose and direction in the school'.
3 Work with a small group of children of the same age (say three or four children playing a game) within a larger teaching group managed by the teacher, gives the helping adult an idea of the noise toleration, the way the teacher handles the children, and it helps the adult experience at first-hand the demands that young children make and their boundless vitality.
4 Sometimes it may be felt that parents should join their child's class because individual difficulties have arisen. For example, a child had an operation on her feet which meant that unless her mother came to sit with

her in the classroom and accompanied her about the school the child
would need to stay at home for several weeks. A teacher may be continually asked about how a child behaves in school. The answer might be
to invite the parent in to see, although there is a danger that the child will
behave differently with the parent in the room.

THE CONTENT AND PRESENTATION OF THE CURRICULUM
There are two possible outcomes of inviting parents to share the management of the children in the classroom: one is the advantages for the
children of another adult's time and expertise; the other is the insight it
gives parents into classroom activities.
1 Parents do not just 'pick up' the intentions of the teacher – on the
contrary they know they need guidance and are usually eager for it.
Explicit explanation of the reason for activities is both needed and wanted.
How can it be provided?
2 Classroom experience with a small group of children can be followed up
by discussion, workshops, films, talks, displays. The ideal is for the parent
and teacher to have a few minutes 'recap and discussion' at the end of the
school session while it is still fresh in both their minds.
3 Help on a trip needs to be talked through and carefully organized, as do
activities in the classroom. Teachers need to ask themselves whether there
are some experiences they would like the parents to participate in but
others they would prefer to keep to themselves. Some teachers feel it is
inappropriate for parents to 'hear reading'. If the teacher sees a parent
using inappropriate techniques then she must say so (e.g. if a parent hands
children scissors incorrectly, this can be gently pointed out).

It is by modelling themselves on the teacher, discussing the activities,
gaining first-hand experience of children's needs and reactions that
parents become active supporters, true partners in the learning process.
When individual children have specific difficulties it is sometimes appropriate for the parents to join the teaching group for a session and then
borrow equipment to continue the activity at home.
Evening and after-school sessions on aspects of the curriculum, explaining the overall plan, showing children's work, and particularly workshop
sessions where the parents participate themselves need careful management and are best tackled in small groups of parents who already know
each other.

CONTRIBUTIONS BY PARENTS
Sometimes parents have expertise that fits the current interests in the
classroom.

1 A science project on 'Myself' might be enhanced by a talk from the local
doctor.
2 In a multi-racial school parents might help to prepare a special meal.
3 One part of the school or classroom might become the sole

responsibility of a parent, for example the woodwork bench.

4 Teachers may find parents can suggest clever ways of storing equipment, displaying children's work or may donate unusual materials.

5 Often parents follow a child's progress at a particular task over several days or weeks and take a genuine pride in his achievements.

Schools staffs must decide whether parents are invited into their child's own class or whether it is more beneficial for them to work in another class. After all, children have no redress if they do not want their mother in the classroom – they have to abide by the joint decision of parent and teacher. Also, children whose mothers cannot come may feel deprived and so may their parents.

Joint projects

1 A 'Home and School Week' might grow from modest beginnings. During the week the school could be open to visitors at selected times and a programme of displays, concerts, talks and slides or films could be arranged.

2 If the receiving school, or all schools concerned, can synchronize their 'Home and School' week the result is very satisfying for staff and parents alike.

3 A stall showing parents' hobbies, competitions, a sale of goods where the parents keep the proceeds, a Cub-Scout display, are a few ideas. Perhaps the week could end with a supper or concert.

4 A special lunch, cooked by the children to which their parents are invited, is another exciting venture.

Two-way traffic

Just as the parents need to know about what is happening in school, how it is happening, and why, so the teacher needs to know about home. A simple way of doing this is a school/home notebook in which messages can be written. In one reception class, after the children had been in school a few days, they had a 'secret message for mummy' written on a gummed address label attached to their dress or jumper. The children chose their own messages which ranged from 'I have been a good boy' to 'We did drawings'. They put on their coats and kept the secret till they got home and then showed it with glee.

Single consultations with parents and a record of who came, reinforced by home visits, can be very helpful. For example a little girl needed to be X-rayed but made a great fuss at the hospital, so much so that the mother became very distressed. Fortunately the child's teacher was able to accompany her next time, and the child was much calmer and the mother reassured. If the value of sharing experiences with the parents about the children has been accepted many opportunties will present themselves. Something as mundane as giving a mother a roll of Sellotape so that she can fasten a child's lunch box to prevent him eating the contents on the way to school is a useful shared experience.

The role of the teacher

Teachers who have not had the experience of working with parents in the classroom need the opportunity to express their doubts and anxieties about the success of such a scheme. School-based in-service meetings and outside courses will help teachers to clarify their own role in working with parents. The following areas can be discussed:

1 Delegation of suitable jobs – the teacher's role in preparing parents for their work.

2 The selection of adults to do particular jobs – how to accommodate everyone without giving offence: the benefits to the teacher of using particular expertise, e.g. requesting a sensitive parent to observe a small group of children playing and using the information gained.

3 Insights into parents' perceptions of the teacher working. Such discussions should aim to stress the practical benefits for the teacher in having adult help: the benefits ascribed to parents: the increased complexity of the teacher's professional task in managing both adults and children in her class.

Learning together

Open University groups, a series of talks or workshops on a mutually interesting topic (e.g. wine making) or an evening purely for enjoyment (such as a fashion show), are all events which can be shared between teachers and parents. Much will depend on the catchment area but a good choir with some audience participation, mince pies and punch makes a fine evening. Similarly, in areas where young mothers are isolated on a large housing estate and finance is short, an evening at school with chat and refreshments (and no talk about children!) is a welcome relief from household chores. A regular club for these kinds of evenings is an occasion to which young housebound parents may look forward.

The community, the school and the children

SHARING THE SCHOOL WITH THE COMMUNITY

1 *Invitations* A first school at Christmas is a haven of delight and some ratepayers have not been inside one for years. They could be invited in to see the trimmings in the evening.

An invitation for the elderly of the district, for local groups such as the Townswomen's Guild, to a concert, or harvest thanksgiving is much appreciated. Sometimes individual friendships grow up and letters pass back and forth.

2 *Events* Children may sing, play instruments, dance or prepare a short list of items for the local old folk's home; dance at the local fête; sing carols outside the supermarket and generally contribute to community life.

3 *Charities* The children and teachers can organize small fund-raising activities, competitions, and supportive events for local causes.

SHARING THE COMMUNITY WITH THE SCHOOL

1 *Individual needs* Often the headteacher is alerted to societies and groups

that are set up to help children with special needs. She can foster this relationship by inviting a speaker from the group to talk to all the children, and by this show both her concern and support.

2 *Multi-ethnic cultures* Books, teaching materials, curricular emphases (care in selecting types of play which will not offend many Asian parents) need to be chosen against a background of informed discussion. Not only parents but local ethnic leaders could be invited into school and given direct information and experience of the way the children are handled, and the activities provided. They can then offer help to teaching staff.

3 *Expanding horizons* It is possible sometimes to arrange for groups of people to come into the school (e.g. the Morris Men to dance for the children, or the local chiropodist to talk about feet). It is always wise for the head or class teacher to 'rehearse' the visit and go through the talk or display beforehand.

4 *Trips* Unambitious outings into the local environment, e.g. a visit to a local library, dairy, even a spacious garden with amateur aviary. A local visit with thank-you letters and an invitation into school to see the resulting painting, writing, mathematics, science, forges a link with the local community which often brings most welcome but unexpected results.

SHARING DECISIONS

Sharing decisions about the school and children with the parents

A helpful technique can be to select a few parents and 'test the response', either at a coffee morning, or toddlers' club, or even in the school cloakroom. The parent governor is a particularly good source of parental feedback. For example, if the teachers want to take the oldest children to London to see the dinosaurs in the Natural History Museum, and are rather dubious as to whether the journey would be too long, it might be helpful to ask ten or twelve mothers for their views.

If changing the time of beginning or closing the school session is contemplated then parents have a valuable part to play in the decision-making. Teachers might need to ask themselves whether an activity which is very unpopular with parents should be dropped, e.g. young children painting on glass.

In one school the mothers wanted to cook sausages and chips for the Christmas party instead of sandwiches and cakes. The teachers agreed, and it was a great success. These may seem trivial decisions, but they are a genuine form of working in partnership. Joint decisons about the fabric and organization, even the school calendar, can be helpful for teaching staff. Parental support is firmer when the parents have had a share in the decision-making.

A sharing of decisions will mean that not only do teachers influence the parents, but parents will influence the teachers and the school. This is not so frightening as it might at first appear, especially if it relates to individual children, or children in a short-term programme. The success of the Haringey Reading Project is an encouragement to the whole profession but a more modest parental involvement (perhaps about a child's reading, with parents and teacher making daily joint decisions about progress and further activity), is a welcome beginning and usually yields observable and swift results.

Sharing decisions with the community about the school and the children

THE GOVERNING BODY
An open, direct approach which keeps the governors informed and genuinely involved in school management, backed up by visits while the school is in session, results in mutual decision-making. This applies not only to appointment of staff, but also to use of resources, and proposed future developments. Many governors have community interests and are local community leaders. They can add a fresh dimension to debate on school issues.

USE OF PREMISES AND ENQUIRIES FROM ORGANIZATIONS
Sometimes a local group (e.g. the National Housewife's register) will want to compile information about schools. Such requests from local groups and ethnic minorities should be discussed in an atmosphere of mutual tolerance and goodwill.

SELF-HELP GROUPS
It is possible, given a suitable leader, to form a group in the local community which will help parents and children who are referred to it by the school. For example a mother could look after another mother's toddler and baby to relieve her if she is ill; hospital appointments can be covered in this way; urgent journeys made for the cost of petrol only; physical or emotional support given in the home.

BACK-UP SERVICES
The school can draw together the services outside education and provide not only the meeting place but the initial will to gel the services together and share experience. (Bate, Hargreaves and Wilson's *Liaison Groups in Early Education* is an excellent example of such an endeavour.)

HOME/SCHOOL LIAISON TEACHER
The job specifications should include listening to the parents' wishes, and if possible changing to accommodate them. However, the teacher who has this role should have the means to carry out the responsibilities, e.g. status and backing to talk with parents, opportunity to visit playgroups etc.

ATTITUDES
The most important requirement of a community school is that it should keep an open mind, receive approval, suggestions, criticisms in an equally phlegmatic manner but, after discussions and careful consideration, act

upon them for the benefit of children, parents and the community.

Hopefully, the time will come when parents will be as familiar with their children's school as they are with the local supermarket. They will look on school as part of the fabric of daily living, not something set apart for the young, but a continuing source of family and community strength.

APPRAISAL QUESTIONS

SHARING INFORMATION

Are there opportunities in the school day for parents to speak with me individually or do they need to make an appointment?

Do I feel at ease when I am talking with parents?

Are there any parents I have never met? Am I making a conscious effort to meet them?

Is there a child in my class about whom I am uneasy? Have I talked to his parents about him?

When did I last send a message or piece of work home to congratulate the child and encourage the parents?

Has there been an occasion this term when information I have received about a child in his family has made me reconsider his behaviour in school?

SHARING EXPERIENCES

Have I had any unexpected or surprising feedback from parents working alongside me in the classroom?

What kinds of activities do I ask them to undertake?

Do I plan the activity, provide the materials, discuss the results and display the children's work or do I leave all or some of this to the parents' discretion?

Is my working relationship with the parents a growing one? How can I tell?

Do I discuss with them the reasons for activities and the rationale behind the management of the children?

Have I had any recent successes with shy, reluctant or awkward parents?

Has my own confidence in handling parents increased?

In what ways would I feel a sense of loss if I did not have parents in my classroom?

Have I any forward plans for parent/home involvement?

SHARING DECISIONS

Would I enjoy living in the catchment area? If not, why not?

Can I name clubs, associations, community ventures, that are operating in the district?

Have I changed any of my classroom routines or techniques in view of what I know about the children's life out of school?

Have I made a conscious effort to help any child in his family since I have had this class? Was it successful?

Do I find myself thinking more and more about the parents in their individual situations and putting myself in their position?

Do I ever wonder how I must appear to parents? Do I ever consciously try to change this image? Do I think it wise to try?

Have I received any criticism from a parent recently? How did I react? do I wish I had reacted differently?

Do I yearn for more time and resources to forward home/school relationships or do I feel I am doing all that is required?

FURTHER RESOURCES

ACE (1981) *One Thousand Children* Heffer

BALL, C. and MOG, M. (1973) *Education for a Change: Community Action and the School* Penguin

BURGESS, T. (1973) *Home and School* Penguin

COSIN, B. R. (1971) *School and Society* Routledge & Kegan Paul for the Open University

CULLEN, K. (1969) *School and Family* Macmillan

DOUGLAS, J. (1964) *The Home and the School* MacGibbon & Kee

GARNER, N. (1973) *Teaching in the Urban Community School* Ward Lock Educational

DES (1972) *Educational Priority Vol. I* (The Halsey Report) HMSO

HALSEY, A. H., HEATH, A. F. and RIDGE, J. M. (1980) *Origins and Destinations* Clarendon

HOLT, J. (1971) *The Underachieving School* Pelican

HOLT, J. (1965) *How Children Fail* Penguin

HUGHES, MAYALL, MOSS, PERRY, PETRIE and PINKERTON (1980) *Nurseries Now: A Fair Deal for Parents and Children* Penguin

JONES, E. and BRAZENDALE, T. (1974) *Determinants of Learning* Ward Lock Educational

KEDDIE, N. (1973) (ed.) *Tinker, Tailor, The Myth of Cultural Deprivation* Penguin

MIDWINTER, E. (1974) *Pre-school Priorities* Chaucer Press

MILLER, G. W. (1971) *Educational Opportunity and the Home* Longman

MORRISON and MCINTYRE (1971) *Schools and Socialization* Penguin

MUSGROVE, F. (1966) *The Family, Education and Society* Routledge & Kegan Paul

RAYNOR, J. and HARDEN, J. (1973) *Cities, Communities and the Young: Readings in Urban Education Vol 1* Routledge & Kegan Paul for the Open University

RAYNOR, J. and HARDEN, J. (1973) (eds.) *Equality and City Schools: Readings in Urban Education Vol 2* Routiedge & Kegan Paul for the Open University

WATSON, L. (1978) *The School and Community* Sheffield Papers in Educational Management

WHITESIDE, T. (1978) *The Sociology of Educational Innovation* Methuen

PERIODICALS
Outlines: A Source Pack for Community Education (34 leaflets) published by Community Education Development Centre, Burton Road, Coventry CV2 4LF.

Journal of Community Education Community Education Development Centre, published quarterly.

Education 3–13 Studies in Education, Nafferton, Driffield, N. Humberside YO25 0JL. Published twice yearly, spring and autumn.

COURSES

Educational Studies: A Third Level Course (E351 Urban Education) Open University Press 1974.

Block 1 Issues in Urban Education
Block 2 The Urban Context
Block 3 People in Cities: An Ecological Approach
Block 4 Education in Urban Communities
Block 5 Alternatives for Urban Schools
Block 6 Whose Schools?

ABSTRACTS

BOND, G. (1974) *Voluntary Helpers in Schools* A Home and School Council Publication

BROOKS, ST. J. (1981) Parents in Class *New Society* 58, 991, pp.281–2

PROSSER (1981) Teaching reading skills: the role of the parents – the myth of parental apathy *Times Educational Supplement* 16 October 1981, pp.22–3

UNIVERSITY OF SOUTHAMPTON *How to organize a home and school week* Schools Council Parents and Teachers Project: Paper II An interim report by the School of Education and Department of Extra Mural Studies

THE SOUTH EAST LONDON GROUP OF THE NATIONAL COUNCIL FOR CIVIL LIBERTIES *the Case of Lee Manor School* A report with recommendations, September 1972

POSTSCRIPT
The Child's Viewpoint

In this book we have tried to help the teacher look at her rationale for working, her organization, and the steps she takes to deepen and broaden her understanding of the job. Although we have emphasized throughout the need for a theoretical backdrop to the successful practice of education, and the necessity for theory and practice to go hand in hand, the basic need is to try and see it all through the eyes of the child. After all the ultimate test of a teacher's success lies in how the child responds to all the school offers him.

And yet in spite of everything children remain delightfully true to themselves. What they take from school is unique – and unpredictable, as the following quotation from Leila Berg's *Look at Kids* (Penguin 1972) reveals. Leanne has just started at primary school. She is lively, intelligent, talkative and sociable.

'Did you like school?' I asked her.
'Yes, it was lovely.'
'What did you like best? . . . The new teaching methods? The paintings on the walls? The story writing? The young teacher?'
'What I liked best was . . . two lovely juniors. They're called Martin and Terry. They came in our playground.'
'Is that allowed?'
'No. And Martin gave me a bottle of perfume.'
'What did he say?'
'He said, "It's for you."'
'And what did you say?'
'I said, "Is it really, I can't believe it . . . I like Martin best, but they're both lovely."' She went on drawing a picture. 'That's what was best.'

INDEX